MEMOIRS

OF

MARMONTEL,

WRITTEN BY HIMSELF:

CONTAINING

HIS LITERARY AND POLITICAL LIFE,

AND ANECDOTES OF THE PRINCIPAL CHARACTERS
OF THE EIGHTEENTH CENTURY.

IN TWO VOLUMES.

VOL. I.

LONDON, 1827.
PRINTED FOR HUNT AND CLARKE,
YORK STREET, COVENT GARDEN.

This scarce antiquarian book is included in our special *Legacy Reprint Series*. In the interest of creating a more extensive selection of rare historical book reprints, we have chosen to reproduce this title even though it may possibly have occasional imperfections such as missing and blurred pages, missing text, poor pictures, markings, dark backgrounds and other reproduction issues beyond our control. Because this work is culturally important, we have made it available as a part of our commitment to protecting, preserving and promoting the world's literature. Thank you for your understanding.

MARMONTEL.

Published by Kent & Clarke, Paternoster Row, Covent Garden.

CONTENTS

OF THE

FIRST VOLUME.

BOOK I.

	PAGE
Editor's Preface	5
Intention of the author in writing his Memoirs	7
Description of the town of Bort, where he was born in 1722, and its environs	8
Manners of the inhabitants	9
The author's childhood	10
His first education	11
His father would not allow him to pursue his studies	ib.
Eulogium on his mother	ib.
Description of all his family	ib.
Their mode of life	12
His father takes him to the little college of Mauriac. examination and admission to this college	14
Reflections on his first studies	15
An old Jesuit, who continues *Vanière*	16
Manners of the scholars of Mauriac; way of living; occupations, amusements	18
The virtuous scholar of Mauriac	20
Eulogium on the custom of confession for children	21
Behaviour of the author with his fellow students	22
Quarrel with the master	23
The author gains his form over to his party against the master	24
Portrait of the professor of rhetoric	25

CONTENTS.

	PAGE
First studies of the author after his rhetoric	26
Holidays	29
First inclinations	34
His father designs him for trade	38
His departure for Clermont	39
He writes to his father that he believes himself called to the ecclesiastical state	40
His reconciliation with his master	41
His admission into philosophy at Clermont	42
He threatens to go to Riom to the Oratorians, upon which they give him some scholars	45
Walk to the country seat of Massillon, and conversation with that prelate	48
First holidays in the ecclesiastical costume	ib.
Second year of philosophy	49
Death of his father	ib.
His grief; his arrival at the paternal roof	50
He goes to divert his thoughts at the house of a curate, one of his friends	51

BOOK II.

Description of the new abode of the author; his occupations, his plans; his residence at the house of M. de Linars	52
Retirement to the seminary of Limoges for the tonsure	53
Conversations in which he astonishes the directors of the seminary	55
He is presented to the bishop (M. de Coetlosquet); good reception; promises of that prelate	57
Error which throws his mother into despair	58
His precipitate departure to console his mother	ib.
Hospitality of a country curate and his niece	60
Anecdote of the policy of the Jesuits	63
Visit of a Jesuit to persuade him to enter his order	65
Journey from Bort to Toulouse; proposal of marriage	68
Arrival at Toulouse; visit to the Jesuit who came to see him at Bort, and who presses him to enter his noviciate. His mother's eloquent letter to dissuade him from becoming a Jesuit	72
At the age of fifteen years, he heads the form of philosophy among the Bernardins	74
Opening of his course	76

CONTENTS.

	PAGE
He obtains a purse from the college of St Catharine	77
Origin of his connections with Voltaire	78
He obtains prizes at the Floral Games	ib.
Pomp of the distributions of these prizes	79
Affecting recognition in the middle of his academic triumph	80
Officiates occasionally for the professor of philosophy	81
Thesis dedicated to the Academy of Toulouse	82
Inconceivable effects of a failure of memory	ib.
Brilliant success of the thesis; offer of a place of assistant at the Academy	83
He sends for one of his brothers to Toulouse	84
Causes which disgust him in the ecclesiastical state	85
Disputes of a fellow of St Catharine with a grand vicar of Toulouse	ib.
Bad reception of the cardinal de la Roche Aymond	87
Voltaire advises him to come to Paris; his difficulty in the choice of a profession	88
Last journey to the place of his birth	ib.
Kind and flattering reception of his friends and townsmen; entertainments they give him	89
Happiness of seeing his mother again blended with much uneasiness for her health	ib.
Conversation with his mother on his aversion for the ecclesiastical state	90
His mother's physician insists on his quitting her; affecting farewell	91
Voltaire's note, which decides the fate of the author	92
He arrives at Toulouse to complete his studies	95
His journey from Toulouse to Paris with a young coxcomb	ib.
His occupations during his journey	96

BOOK III.

Arrival of the author at Paris (1745); first visit to Voltaire; hopes dispelled	ib.
Conversation with Voltaire	99
First lodging; first resources	99
His studies	100
First choice of a subject for a tragedy	101
He obtains his entrance at the Theatre Français	ib.

CONTENTS.

	PAGE
He writes upon Dionysius the Tyrant	101
On Vauvenargue	ib.
His first connections; his way of life	102
He projects a journal which has little success	103
He obtains a prize at the French Academy (1746)	ib.
Great penury	ib.
Voltaire sells the author's poem to the court; crowned at the Academy	ib.
He undertakes the education of madame de Harenc's grandson	107
Charming society of this lady	106
He again obtains the prize for poetry (1747)	107
His mother's death; consolations bestowed on him by madame de Harenc	ib.
He requests the actors to hear the reading of his tragedy	108
He successfully alters an act in three days	ib.
His embarrassment in the midst of the claims of mademoiselles Gaussin and Clairon for the principal character	109
Distribution of the other characters; rehearsals	112
Amusing description of a meeting of amateurs and of their criticisms; d'Argental, Chauvelin, de Praslin, Thibouville	113
Trick of a sharping Gascon; brief of a Toulousian lawyer, Favier	116
Instance of friendship in madame de Harenc	120
First representation of Dionysius the Tyrant (5th February 1748); agonies of the author	121
Complete success. Author called for on the stage for the second time	122
Meeting at madame de Harenc's to celebrate his triumph	123
He dedicates his piece to Voltaire	ib.
Death of Vauvenargue (1747); the author celebrates it in an epistle to Voltaire	ib.
His fellow lodgers; his society; madame Denis	124
Vortex into which his success throws him	125
Mademoiselle Navarre, mistress of marshal de Saxe; the author's acquaintance with her; her seduction, her charms	ib.
She invites the author to go with her to a little village in Champaign	127

CONTENTS.

	PAGE
He conceals his departure from his friends; society of madame Denis	128
Violent passions; its storms, its torments	129
He returns to Paris. A song reveals his adventure. Reproaches of his friends	132
First letters of mademoiselle Navarre	134
Uneasiness, grief, despair of the author; he falls sick; visit of the chevalier de Mirabeau	135
Visit of mademoiselle Navarre, and of the chevalier de Mirabeau; their plans; they consult the author	ib.
Uneasiness, ennui; mademoiselle Clairon consoles him	140
Revival of *Dionysius*	141
Mademoiselle Clairon	ib.
She tells him he has a successor	ib.
Mademoiselle B...., object of his first inclination, fulfils her promise of informing him before she marries	142
Madlle. Clairon wishes to be reconciled; he refuses	ib.
Aristomène	142
Duke de Duras; his kind behaviour to the author	144
He reads *Aristomène* to Voltaire	145
First representation (April 30, 1749)	146
Voltaire in the author's box	ib.
Complete success; paternal joy of Voltaire	ib.
The author again appears on the stage	147
The illness of an actor interrupts the performances	ib.
Roselli's acting in *Aristomène*	ib.
Revival; success; refuses to appear on the stage	148

BOOK IV.

Connection of the author with mademoiselle Verrières, marshal de Saxe's mistress; he gives her lessons in declamation	149
He had read *Aristomène* to marshal de Saxe	ib
Character of the marshal; his other mistresses	ib.
More intimate connection of the author with mademoiselle Verrières; anger of the marshal	150
The author renounces all connection with mademoiselle Verrières	ib.
Returns to some imprudences of conduct	151

CONTENTS.

	PAGE
Epitaph on the marshal de Saxe, who died in 1760	153
Residence of the author with M. de la Poplinière. History of the marriage of that financier	ib.
Mode of life in his house	155
The author reads *Aristomène* at the house of mademoiselle de Tencin, in the presence of Fontenelle and Montesquieu	157
He refuses to go to mademoiselle de Tencin's dinners	ib.
Guests who were there,—Fontenelle, Montesquieu, Mairan, Marivaux	158
Growing intercourse of mademoiselle Geoffrin	ib.
Rupture of M. de la Poplinière with his wife; her retirement; her unhappy end	160
Amusements, diversions, enchantments of every species, in the country-house of M. de la Poplinière	164
The author complains of so many seductions	165
He finishes his *Cleopâtra* and causes it to be played (May 20, 1750)	166
He chooses a new subject, *Les Heraclides*	167
Cabal against the success of his piece. First representation (May 24, 1752); anecdote of mademoiselle Dumenil	ib.
Acquaintance with d'Alembert, mademoiselle l'Espinasse, Diderot, Grimm, J. J. Rousseau, at the house of the baron d'Holbach	170
J. J. Rousseau; reflections on his owing his talent to the wisdom of beginning to write late	171
Cause of the favour the author received from madame de Pompadour	172
His visits to this lady with the abbé de Bernis and Duclos	173
He asks her for a place in a public office	ib.
She engages him in new dramatic attempts	ib.
He takes for a subject *Les Funerailles de Sesostris*	174
Toilet of madame de Pompadour. Anecdote	ib.
Downfall of his piece (1753)	175
He informs madame de Pompadour, who, to console him, proposes a place to him	176
He accepts it, and quits M. de la Poplinière; affectionate regrets of the latter	ib.
A fresh glance on the brilliant society of M. de la Poplinière	177
The count (since prince) de Kaunitz	ib.

CONTENTS.

	PAGE
Lord Albemarle	178
His mistress Lolotte (model of the Shepherdess of the Alps)	179
History of Lolotte after the death of his lordship; her marriage; her griefs; her sad end	ib.
Madame de Tencin; her disposition, her wit, her conversations, her advice, her maxims	181
Rameau. The author writes for him *Acanthe et Cephise* (1751)	183
La Guirland et les Sybarites (idem)	184
Forsaken by Rameau for Italian music	ib.
Fellowship of the comptrollers of the private expenses, Cury, Thibon	185
Geliote; his talents, his success in every department	ib.
Contrast of these fellowships with those of the philosophers	187
Voltaire; his sensibility on the occasion of the death of madame Duchâtelet. His mobility.	188
Desire of Voltaire to be a courtier	189
Voltaire succeeds with madame de Pompadour	190
He never can please the king	ib.
They oppose Crébillon to him	191
Madame de Pompadour obtains a pension of a hundred louis for Crébillon; he comes to thank her. Anecdote	192
Representation of *Catiline* (Crébillon's) December 10, 1748. Voltaire wishes to re-write all the pieces of Crébillon	193
Semiramis (played August 29, 1748)	194
Oreste (played January 12, 1750)	195
Rome Sauvée, (played February 24, 1752)	ib.
Voltaire experiences some disagreeables, the true motives of his journey to Prussia	ib.
Difficulty concerning the expenses of the journey	ib.
Amusing fury of Voltaire	196
Another anecdote	197
Voltaire departs (June 1750) displeased with Louis XV.	199
The author goes to settle at Versailles; he enters upon a more calm life	ib.

BOOK V.

The author, on arriving at Versailles, goes to thank madame de Pompadour	200

	PAGE
Portrait of M. de Marigny. The author's intercourse with him	ib.
Admirable firmness of M. de Marigny in the discharge of the duties of his situation	201
Life of the author while at Versailles, Fontainbleau, Compeigne. His new studies in literature	203
Gaming of the king at Marly	204
Society of the author at Versailles. The abbé Delaville	205
The first commissary of war, Dubois, Cromot, madame Filleul, Bouret	ib.
Marriage of Marmontel's eldest sister with M. Odde	206
Bouret obtains a place for his brother-in-law	207
Madame de Pompadour promises him another place for M. Odde. She forgets her promise; the author compels her to keep it	209
His connection with madame de Chalut; influence of this lady with the dauphiness, who loved her tenderly	210
The author never asks her for anything	211
He composes some verses on the convalescence of the dauphin	212
He attends the dinners of the prince and princess, who wish to thank him, yet dare not	212
The author causes a daughter of the marshal de Saxe to be acknowledged	213
Madame de Pompadour's physician, Quesnay	214
Dedication of the work of Patulo the Irishman	ib.
Noble action of Quesnay	215
The countess d'Estrade	ib.
Intrigue of M. d'Argenson to give the king a mistress	216
Dinners at Quesnay's with Diderot, Helvétius	217
Madame de Marchais (since madame d'Angiviller); her portrait; her eulogium; her society	ib.
M. d'Angiviller. His conduct towards his wife before and after his marriage	128
Alteration in the art of declamation effected by mademoiselle Clairon	220
Fresh observations on the connections of the author with M. de Marigny	222
Impolicy of the government in keeping Voltaire in exile	223
The author demands an audience of madame de Pompadour, and gives her some patriotic advice	224

CONTENTS.

	PAGE
The abbé (since cardinal) de Bernis	227
His first connection with madame de Pompadour	229
His success in every department	ib.
He employs the author in an important affair	230
He offers him his services	ib.
Remark of an old commissary on the abbé de Bernis when he became minister for foreign affairs	231
Project of working on the archives of this department	ib.
The minister appears much pleased with it, and forgets the author	232
Singular disease, singularly cured	233
The author is consulted concerning the pensions of the *Mercure*	237
He is the cause of the privilege of this journal being given to Boissy	ib.
Lively gratitude on the part of the latter	238
He has recourse to the author. Origin of the *Contes Moraux*	240
Death of Boissy. The commission of the *Mercure* is granted to the author	ib.
The count de Gisors offers him a place; he proposes it to his friend Suard, who refuses it	241
This place is given to Delaire. Death of the count de Gisors	242
The author resigns his secretaryship; he returns to Paris, and lodges at the house of madame de Geoffrin	243

BOOK VI.

Of what the *Mercure* was composed; plan of the author to rearrange it; his prospectus; his principles of criticism. First attempts of the abbé Delille, Thomas, Mafilatre, Lemierre, &c.	244
Literary correspondence with the provinces	247
Departments of arts and sciences in the *Mercure*	ib.
Saloon of arts, 1759	248
Eulogiums on great men, proposed as subjects for the prizes of the French Academy	ib.
Prospectus of the provincial Academies	249
Defence of the stage. Answer to J. J. Rousseau	ib.

CONTENTS.

	PAGE
Gallet. Panard; his talent, his disposition, his manner of life	250
Madame Geoffrin; her disposition, her prudence, her varied society, her maxims, her principles	252
D'Alembert. Mairan	256
Marivaux	257
Chastellux	ib.
The abbé Morellet	258
St Lambert	ib.
Helvétius	ib.
Thomas	259
Mademoiselle Lespinasse	260
The abbé Raynal	ib.
The abbé Galiani	262
Carracioli	ib.
The count de Creutz	263
Behaviour of the author towards madame Geoffrin	264
The dinner of artists at the house of madame Geoffrin Carle Vanloo, Vernet, Soufflot, Boucher, Lemoine, Latour	265
The count de Caylus	266
Suppers at the house of madame Geoffrin, with mesdames de Brionne, de Duras, d'Egmont, the prince Louis de Rohan. There the author reads the sketch of his Tales	267
The society is much freer at the house of Pelletier	270
The 'Gentil' Bernard	271
Cury; his country seat; his quarrel with the gentlemen of the bedchamber	273
Parody on Cinna, written by Cury against the duke d'Aumont. Great event in the life of the author	276
The author recites it at a party at the house of madame Geoffrin	278
They accuse him of having written it. He writes to the duke d'Aumont. He obtains an audience of the duke de Choiseul; he justifies himself, but refuses to name him who actually wrote the parody	279
He is sent to the Bastille. His entrance into and residence in this prison	282
Eulogium of M. Abadie, the governor	287
Inscriptions on the walls of the Bastille	288
Event which renders the author very uneasy	ib.

	PAGE
He receives a letter from mademoiselle S., (since madame San...), to whom he was to have been married	289
They announce to him his enlargement on the eleventh day	290
First visit to his friends: to madame Geoffrin; she scolds him, repents of it, and evinces much sensibility	ib.
Interview of the author with the duke de Choiseul, in which he makes his defence; very affecting discourse. M de Choiseul wishes to serve him	ib.
The author sees madame de Pompadour; who also shows him some kindness; but the *Mercure* is is taken from him	293
What the duke de Choiseul said to the author on this subject ten years afterwards	300

BOOK VII.

Recapitulation. Effects of the late events. Fortune of the author produced by what he imagined would have ruined it	301
His situation; that of his family	302
They propose to him, while dining, a journey to Bourdeaux, to which he immediately consents	ib
Details of this journey. Manners of the inhabitants of Bourdeaux	304
Ansley, the philosophic merchant	306
Digression on Lefranc de Pompignan	307
In returning to Paris, the author completes the tour of the south of France, Toulouse, Beziers	ib.
The canal of Languedoc	309
He meets at Beziers with an old Parisian acquaintance	312
Digression on his last intercourse with M. de la Poplinière	ib.
Montpellier. Nismes. Avignon. Vaucluse. The isle of Aix; reception by the governor. Marseilles. Toulon	314
Procession of the king René to Aix	317
M. de Monclar	ib.
Arrival at Ferney; residence with Voltaire	318
Anecdotes; conversations; reading. The Genevese	319

xii CONTENTS.

	PAGE
Digression on J. J. Rousseau. Conversation with Voltaire. Anecdote of the first discourse of Jean-Jacques	322
Château de Tornay	324
The author speaks of Voltaire; of madame de Pompadour	325
He reads *Tancrède*, which Voltaire had just finished	ib.
Last evening spent at Ferney. Affecting farewell	326
Return to Paris. Enemies of the author	328
History of the academic meetings, where the *Epître aux Poëtes* was crowned (in 1760)	ib.
The author publishes his *Pharsalie* (in 1760)	330
Origin of the story of *Annette et Lubin*	ib.
Divers country seats where the author passes the summer. Malmaison. Croix Fontaine. Sainte Assise. Saint Cloud	331
Family of madame de Montulé. Tender friendship of madame de Chalut	332
Generosity of Bouret	334
Madame Gaulard drawn in one of the *Contes de la Veillée*	ib.
The author passes a whole year at Maisons, the country seat of this lady. What detained him there	335
Impatience of his friends on account of his indifference with regard to his reception at the French Academy	ib.
Origin of M. de Praslin's hatred for the author	336
That minister endeavours to remove him from the Academy	ib.
The author tries to secure the consent of the king	337
He pays the customary visits on the death of Marivaux (in 1763)	ib.
He retires, on hearing that the abbé Radouvilliers was his competitor	338
Anecdote of a ballot for an election at the French Academy	ib.
The author dedicates his *Poëtique* to the king	340
D'Alembert is reconciled with Duclos, that he may secure the author's election	341
They wish to oppose Thomas to him	343
Generous conduct of Thomas. The author is chosen at the French Academy in 1763	344

EDITOR'S PREFACE.

The general character of the Memoirs of Marmontel is so well known, that little in the way of preface is necessary to the early introduction of a new edition in the present collection. Of that class of autobiography, the charm of which is universally acknowledged, they advance a claim to priority on the double ground of their own attraction, and the fact that the remnant of the last edition in four volumes, is becoming scarce. In respect to the first of these points, it is scarcely necessary to say that the genius of Marmontel especially adapted him for that light, easy, mild, yet pointed species of narrative and portrait painting, which form the distinctive features of his Memoirs, and render them so delightful. Immersed, as this ingenious and industrious writer was, in the high tide of Parisian society, his mind was yet deeply imbued with the primary elements of both the morals and the affections, a tendency which has enabled him to throw an air of most attractive simplicity over the very piquant communications of a veteran man of the world. The same amenity and chastened humour which adorn his Tales, are predominant in his account of his own life; and while his details exhibit little of those deep ploughings up of the bosom, which, in the manner of the ancient sacrifices, expose the palpitating heart of the victim to minute inspection and general gaze, they form an exquisitely pleasing sketch of the life of a French man of letters, during the variegated era which immediately preceded the revolution. Possibly no other source of information can vie with this narrative of Marmontel, in affording a due notice of the genuine *savoir-vivre* of the French capital, in respect to the easy intercourse between science and literature, and rank and opulence, which, at the period alluded to, had become systematised into its principal distinction. In society thus modified, all eminent men must necessarily be acquainted with each other; and hence a spirit in the French literary etching of character, which is scarcely to be in any other manner obtained. Marmontel is peculiarly happy in this way; and, when it is recollected that he himself was one of the latest members of the Voltairean circle, the materials for the exercise of his skill must be regarded as abundantly ample. At the same time, while forming no part of his direct object to develop the springs which led to the momentous event of the revolution, he throws innumerable incidental lights on the gross and excessive corruption of morals and of manners in the court and the capital of France, which, added to weak and unprincipled government, and the searching exposure of intellect, rendered it inevitable. The opening of that grand conflict of human interests and passions, is also traced with a light but skilful hand; and, to conclude, in respect both to information and entertainment, few works of a similar unpretending nature excel the Memoirs of Marmontel, or will more certainly take their place on the most frequented bookshelf of the general reader, for many ages to come.

MEMOIRS

OF THE

LIFE OF MARMONTEL.

BOOK I.

It is for my children that I write the history of my life : it was their mother's wish. Should it meet the eyes of a stranger, let him pardon details which to him must appear minute and trifling, but which to them I think necessary. It may be useful to my children to collect the lessons that time, opportunity, example, and the various scenes through which I have passed, have afforded me. I could wish them to learn from me never to despair of their own powers, but never to be too confident of success ; to fear the rocks of good fortune, and to pass with courage the straits of adversity.

I have had an advantage over them in being born in a place where inequality of birth and fortune were scarcely felt. A small property, some industry, or some small trade, constituted the chief wealth of the inhabitants of Bort ; a little town in Limosin, where I was born. Mediocrity prevailed, not riches : for here all were free and usefully employed. Thus the independence, frankness, and native nobility of the mind were perverted by no servile manners; for no where was stupid pride worse received, or sooner corrected. Hence I may say that, during my childhood, although born in obscurity, I knew only my equals; and hence perhaps a little stiffness arose, which has ever made a part of my character, and which even reason and age have never sufficiently softened.

Bort, seated on the Dordogne between Auvergne and Limosin, presents at the first view a fearful picture to the traveller, who, at a distance, from the top of the hill, sees it at the bottom of a precipice threatened with inundation by the torrents that the storms occasion, or with instant annihilation by a chain of volcanic rocks, some planted like towers on the height that commands the town, and others already hanging and half torn from their base. But Bort assumes an aspect more gay, as these fears are dissipated, and the eye extends itself along the valley. On the verdant island, that lies beyond the town, surrounded by the stream, and animated by the noise and motion of a mill, is a grove filled with birds. On each bank of the river, orchards, meadows, and cornfields, cultivated by a laborious people, form the varied landscape. Below the town, the valley opens, presenting on one side an extensive meadow watered by continual springs, and on the other fields crowned by a circle of hills, whose gentle slope forms a pleasing contrast with the opposite rocks. Farther on, this circle is broken by a torrent, which, descending from the mountains, rolls and bounds through forests, among rocks, and over precipices, till it falls into the Dordogne, by one of the most beautiful cataracts of the continent, both for the volume of water, and the height of its fall; a phenomenon which only wants more frequent spectators to be renowned and admired. It is near this cataract that the little farm of St Thomas lies, where I used to read Virgil under the shade of the blossoming trees that surrounded our bee-hives, and where their honey afforded me many a delicious repast. It is on the other side of the town, beyond the mill, and on the slope of the mountain, that the garden lies, where, on welcome holidays, my father used to lead me to gather grapes from the vines which he himself had planted, or cherries, plums, and apples, from the trees he had grafted. But the principal charm that my native village has left on my memory arises from the vivid impression I still retain of the first feelings with which my soul was imbued and penetrated, by the inexpressible tenderness that my parents showed me. If I have any kindness in my character, I am persuaded that I owe it to these gentle emotions; to the habitual happiness of loving and being loved. Ah! what a gift do we receive from heaven, when we are blessed with kind, affectionate parents!

I also owed much to a certain amenity of manners that then distinguished my native place; and indeed the simple, gentle life we led there must have had some attraction, since nothing was more rare than to see it deserted by the natives. Their youth were well instructed, and their colony held a distinguished rank in the neighbouring schools: but they returned again to their town, like a swarm of bees to the hive, with the sweets they had collected. I learned to read in a little convent of nuns, the good friends of my mother. They taught only girls; but in my favour they made an exception to this rule. A lady of birth, who had long lived retired in this convent, had the kindness to take care of me. I ought indeed to cherish her memory, and that of the nuns, who loved me as their child. I passed from the convent to the school of a priest in town, who voluntarily, and without any gratuity, had devoted himself to the instruction of children. The only son of a shoemaker, and the worthiest man in the world this divine was a true model of filial piety. How well do I recollect the becoming respect and mutual attentions that this old man and his son had for each other; the former never forgetting the dignity of the priesthood, nor the latter the sanctity of the paternal character. The abbé Vaissière (this was his name) after having fulfilled his duties at church, divided the rest of his time between reading and the lessons he gave us. A short walk, when it was fine, for exercise, or amusement with a game at bandy in the meadow, were his sole recreations. He was serious, severe, and of an imposing countenance. Two friends, men much esteemed in our town, were his only companions. They continued to live together in the most peaceful intimacy, meeting every day, and finding each other every day the same, without change, without diminution in the pleasure of each other's society: and, to crown all, they died nearly at the same period. I have scarcely seen an example of so mild and constant an equality in the course of human life.

At this school I had a schoolfellow, who, from my infancy, was an object of my emulation. His sage and steady air, his application to study, the care he took of his books, in which I never saw a single spot, his fair hair always so well combed, his coat always clean in its simplicity, his linen always white, were for me an impressive example; and one child rarely inspires another with the esteem I had for him. His name was Durant; his father, a labourer in a neighbouring village, was acquainted with mine: I used to walk to see him with his son. How kindly he received us, the good old grey-headed man! the delicious cream, the sweet milk, the excellent brown bread he gave us! and the happy omens he was pleased to say he saw in my respect for his age! Still could I delight to scatter flowers on his grave! His ashes ought to sleep in peace, for his life was spent in doing good. Twenty years afterwards, his son and I, pursuing very different routes, met at Paris, and I recognised in him the same sage and correct character that distinguished him at school: I stood godfather to one of his children, which was no trivial satisfaction. Let us return to my early years.

My Latin lessons were interrupted by a singular accident. I had a great desire to learn, but nature had refused me the gift of memory. I had enough to retain the sense of what I read; but the words left no traces on my mind: I took infinite pains to fix them there, but it was like writing on a quicksand. I obstinately endeavoured by perseverance to supply the defect; and this labour exceeded the powers of my age, so that my nerves were affected. I became unable to take proper rest: in the night, when fast asleep, I used to sit up in my bed, and, with my eyes half open, repeat aloud the lessons I had learned. He will be mad, said my father to my mother, if you do not make him leave off that unfortunate Latin; and I refrained from the study: but at the expiration of eight or ten months it was resumed; and, when I had completed my eleventh year, my master, thinking me sufficiently advanced to be admitted into the fourth class, my father consented, though with regret, to take me himself to the school of Mauriac, which was the nearest to Bort.

This regret of my father was that of a prudent man, which it is my duty to show. I was the eldest of a great number of children: my father, a little severe, but essentially kind, under a rough and stern exterior, loved his wife to adoration: and with reason; my tender mother was the worthiest and most interesting of women, and truly amiable in her family. I never could imagine how, with the simple education of our little convent at Bort, she had acquired so much polish of mind with such elevation of soul, and, particularly in her language and style, a feeling of propriety so just, so delicate, so refined, that it appeared in her to be the pure instinct of taste. My good bishop of Limoges, the virtuous Coetlosquet, has often spoken to me, at Paris, with the tenderest interest, of the letters my mother had written to him to recommend me to his kindness.

My father had no less veneration than love for her. His only cause of reproach was her weakness for me, and this weakness had one excuse : I was the only one of her children that she had suckled ; her ill health did not again permit her to fulfil so sweet a duty. Her mother was not less fond of me ; I think I now see the good little old woman : what a charming temper! what sweet and smiling gaiety ! She was the housekeeper, the mistress of the family, and gave us all an example of filial tenderness; for she too had a mother and her husband's mother, on whom she lavished her attentions. I am going rather far back when I talk of my great-grandmothers, but I well remember that, at the age of eighty, they were still living, drinking their glass of wine by the fireside, and recollecting old times, of which they told us wonders.

Add to the family three sisters of my grandmother, and an aunt, the sister of my mother, who is still living: my father was the only man, among all these women, and a swarm of children.

The property on which we all subsisted was very small. Order, domestic arrangement, labour, a little trade, and frugality, kept us above want. Our little garden produced nearly as many vegetables as the consumption of the family required : the orchard afforded us fruit ; and our quinces, our apples, and our pears, preserved with the honey of our bees, were, in winter, most exquisite breakfasts for the good old women and children. They were clothed by the small flock of sheep, that folded at St Thomas. My aunts spun the wool and the hemp of the field that furnished us with linen; and on the evenings, when by the light of a lamp, supplied with oil by our nut trees, the young people of the neighbourhood came to help us to dress our flax, the picture was exquisite. The harvest of the little farm secured us subsistence; the wax and honey of the bees, to which one of my aunts carefully attended, formed a revenue that cost but little; the oil pressed from our green walnuts had a taste and smell that we preferred to the flavour and perfume of that of the olive. Our buckwheat cakes, moistened, smoking hot, with the good butter of Mont d'Or, were a delicious treat to us. I know not what dish would have appeared to us better than our turnips and our chesnuts; and on a winter evening, while these fine turnips were roasting round the fire, and we heard the water boiling in the vase where our chesnuts were cooking, so relishing and so sweet, how did our hearts palpitate with joy! I well remember too the perfume that a fine quince used to exhale when roasting under the ashes, and the pleasure our grandmother used to have in dividing it among us. The most moderate of women made us all gluttons. Thus, in a family where nothing was lost, trivial objects united made plenty, and left but little to expend in order to satisfy all our wants. In the neighbouring forests, there was an abundance of dead wood, of little value; there my father was permitted to make his annual provision. The excellent butter of the mountain, and the most delicate cheese, were common and cost but little; wine was not dear, and my father himself drank of it soberly.

But however, though extremely moderate, the expense of the house did not fail to be nearly the measure of our little revenue; and, when the time came to place me at college, my father dreaded the expense of my education; beside he considered the time that was given to study as but ill employed: he used to say that Latin only made sluggards. Perhaps too he had some presentiment of the misfortunes we afterwards experienced when deprived of him by a premature death; and, by making me early embrace a profession the utility of which would be less tardy and less uncertain, he might hope to leave in me a second father to his children. Yet, pressed by my mother, who was passionately desirous that at least her eldest son should receive a classical education, he consented to take me to the school at Mauriac.

Loaded with caresses, bathed with gentle tears, and breathing endless benedictions, I sat out with my father: I rode behind him, and my heart beat with joy; but it beat too with alarm when my father said to me: " They have promised me, my dear boy, that you shall be admitted into the fourth class; if you are not, I shall bring you back again, and all will be over." Judge how I trembled when I appeared before the master who was to decide my fate! Fortunately, it was the good father Malosse, to whose kindness I am so much indebted: there was in his look, in the sound of his voice, and in his physiognomy, a character of benevolence so natural, and so feeling, that his first approach announced a friend to the stranger who addressed him. After having received us with graceful suavity, and invited my father to come back and learn the success of the examination I was about to undergo, seeing me still timid, he began by encouraging me; he then gave me a trial exercise; but this, alas! abounded in difficulties that were to me insoluble. I did it ill; and after having read it, " My good boy," said he, " you are very far from being fit to enter this class; you will even find it difficult to be admitted into the fifth." I began to cry. " Then I am lost," answered I: " my father has no desire to let me continue my studies; he has brought me hither only out of complaisance to my mother, and declared to me on the road that, if I were not admitted into the fourth class, he would take me home again: that would be very hard on me, and very afflicting to my mother. Ah! for pity's sake, take me; I promise you, good father, to study so hard that you shall shortly be fully satisfied with me." The master, affected by my tears and my ardour, admitted me; and told my father not to be unhappy about me, for he was sure I should do well.

I was lodged, as was the custom of the school, with five other scholars, at the house of an honest mechanic; and my father, sad enough to return without me, left me there with my packet and provisions for the week: these provisions consisted in a large loaf of rye bread, a little cheese, a piece of bacon, and two or three pounds of beef; my mother had added to them a dozen apples. This was the weekly provision of the best-fed scholars of the school. The mistress of the house cooked for us, and for her trouble, her fire, her lamp, her beds, her house-room, and even including the vegetables of her little garden which she used for our soup, we gave her twelve pence halfpenny a piece per month.; so that reckoning everything, except my clothes, I might cost my father between four and five pounds a year. This was much to him, and an expense of which I was very anxious to see him relieved. The day after my arrival, as I was going in the morning to my lesson, I saw my master at his window, who beckoned to me to his chamber. "My son," said he, "you have need of private instruction and much study, to overtake your fellow students: let us begin with the elements, and come hither half an hour before lectures, every morning, to repeat the rules you have learned; in explaining them to you, I will point out their use." On that day, also, I wept; but it was with gratitude, when, returning thanks for his kindness, I entreated him to add that of sparing me, for some time, the humiliation of hearing my exercises read aloud in the lecture room. He granted my request, and I went to my studies.

I cannot express with what tender zeal he undertook the care of instructing me, or the charm he had the art of giving to his lessons. At the bare name of my mother, of whom I sometimes spoke, he seemed to breathe her very soul; and, when I communicated the letters, in which maternal love expressed its gratitude to him, the tears have flowed from his eyes.

From the month of October, in which we then were, to the Easter holidays, there was neither amusement nor relaxation for me; but after that half year, familiar with all the rules, firm in their application, and as it were disengaged from the thorns of syntax, I proceeded with more freedom. After that period, I was one of the best scholars in the class, and perhaps the happiest; for I loved my task, and, almost certain of doing it tolerably well, it was only a recreation. The choice of words and their appropriate use, in translating from one language to another, with even some elegance in the construction of phrases, began already to occupy my mind; and this study, which necessarily induces us to analyze our ideas, fortified my memory. I perceived it was the associations attached to a word that fixed it in my mind; and reflection made me soon feel that the study of languages is also the study of the art of discriminating the shades of ideas, of decomposing them, of forming their texture, and of seizing with precision their characters and their relations. I perceived, that with new words new thoughts were introduced and developed in the young mind; and that our classical lectures were a course of elementary philosophy, much more rich, more extensive, and more eminently useful than those persons imagine, who complain that nothing is taught in schools but Latin.

This exercise of the mind in the study of languages was remarked to me by a man to whom my master had recommended me. Father Bourges, an old jesuit, was the person: he was one of the best Latin scholars of his time. Charged with continuing and completing the work of father Vanière, in his poetical Latin dictionary, he had humbly asked to teach the fifth class in this little school in the mountains of Auvergne. He took an interest in my improvement, and invited me to come to him on holidays. You will easily believe I did not fail, and he had the kindness to dedicate occasionally whole hours to my instruction. Alas! the only service I could render him was to wait on him at mass; but that was a merit in his eyes, and for the following reason.

When this good old man was praying, he was perpetually anxious lest his attention should be diverted from his prayers; which he could only prevent by a most painful attention of mind. While saying mass, he exerted every effort to fix his thoughts on each sentence he pronounced; and, when he came to the words of the sacrifice, drops of sweat fell from his bald forehead as he bowed. I have seen his whole body tremble with respect and terror, as if he had beheld the roof of heaven open, and the living God descend. Never was there an example of a more lively and profound faith: so that, by the performance of this sacred duty, he was almost exhausted. He used to revive himself with the pleasure he had in teaching me, and with that which I felt in receiving his instructions. He it was who instructed me in ancient literature, that inexhaustible source of riches and beauty, and who inspired me with a thirst for it that sixty years of study have not yet extinguished. Thus, in an obscure school, had I the good fortune to be guided in my pursuits by one of the most learned men that perhaps the world knew: but this was an advantage I did not long enjoy; father Bourges was removed, and six years afterwards I found him in a monastery at Toulouse, infirm and almost abandoned. What an odious vice, in the institutions and customs of the jesuits, was that of forsaking and neglecting their aged members! The most laborious of men, he who had been longest useful, as soon as he ceased to be so, was rejected as refuse; a cruelty as extravagant as inhuman, among beings all of whom are hastening to age, and by whom each in his turn must thus be repulsed.

With respect to our school, it was particularly characterised by a police, which the scholars themselves exercised. Those who lodged in the same chamber consisted of scholars of different classes, and among them the authority of age or talent, naturally established, put order and rule into our studies and our manners. Thus the boy, who, far from his family, appeared, when out of school, to be abandoned to himself, did not fail to find monitors and censors among his fellow students. They studied together round the same table; it was a circle of witnesses, who, under each other's eye, reciprocally imposed silence and attention. The idler wearied himself with mute immobility, and was soon tired of his indolence: the dull boy, if diligent, was pitied, aided, encouraged; if they could not admire his talents, they esteemed his willingness; but there was neither pity nor indulgence for the incurable sluggard; and, if all who lodged in the same chamber were affected with this vice, they became dishonoured; the whole school despised them, and parents were advised not to put their children there. The inhabitants themselves had therefore a great interest in lodging only studious boys; and I have seen some turned away solely for their indolence and want of discipline. Thus in scarcely one of these groups of children was idleness tolerated; never did amusement or recreation precede study.

A custom, which I have never seen but in this school, gave, toward the end of the year, redoubled fervour to our studies. To rise from one class to another, it was necessary to undergo a severe examition, and one of the tasks we had to accomplish, was a work of memory. According to the class, in poetry, some lines of Phædrus, Ovid, Virgil, or Horace, were to be studied; and, in prose, parts of

Cicero, of Livy, of Quintus Curtius, or of Sallust: the whole, to be retained by rote, formed a very considerable mass of study. We began it long before the examination, and, that it might not trench on our usual studies, it employed us from daylight to the morning's lesson. We used to learn it in the fields, where, divided into bands, each his book in his hand, we went humming along like swarms of bees. It is painful, in early youth, to tear ourselves from the morning's sleep; but the most diligent of the band roused the more tardy: I myself have frequently been pulled from my bed, while still asleep; and, if I have since had a little more suppleness and docility in my memory, I owe it to this exercise.

Our scholastic habits were not less distinguished by a spirit of order and domestic economy than by a taste for study. The new comers, however young, learned from the elder boys to be careful of their clothes, their linen, their books, and their provisions. All the morsels of bacon, beef, or mutton, that were put into the boiler, were neatly strung, like the beads of a chaplet; and, if, in the mixture, any debates arose, the mistress of the house decided. As to the more delicate bits that on certain festivals were sent us by our families, the treat was common; and those who received nothing were not the less invited to partake. I recollect with pleasure the delicate attention that the more fortunate of our little troop always observed, to prevent the others from feeling this afflicting inequality. When one of these presents arrived, the mistress of the house announced it to us, but she was forbidden to name him who had received it, and he himself would have blushed to have made the boast. This modest caution was the admiration of my mother, when I told it her. Our amusements were chosen from ancient games: in winter, on the ice, and amid the snow; in fine weather, far out in the country, in the heat of the sun; and neither racing, wrestling, boxing, nor the game of quoits, nor the sling, nor the art of swimming, were strangers to us. In the heat of summer, we used to go and bathe more than a league from the town: to the little boys, searching for cray-fish in the rivulets, and to the great, fishing for eel and trout in the rivers, or catching quails with nets after harvest, were our most lively pleasures; and, on our return from a long ramble, woe to the fields where the green peas were yet to be gathered. Not one of us could have been guilty of stealing a pin; but, in our moral code, it had passed into a maxim that what could be eaten was no theft. I abstained as much as possible from this species of pillage; but, when I did not co-operate, it still is true that I shared, first in contributing my contingent of bacon for cooking the peas, and afterward in eating them with all the accomplices. To do like the rest appeared to me a duty, from which I dared not deviate; but I capitulated afterward, with my confessor, by restoring my part of the theft in alms.

I perceived, however, in a class above mine, a boy whose prudence and virtue were unalterable, and I owned to myself that the good example ought to be followed; but, while I regarded him with the eyes of envy, I did not dare to suppose I had the right like him to make myself singular. Amalvy had so many titles to consideration in the school, and was so far superior to us all, that the kind of distance at which he left us was considered as just and natural. In this rare youth, all the excellencies of mind and heart appeared to have been united, to render him perfect. Nature had given him that exterior which it seems should only be reserved for merit. His countenance was mild, yet noble, his figure tall, his deportment grave, his air serious, yet serene. I used to see him enter the school perpetually surrounded by some of his school-fellows, who were proud to be in his company Sociable, yet not too familiar, he never divested himself of that dignity which arose from the long habit of surpassing his fellows. The cross, which was the mark of this priority, never quitted his button-hole; of this no one dared pretend to deprive him. I held him in admiration: to look on him was to me a pleasure; and, as often as I saw him, I returned dissatisfied with myself. Not that I was not sufficiently distinguished in my class, from the time I entered the third: but I had two or three rivals; Amalvy had none. I had by no means acquired that invariable success which astonished us in his compositions; and I had still less of that facile and sure memory with which Amalvy was gifted. He was older than I; this was my only consolation: and my ambition was to equal him when I should arrive at his age. In analyzing as much as possible what used to pass in my mind, I may say with truth that this sentiment of emulation was unmixed with any malignant thought of envy; I was not sorry that an Almalvy existed, but I would have prayed to heaven that there might be two, and that I might be the second.

The spirit of religion, which was carefully maintained in the school, was an advantage still more precious than emulation. How salutary a preservative, for the morals of youth, is the custom and obligation of going every month to confession! That modest, chaste, and humble avowal of our most secret faults prevented perhaps a greater number of them than all the most holy motives.

It was then at Mauriac, from the age of eleven to fifteen, that I pursued my classical studies; and in rhetoric I almost habitually kept my place as first in my class. At this, my kind mother was charmed; and, when my dimity waistcoats were returned to her, she eagerly looked to see whether the silver chain that used to suspend the cross had blackened my buttonhole: if she perceived that mark of my triumph, all the mothers of the neighbourhood were told of her joy; our good nuns returned thanks to heaven; and my dear abbé Vassière shone with resplendent glory. The dearest of my recollections to this hour, is that of the happiness I gave my mother; but I had as much care to dissemble my griefs as I had pleasure in telling her of my success; for I had some sorrows that were vivid enough to have afflicted her, if the least complaint had escaped me. Such was the dispute I had, when in the third class, with Father Bis, the head master of the school, about the dance of Auvergne; and such was the danger I ran of being flogged, when in the second class, and in that of rhetoric, once for having dictated a good theme, and another time for having been to see some clock-work. Fortunately, I extricated myself from these errors without accident, and even with some glory.

It is well known what envious malignity favourites attract at the courts of kings: it is the same at schools. The particular care that the master of the fourth class had taken of me, and my assiduity in going to see him every morning, made my companions look on me with a jealous and suspicious eye; and from that time I made it my study to show myself a better and more faithful comrade than any of those who accused me of not being so, and who chose to distrust me. When I afterward became frequently the first of my class, a dignity to which the unwelcome office of censor was attached, I made it a rule to mitigate my censure; and, in the master's absence, during the half hour I presided singly, I began by granting a moderate liberty: they used to talk, laugh, and amuse themselves without being noisy, and my notes said nothing. This indulgence, which made me beloved, became every day more extended. Licence succeeded liberty, and I suffered it; I did more, I encouraged it; such was the charm that public favour had for me. I had been told, that at Rome the rich who were desirous of gaining the multitude gave them public shows; it took my fancy to imitate them. One of our school-fellows, whose name was Toury, was mentioned to me as the best performer of the Auvergnian dance that the mountains could boast; I gave him leave to dance, and certainly he made some marvellous jumps. When they had once tasted the pleasure of seeing him bound in the middle of the school-room, they could not be contented without it; and I, more and more obliging, called again for the dance. It must be observed, that the wooden shoes of the dancer were capped with iron, and that the room was laid with slabs of stone that resounded like brass. The master, who was going his rounds, heard this prodigious noise; he hastened to us; but the noise instantaneously ceased, and each was in his place; Toury himself in his corner, his eyes fixed on his book, only presented an image of heavy immobility. The master, boiling with rage, came to me, and demanded the note: no note was written. Judge of his impatience: finding no one to punish, he made me suffer the pains of the guilty by the tasks he gave me. I submitted without complaining; and he found me as docile and as patient in what concerned me personally, as he had found me resolute and obstinate in not giving pain to my companions. My courage was sustained by the honour of hearing myself called the martyr and even sometimes the hero of my class. It is true that, in the second class, the liberty I gave became less noisy, and the resentment of the headmaster appeared to soften: but in the midst of the calm, I felt myself assailed by a new storm.

Father Malosse, who had been so fond of me, was no longer master of the second class: it was one father Cibier, as dry and as sour as the other was engaging and gentle. Without much talent, and I believe without much learning, Cibier did not fail to conduct his class well enough. He had singularly the art of exciting our emulation, by provoking our jealousy. If an inferior scholar did at all better than usual, he extolled him with such an air as to make the best fearful of a new rival. It was in this spirit that, recollecting one day a certain theme that an indifferent scholar was said to have composed, he defied us all to equal it. Now it was known who had written this theme, which was so excessively praised. It was kept secret, because it was severely forbidden in the class to do the exercise of another. But the impatience at hearing borrowed merit commended to excess could not contain itself: "The theme, father, that you are thus extolling to us, is not his own," cried some one. "And whose is it then?" asked he angrily. All were silent. "It is you then who must tell me, continued he," addressing himself to the boy who was saying his lesson: he cried and named me. I was forced to confess my fault, but I begged the master to hear me, and he listened. "It was," said I, "on St Peter's day, his birth-day, that Duriff, our school-fellow, invited us to dine with him: entirely occupied with feasting his friends, he had not been able to finish the duties of his class, and he was most truly anxious about his theme. I thought it allowable and just to spare him the pains, and I offered to employ myself for him while he employed himself for us."

There were at least two in the fault; the master would see but one, and his anger fell upon me. Confused, mad with rage, he ordered the corrector to be called to flog me, as he said I deserved: at the name of the corrector, I made up my packet of books and was going to quit the school. From this time my studies were at an end, and my destiny assumed a new character. But that sentiment of natural justice, which in early youth is so lively and so prompt, did not permit my companions to leave me abandoned. No, exclaimed the whole class, this punishment would be unjust, and if they oblige him to go away, we will all go. The master was appeased, and pardoned me; but he pardoned me in the name of the class, and justified himself by the example of the dictator Papirius. All the school approved his clemency, with the exception of the head-master, who maintained that it was an act of weakness, and that nothing should ever be yielded to rebellion. He himself, a year afterward, wanted to exert over me the rigour that he had made his law; but he learned that justice at least should precede severity.

We had but one month more to employ in the study of rhetoric, in order to be wholly released from his authority, when he found me in the list of boys that he was about to punish for a fault devoid of probability, and of which I was wholly innocent. In the tower of the Benedictines, two steps from the school, the clock was under repair: curious to see its mechanism, some boys from the different classes went up the tower. Owing to the unskilfulness of the workmen, or to some accident of which I am ignorant, the clock did not go. It would have been as difficult for children to have deranged those massive wheels of iron as for mice to have eaten them away: but the clock-maker accused them of it, and the head-master received his complaint. The day after, at the hour of the evening lesson, he sent for me: I went to his chamber; I found there ten or twelve of the scholars ranged in a line around the wall, and in the middle the corrector and this terrible master, who had them successively flogged. On seeing me, he asked me if I were of the number of those who had gone up to the clock; and having answered that I was, he pointed out my place in the circle of my accomplices, and turned to continue his cruelty. You will easily believe that my resolution to escape was soon formed. I took the opportunity when he was holding one of his victims, who struggled with him, suddenly to open the door and run. He rushed forward to catch me, but missed his prey, and I escaped with a rent in my coat.

I took refuge in the school-room of my class, whither the master was not yet come; and my torn coat, my confusion, with the alarm or rather the indignation that inspired me, served instead of exordium to command attention. "My friends," cried I, "save me, save yourselves, from the hands of a madman that pursues us! It is my honour, it is your own, that I recommend and put under your protection: that violent and unjust man, that father Bis, had nearly done you the basest outrage in my person, by dishonouring the class of rhetoric with the rod: he has not even deigned to tell me why he wanted to punish me; but, amid the cries of the children he was flaying, I understood we were accused of having deranged a clock; an absurd accusation of which he felt the falsehood; but he delights to punish, he loves to drink plentifully of tears; and the guilty and the innocent are alike to him, provided he exercises his tyranny. My particular crime, a crime indelible, and which he can never pardon me, is that of having uniformly refused to betray you, in order to please him; and of preferring to endure his severity rather than to expose my friends. You have seen with what obstinacy he has laboured, for three years, to make me the spy and accuser of my class. You would be frightened at the mass of study he has loaded me with, in order to wrest from me a few notes that might give him every day the pleasure of molesting you. My constancy has conquered his; his hatred has appeared to subside; but he was watching the moment to revenge himself on me, and on you, for the fidelity I have observed. Yes, my friends, had I been fearful or feeble enough to have suffered him to lay hands on me, we should have been lost, the class of rhetoric would have been for ever dishonoured. It was this at which he aimed: he desired to have it said that rhetoric had bent under his mastership, and under his humiliating rod. Thank heaven, we are saved! No doubt, he is coming to require you to give me up, and I am well assured beforehand of the tone in which you will answer him: but, had I companions base enough not to defend me, I would singly sell my honour and my life most dearly to him, and would die free rather than live disgraced. No, far from me be this idea; I see you all determined, like myself, not to rest under such a yoke: in a month from this time, our course of rhetoric is to finish, and our vacation commence: a month retrenched from the course of our studies does not merit our regret: let to-day then be the end and close of the labours of our class. From this moment we are free, and that proud, that cruel, that ferocious man is baffled and confounded."

My address had excited great indignation, but the conclusion had more effect than all the rest. No peroration ever led captive the minds of its hearers with so much rapidity. The great majority answered me with acclamation: "Yes, no more rhetoric! Vacation! and let us swear, before we leave the room, let us swear on this altar (for there was one there) never to set foot in it again."

After the oath had been pronounced, I resumed— "My friends," said I to them, "it would not become us to quit this room either as libertines or as fugitive slaves; let the head-master never say that we fled: our retreat should be peaceful and decent: and, to render it more honourable, I would propose to signalize it by an act of religion. This room is a chapel; let us return thanks to God, in a solemn *Te Deum*, for having acquired and preserved, during the course of our studies, the good-will of the school, and the esteem of our masters."

In an instant I beheld them all ranged round the altar, and, amidst a profound silence, one of our companions, Varlarché, whose voice vied with that of the bulls of Cantal, where he was born, chanted the hymn of praise: fifty voices answered his, and the astonishment of the whole school, at the extraordinary and sudden noise of this concert of voices, may easily be imagined. Our master was the first who arrived, the head-master came down, and the provost himself advanced gravely to the door of the school-room. The door was shut, and was not opened till the *Te Deum* had been sung: then, ranged in a semicircle, the little boys by the side of the great ones, we suffered them to approach. "What's this disturbance?" demanded the furious head-master, as he advanced among us.—"What you call a disturbance," said I, "is but a thanksgiving, father, that we render to heaven, for having permitted us to complete our first studies without falling into your hands." He threatened to inform our parents of this criminal revolt; and, looking on me with a menacing and terrible eye, he predicted that I should be the chief of some faction. He knew me but ill: and his prediction has not been accomplished. The provost, with more gentleness, wanted to reclaim us: but we begged him not to insist against a resolution that an oath had consecrated; and our good master remained alone with us: yes, good; I owe him this praise; and, though with a temper of mind less flexible and less gentle than that of father Malosse, he might vie with him at least in goodness of heart. According to the idea that is usually entertained of the political character of this society, so lightly condemned and so harshly abolished, no jesuit was less severe in his heart than father Balme: that was his name. His character was firm and open: the impartiality, the rectitude, the inflexible equity with which he conducted his class, and the noble and tender esteem that he showed his scholars, had gained him our respect, and conciliated our love.

Through the austere decorum of his order, his native sincerity would sometimes force its way, and exhibit features of power and boldness that would have harmonized better with the courage of the soldier than with the spirit of a monk. I remember, one day, a rude boy of our class having answered him improperly, he rushed from his desk, and, tearing up an oak plant from the floor of the room, he raised it up, and exclaimed—" Wretch! I will not flog a boy in the class of rhetoric, but I will knock down the insolent who dares to treat me with disrespect." This kind of correction pleased us excessively: we felt obliged to him for the fright that the noise of the broken plank had occasioned, and we beheld with pleasure the culprit on his knees under this club, humbly asking pardon.

Such was the man to whom I had to render an account of what had just passed. I observed him while I told my tale; and, when I stood before him, as one of his scholars, who by force was almost obliged to submit to the rod, I saw his eyes and countenance inflamed with indignation; but, endeavouring to disguise his anger by a smile—" Why did you not cry out," said he, " *Sum civis Romanus!*"— " I did not care to say that," answered I; " I had to face a Verres."

However, that he might not incur reproach, father Balme did all that his duty required to retain us: reason and sentiment were both employed. His efforts were fruitless: he did not esteem us the less for it, and he loved me the more. " My son," whispered he, " to whatever school you go, my attestation may be of some service to you: it is not now the moment to offer it; but come in a month and take it; I will give it you with a sincere and willing heart." Thus finished my rhetoric.

This year, then, my holidays were considerably prolonged; but very fortunately I found in my native town an old country curate, a distant relation, a man of some learning, who taught me the logic of Port-Royal, and who beside took the pains of exercising me in speaking Latin, not choosing, in our walks, to employ any other language with me than that; which he spoke fluently. This exercise was an invaluable advantage to me when, in philosophy, the course of which was given in Latin, I found myself as in a country where I had been already naturalized. But, before I pass thither, I would willingly again cast an eye over the years I have just seen elapse: I would speak of the vacations that, every year, brought me back to my home, and that recompensed my labours and my pains with such gentle repose.

The short vacations at Christmas were passed by my parents and myself in the mutual enjoyment of tenderness, without any other diversion than that afforded by the duties of kindness and affection. As the season was sharp, my liveliest pleasure was that of finding myself at my ease by a good fire; for at Mauriac, even during the severest cold, when surrounded by ice, and when in going to school we had every morning to trace our way in the snow, we found at the house where we lodged no other fire on our return than a few half-burnt billets that hissed at each other under the boiler, and at which we were scarcely permitted in turn to thaw our fingers. Frequently, as our hosts sat and surrounded the chimney, it was a favour to let us approach. In the evening too, when studying, and our fingers benumbed with cold refused to hold the pen, the lamp afforded the only flame at which we could revive them. Some of my companions, who, bred on the heights, and hardened to cold, endured it better than I, used to accuse me of delicacy; and, in a chamber where the cold wind blew in at the cracks in the windows, thinking it ridiculous that I should be chilled, they mocked at my shivering. I also used to reproach myself for being so chilly and tender, and often accompanied others, on the ice and in deep snows, to accustom myself, if possible, to the severity of winter: I conquered nature, but did not change it I only learnt to suffer. Thus, when I went home, and, in a good bed or by the corner of a good fire, I felt myself revived, it was one of the most delicious moments of my life; an enjoyment that luxury would never have taught me.

In these Christmas holidays, my good grandmother used to confide to me, with all due mystery, the secrets of the house. She used to show me, as so many treasures, the provision she had made for the winter. Her bacon, her hams, her sausages, her pots of honey, her vases of oil, her piles of buckwheat, of barley, of peas and beans, her heaps of turnips and chesnuts, and her beds of straw covered with fruits. "See, my dear," would she say, "these are the gifts Providence has sent: how many honest families have not received so much as we! and what thanks ought we to return for these favours!"

For herself, nothing could be more moderate than this prudent housewife; but her happiness consisted in seeing abundance reign in the house. The treat she used to give us with the most lively joy was that on Christmas night. As it was every year the same, all expected it, but care was taken not to appear to do so; for she flattered herself every year that the surprise would be new, and this was a pleasure we were careful not to deprive her of. While all were at midnight mass, the green cabbage soup, the pudding, the sausage, the piece of salt pork of the brightest red, the cakes, the apple fritters fried in lard, all were mysteriously prepared by her and one of her sisters: and I, the sole confident of all these preparations, said not a syllable to any one. After mass, the family all returned; and finding this excellent collation on the table, they exclaimed at the magnificence of the good grandmother. This exclamation of surprise and joy was to her a complete triumph. Beans, on Twelfth-day, afforded us another subject for rejoicing; and, when the new year came, the whole family presented such a scene of continued embraces, and such a concert of tender wishes, that it would, I think, have been impossible to witness it without being moved. Figure to yourself the father of a family amidst a crowd of women and children, who, with their hands and eyes all raised to heaven, were calling down blessings on him, while he answered their prayers by tears of affection, that presaged, perhaps, the ill that threatened us: such were the scenes that my vacations presented.

That of Easter was somewhat longer; and, when the weather was fine, I had time for some amusements. I have already observed, that in my little town the education of the boys was carefully conducted; their example became to the girls an object of emulation. The instruction of the one influenced the spirit of the others; and gave to their air, their language, and their manners, a tint of politeness, decorum, and agreeableness, that nothing has made me forget. An innocent freedom reigned among us all: the girls and the young men used to walk together in an evening by the light of the moon. Their usual amusement was singing; and it seems to me that these young voices, united, used to form sweet harmony and charming concerts. I was admitted early into this society; but before the age of fifteen it did not at all diminish my taste for study and solitude. I was never happier, than when, in the bee-garden at St Thomas, I passed a fine day in reading the verses of Virgil on the industry and police of those laborious republics, that prospered so happily under the care of my aunt. she had observed still better than the poet their labours and their habits; and instructed me in them better than Virgil, by making me see with my own eyes, in the wonders of their instinct, marks of intelligence and wisdom that had escaped the divine poet, and with which I was charmed. Perhaps there was some delusion in the affection of my aunt for her bees, as there is in all affections, and the interest she took in their young swarms very much resembled that of a mother for her children: but I should say too that she appeared to be beloved by as much as she loved them. I used to think I saw them pleased to fly around her, to recognise, to listen to, and to obey her voice: they had no sting for their beneficent mistress: and when, in a storm, she used to take them to her, wipe them and warm them with her breath and in her hands, it seemed that, on reviving, they gently hummed their gratitude around her. No fears disturbed the hive when it was visited by their friend; and if, on seeing them less diligent than usual, or sick, or feeble from fatigue or age, her hand poured a little wine by the hive to restore them to strength and health, the same gentle murmur seemed to return her thanks. She had surrounded their little domain with fruit trees, and with those that flowered in early spring; she had also introduced a little stream of limpid water, that flowed on a bed of pebbles; and, on its borders, thyme, lavender, and marjorum: in short, the plants in which they most delighted offered them the first gifts of summer. But when the uplands began to blossom, and the aromatic herbs to spread their perfume, our bees, not deigning to amuse themselves longer with the produce of their little orchard, went forth to seek more ample riches at a distance; and, as they returned, loaded with stamina of different colours, purple, azure, and gold, my aunt named to me the flowers that had afforded their spoil.

What passed under my eyes, what my aunt related to me, and what I read in Virgil, inspired me with so lively an interest in behalf of this little people, that I forgot myself whilst I observed them, and never quitted them without sensible regret. Since, and even now, I have such an affection for bees, that I cannot without pain think of the cruel custom that exists in some countries, of killing them to collect their honey. Ah! when the hive was full, it was a comfort to them to remove what was superfluous; but we left them an abundant provision for themselves, until the next flower season; and we knew, without hurting a single bee, how to remove the comb that exceeded their wants.

In the long vacations at the end of the year, all my duties fulfilled, and all my tastes satisfied, I had still some time to give to society; and that of the young girls, I confess, became every year more pleasing to me; but, as I have already said, it was not until the age of fifteen that I felt all its charms. The connections that were formed there did not at all disquiet our families: there was so little inequality of condition and fortune, that the parents were almost as soon agreed as their children; and after marriage love did not often languish: but that, which was attended with no danger to my companions, might extinguish my emulation, and make the fruit of my studies abortive.

I saw hearts choosing and forming ties with each other; example inspired me with a similar inclination. One of our young companions, and the prettiest to my taste, appeared to me still disengaged, and, like me, to have only the vague desire of pleasing. In her freshness, she had not that tender and soft brilliancy with which beauty is painted, when it is compared to the rose; but the lively red, the down, and roundness of the peach, afford you an image that very much resembled her. As for wit, with so sweet a mouth, could she be without it? Her eyes and her smile would alone have given wit and grace to her simple language; and from her lips " good-day" and "good-night" seemed to me exquisitely delicate. She might be one or two years older than I, and this inequality of age, that an air of steadiness and prudence rendered still more imposing, intimidated my dawning love; but, by degrees, in trying to make my attentions please her, I perceived they affected her; and from the moment I thought I had won her heart, I loved her in good earnest. Of this I made her a plain avowal, and she as plainly answered me, that her inclinations were not at variance with mine. " But you well know," said she, " that, to be lovers, we must hope one day to be married; and how can we expect it at our age? You are scarcely fifteen: and are not you going to pursue your studies?"—" Yes," I replied, " such is

my determination, and the wish of my mother."—
" Well then! here will be five years of absence before you can be fixed in life, and I shall be more than twenty, without knowing for what you are destined."
—" Alas! it is too true," said I, " that I know not what will become of me; but promise me, at least, never to marry without consulting my mother, nor without asking her whether I have not some hope to offer you." She gave me her promise with a charming smile; and, during the rest of the vacation, we abandoned ourselves to the pleasure of loving each other with the ingenuousness and innocence of our age. Our private walks, our most interesting conversations, were passed in imagining for me possibilities of future success or fortune, that might favour our wishes; but, as these sweet illusions succeed each other like dreams, the one effaced the other, and, after they had delighted us for a moment, we finished by weeping over them, as children weep when a breath overturns the house of cards they have built.

During one of these conversations, and as we were sitting on the slope of the meadow that bordered the river, an incident happened that had nearly cost me my life. My mother had been told of my attachment to Mademoiselle B * * *. She was sorry for it, and feared lest love should diminish my taste and ardour for study. Her aunts perceived she was unhappy, and pressed her so much that she could not dissemble the cause of her sorrow. From that moment these good women, presaging my ruin, exerted themselves to see who could be most bitter against this young innocent girl, accusing her of coquetry, and finding it criminal in her to be amiable in my eyes. One day then, when my mother was enquiring for me, one of my aunts came into the meadow to look for me, and, finding me tête-à-tête with the object of their resentment, she loaded that amiable girl with the most unjust reproaches, without sparing the words indecency and seduction. After this imprudent burst of passion, she quitted us; and left me furious, and my lovely girl disconsolate, and almost suffocated with sobbing, and her eyes full of tears. Judge what impression her grief made on my heart! In vain did I ask her pardon, weep at her knees, and entreat her to despise and forget this injury. "I am indeed wretched," exclaimed she, "for they accuse me of having seduced you, and of wishing to unsettle you! Fly me, see me no more: no, I wish never to see you again." At these words she quitted me, and forbade me to follow her."

I returned home, my air wild, my eyes on fire, my recollection absolutely lost. Fortunately, my father was absent, and my mother was the only witness of my delirium. As she saw me pass and go up to my chamber, she was frightened at my disorder; she followed me: I had locked the door; she commanded me to open it. "Oh, mother!" said I, "in what a situation do you see me! Pardon me! I am desperate; I no longer recognise myself; I am not master of my feelings. Spare me the shame of appearing thus before you." I had beaten my head against the wall, and my forehead was wounded with the blows. What a passion is rage! I felt, for the first time, its violence and transport. My mother, dismayed, pressing me to her bosom, and bathing me with tears, uttered such doleful cries that all the women of the house, except one, hastened to us; and she who dared not appear, and who had just been avowing her fault, was tearing her hair for the grief she had caused. Their desolation, the deluge of tears that I saw showering around me, the tender and timid groans that I heard, softened my heart and made my anger subside. But I could scarcely breathe, my blood had swelled all my veins; it was necessary to bleed me. My mother trembled for my life: while I was bleeding, her mother told her in a whisper what had passed; for in vain she had asked it of me: "Horrid! barbarous usage!" were the only words I could make her understand of my answer; to have told her more, would, at that moment, have been too dreadful for me. But, when the bleeding had relieved me, and a little calm had changed my fury into grief, I made my mother a faithful and simple recital of my love, of the kind and prudent answer of Mlle. B***, and of the promise she had the goodness to make me, never to marry without the consent of my mother. "After that," said I, " what a wound for her heart, what torture for mine, was the unjust and cruel reproach she has just suffered for me! Ah! mother, this is an affront that nothing can efface."—" Alas!" said she weeping, " it is I that am the cause; it is my inquietude about this connection that has disordered the intellect of your aunts: if you refuse to pardon them, you must refuse to pardon your mother too." At these words I threw my arms around her, and pressed her to my heart.

To obey her, I had gone to bed. The effervescence of my blood, though moderated, was not appeased; all my nerves were shaken; and the image of this interesting and unhappy girl, whom I believed disconsolate, was present to my mind, with the features of the most lively and most piercing grief. My mother saw me struck with this idea; and my heart, still more disordered than my brain, kept my blood and spirits in an agitation that resembled a burning fever. The physician, who knew not its cause, presaged disease, and spoke of preventing it by a second bleeding. "Do you think," said my mother, " that this evening will be time enough?" He answered in the affirmative. "Then come again at that time, sir; at present I will take care of him." My mother, having entreated me to try and sleep a little, left me alone; and a quarter of an hour afterward she returned accompanied .... by whom? You, who know nature, ought to foresee. "Save my son, restore him to me," said she to my young love, as she led her to my bed-side. "This dear boy thinks you are offended; teach him that you are not so, that pardon has been asked you, and that you have pardoned." "Yes," said the charming girl; "I have now only thanks to render to your worthy mother; and there is no unhappiness that the kindness she heaps on me would not make me forget."—"Ah! Mademoiselle, it is for me to be grateful for the attentions her love has dictated; it is me she restores to life." My mother made her sit down by my bedside; and while I heard and looked at her, a pure and gentle calm overflowed my soul. She had the kindness too to appear to favour our happy dreams; and while she recommended prudence and piety to us both, "Who knows," said she, "what heaven has in reserve for you? It is just; you are both honestly born; and love may even render you still more worthy of being happy."—"These," said Mlle. B * * *, "are kind consoling words, and proper to calm your thoughts! As for me, you see that I retain neither anger nor resentment. Your aunt, whose vivacity had wounded me, has testified her regret; I have been fully reconciled to her; and will not you, who are so good, embrace her?"—"Yes, with all my heart," answered I; and in an instant the good aunt came, bathing my bed with her tears. In the evening the physician found my pulse still rather quick, but perfectly regular.

My father, on his return from a journey he had just been making to Clermont, informed us it was his intention to take me there—not, as my mother would have wished, to continue my studies, and pursue a course of philosophy, but to learn trade. "He has enough of study and Latin," said he; "it is time to think of giving him some useful employment. I have got a place for him in the house of a rich merchant: the counting-house shall be his school." My mother combated this resolution with all the force of affection, grief, and tears; but I, perceiving that she afflicted my father without dissuading him, persuaded her to comply. "Let me but once get to Clermont," said

I to her, " and I will find means to satisfy you both."
Had I followed only the dictates of my new passion,
I should have been of my father's opinion; for
trade, in a few years, might have put me in a tolerably happy situation. But neither my passion for
study, nor the will of my mother, which while she
lived was ever my supreme law, would suffer me to
take counsel of my love. I set out then with the
intention of reserving, morning and evening, an hour
and half of my time for the continuance of my studies; and by assuring the merchant that all the
rest of the day should be his, I flattered myself that
he would be contented. But he would not hear a
word of this composition, and it became necessary to
choose between trade and study. " What! sir," said
I, " will not eight hours a day of assiduous application in your counting-room suffice? What would you
require from a slave?" He answered, that it depended
on me to go and be more free elsewhere. I did not
give him time to repeat it, and instantly took my
leave.

All my riches consisted of two half-crowns, which
my father had given me for pocket-money, and some
sixpenny pieces that my grandmother had slided into
my hand, as she bade me farewell. But the poverty
that threatened me was the least of my cares. In
quitting the employment to which my father had
destined me, I was acting contrary to his will, and I
seemed to be withdrawing myself from his authority.
Would he pardon me? Would he not exert his authority to reduce me to obedience? And if even, in his
anger, he should abandon me, with what bitterness
would he accuse my mother of having contributed to
my ruin? The bare idea of the vexation I should
cause my mother was an acute punishment. My
mind agitated, and my spirits broken, I entered a
church and betook myself to prayer, the last refuge
of the unhappy. There, as by inspiration, a thought

struck me, that suddenly changed the prospect of my life and my dream of the future.

Reconciled to myself, hoping to be so with my father, by the sanctity of the motion I was about to offer him, I began by securing myself a lodging, and hired a little garret near the college, the furniture of which consisted in a bed, a table, and a chair; the whole for five-pence a week, I not being in a situation to make a longer agreement. To this furniture I added a hermit's vessel, and made my provision of bread, plain water, and plums.

After I was settled, and had made, in the evening, a frugal supper at home, I went to bed; I slept but little, and the next day I wrote two letters; one to my mother, in which I exposed to her the cruel refusal I had experienced from the inflexible merchant; the other to my father, in which, assuming the language of religion and nature, I entreated him, with tears, not to oppose the resolution that inspired me of consecrating myself to the church. The sentiment I thought I felt for that sacred vocation, was indeed so sincere, and my faith in the designs and cares of providence was then so lively, that in my letter to my father I announced the almost certain hope of being no longer any expense to him; and, to continue my studies, I only asked of him his consent and blessing.

My letter was a text for the eloquence of my mother. She thought she saw my route traced out by angels, and beaming with light, like the ladder of Jacob. My father, with less weakness, had not less piety. He suffered himself to be persuaded, and permitted my mother to write me word that he consented to my pious resolutions. At the same time, she sent me some succour in money, of which I made little use, and which I was soon in a situation to return to her just as I had received it.

I had learned that at the school at Clermont,

much more considerable than that of Mauriac, the masters were aided by private tutors: it was on this employment that I founded my existence: but to be admitted to undertake it, I found it necessary, as quickly as possible, to create myself a name in the school, and to gain, in spite of my youth, the confidence of the masters.

I had forgotten to say, that, when the vacation commenced at Mauriac, I had gone there to take the attestation of my master in rhetoric: he had given it me as completely as he could; and, after having embraced and tenderly thanked him, I was going with tearful eyes, when I met the head-master in the corridor, who had treated me so harshly. "Ah! are you there, sir?" said he. "Whence do you come?" —"From a visit to father Balme, sir," answered I: "I have been to take leave of him."—"He has surely given you a favourable attestation."—"Yes, father, very favourable; and I am very grateful for it."—"You don't ask me for mine; you think you shall not want it."—"Alas! father, I should be very happy to obtain it; but for that I dare not hope."— "Come into my chamber," said he; "I will convince you that you have mistaken me." I followed him. He seated himself at his table; and, after having written an attestation more extravagant in praises than that of my master, "Read," said he, as he presented it to me before he sealed it; "if you be not satisfied with it, I will give you one more ample." As I read it, I felt myself overwhelmed with confusion. I stood before father Bis, like Cinna before Augustus. All the odious names I had given him presented themselves to my mind, as so many injuries with which I had blackened him; and the more greatness he showed, the more was I confused and humbled before him. At length, as my eyes, full of tears, dared to raise themselves to his, I perceived that my repentance affected him. "Do you then pardon me, father?" said I, with transport; and I threw myself into his arms. I well know that scenes, which to us are personal, have a private interest, which can only be personally felt; but I am deceived, or this would have been affecting even to the most indifferent.

Fortified with these attestations, I had only to present them to the head-master of the school at Clermont: that would have been sufficient to admit me into the class of philosophy, instantly and without examination: but this was not what I wanted. Verbal praise, however exaggerated, makes but a vague impression; and I wanted something more striking, more intimate; I wanted to be examined.

I addressed myself to the head-master, and without saying where I came from, I asked him permission to enter the class of philosophy. "Where do you come from?" demanded he.—"From Bort, father."—"And where have you studied?"—Here I suffered myself to use some evasion. "I have been studying," said I, "with a country curate." A sign of disdain was visible on his brows and lips; and, opening a book of exercises, he proposed to me one in which there was no difficulty. I did it with a stroke of the pen, and with some elegance. "How!" said he, on reading it, "have you had a country curate for your master?"—"Yes, father."—"This evening you shall translate." It chanced to be part of an oration of Cicero that I had seen when in rhetoric; I therefore translated it without difficulty, and as quickly as I had done the exercise. "And is it, indeed," said he, on reading my translation, "at a country curate's that you have studied?"—"You must plainly perceive it," said I.—"That I may see it still better, to-morrow you shall compose a theme." In this prolonged examination I thought I discovered a curiosity that was favourable to me. The subject he proposed to me was not less encouraging: it was the regret and parting of a boy that leaves his parents for school. What more analogous to my situation, and to the affections of my soul! I would I could recollect the expression I gave to the feelings of the son and the mother. Those words, dictated by nature, and whose eloquent simplicity art can never imitate, were watered with my tears, which the master perceived. But what most astonished him (for there truth itself resembled invention) was the passage where, rising above myself, I made the youth address his father, and tell him of the courage he felt to become, one day, by force of application and study, the consolation, the support, and honour of his old age; and of restoring, to his other children, what his education had cost. "And you have studied at a country curate's!" exclaimed my Jesuit, yet more loudly.—For this time I was silent, and only cast down my eyes. —"And," resumed he, "has your country curate also taught you to write in verse?"—I answered that I had some idea of the art, but very little practice.—"That is what I should be glad to know," said he smiling. "Come this evening before the lecture hour." The subject of the verses was,—"What is the difference between feigning and lying?" This was precisely an excuse that he, perhaps intentionally, offered me.

I studied to represent feigning as a pure joke, or an innocent artifice; an ingenious art of amusing, in order to instruct; sometimes even a sublime art, to embellish truth herself, to render her more amiable, more impassioned, and more attractive, by lending her a thin transparent veil, covered with flowers. In lying, it was easy for me to show the baseness of the mind that betrayed its feeling or its judgment; and the impudence of the crafty knave, that perverts and disfigures truth, in order to impose, and whose language bears the character of trick, malice, fraud and dishonour.

"Now tell me," said the adroit Jesuit, "whether you lied, or feigned, when you told me that a country curate had been your master; for I am almost cer-

tain that you have studied with us at Mauriac."—
"Though both be true, father," said I, "I confess that
I should have told a lie, if my intention had been to
deceive you; but, in deferring to tell you what you
at present know, I had no desire of disguising the
truth, or of leaving you in error. I wanted to be
known to you better than by attestations: I had
good ones to produce to you; and here they are. On
these testimonies, and without examination, you
would have granted me my first request; and I had
one to make you, much more essential to me. While
I study, I must teach; and you must have the kindness to make me gain my living, by giving me scholars. My parents are poor, and their children numerous; I have already cost them too much; I will no
longer be a burden to them; and, till I shall be able
to succour them, I ask of you what every man in
misfortune may ask without blushing—employment
and bread."—" Ah, child," said he, "at your age,
have you the means of commanding attention, obedience, and respect, among your equals? You are
scarcely fifteen."—" True; but, father, do you reckon
for nothing misfortune and its influence? Do you
think it does not advance the authority of reason,
and the maturity of age? Try me; you will perhaps
find my character sufficiently grave, to make you
forget my youth."—" I will consider of it," said he.
—" No, father, no consideration is necessary: I
entreat you to put me from this moment on the list
of private tutors at this school, and to furnish me
with scholars. It is immaterial to me from what
classes; I dare answer for it, they shall do their duty,
and you shall be contented with me." He promised
me, but rather feebly; and, with a note from his
hand, I went to begin my course of logic.

From the next day, I thought I perceived that the
professor had paid some attention to me. The logic
of Port-Royal, and the habit of speaking Latin with
my country curate, gave me a considerable advantage

over my comrades. I hastened to put myself forward, and neglected nothing to make myself remarked. In the meantime weeks elapsed without my hearing anything from the head-master. Not to appear importunate, I waited. I only sometimes placed myself in his way, and bowed to him with a suppliant air; but he scarcely perceived me. But it seemed that, having nothing good to communicate, he affected not to see me I retired very sad; and in my garret that almost touched the clouds, abandoning myself to my reflections, I made my hermit-like supper in tears: fortunately I had excellent bread.

A good little lady, madame Clément, who lived under me, and had a kitchen, was curious to know where mine was. One morning she called on me. "Sir," said she, "I hear you go up to your room at dinner hour, where you are alone without fire, and no one comes up after you. Excuse me, but I am unhappy at your situation." I confessed to her that for the moment I was not much at my ease; but I added, that I should shortly have full enough to live on; that I was capable of keeping a school; and that the Jesuits would provide for me. "Ah!" said she, "your Jesuits. They have something very different in their heads: they will lull you with promises, and leave you to languish. Why don't you go to Riom, to the Oratorians? They will give you fewer fine words, but will do more for you than they promise." I need not tell you that I was speaking to a Jansenist. Touched with the interest she took in me, I appeared disposed to follow her advice, and requested her to give me some information about the Oratorians. "They are," said she, "very honest people, whom the Jesuits detest, and would wish to annihilate. But it is dinner time; come and partake of my soup; and I will tell you more." I accepted her invitation; and though her dinner was certainly very frugal, I never made a better in my life; above all, two or three small glasses of wine that she made me drink revived all my spirits. I there learnt, in an hour, all I wanted to know of the animosity of the Jesuits against the fathers of the Oratory, and of the jealous rivalship of the two schools. My good neighbour added, that if I went to Riom I should be well recommended. I thanked her for the good offices she was willing to render me; and, strong in her intentions and my own hopes, I went to call on the head-master. It was a holiday. He appeared surprised at seeing me, and inquired the object of my visit. This reception completely persuaded me of what my neighbour had told me. " I come, father," answered I, " to take leave of you." —" What! are you going away?"—" Yes, father, I am going to Riom, where the fathers of the Oratory will give me, in their school, as many scholars as I desire."—" What! my son! you are going to quit us! you, educated in our schools, are going to desert us!"—" Alas! 'tis with regret; but you can do nothing for me, and I am assured that those good fathers".... —" Those good fathers have but too much the art of seducing and attracting credulous young men like you. But be assured, my son, that they have neither the credit nor the power that we have."—" Then have the kindness, father, to give me an employment that will maintain me."—" Yes, I am thinking of it, I am endeavouring to do it; and in the meantime I will provide for your wants."— " What do you call providing for my wants, father? Know that my mother would sooner deprive herself of everything, than suffer a stranger to assist me. But I will no longer receive any aid, even from my family; it is on the fruit of my labour that I ask to subsist. Put it in my power to do this, or I must seek elsewhere."—" No! no! you shall not go," replied he; " I forbid it. Follow me. Your professor esteems you. Let us go to him together." And in this way he conducted me to my professor. " Do you know, father," said he, " what is going to become of this youth? he is invited to Riom. The Oratorians, those dangerous men, want to make a convert of him. He is going to ruin himself, and we must save him." My professor took fire at this intelligence, even more sensibly than the head-master. They both told wonders of me to all the masters of the school! and, from that time, my fortune was made: I had a school; and, in a month, twelve scholars, at three shillings and four-pence a-piece, put me in a situation above all my wants. I was well lodged, well fed, and at Easter I could clothe myself decently in the dress of an abbé, which was what I most desired, both for the purpose of better assuring my father of the sincerity of my vocation, and of having a serious existence in the school.

When I quitted my garret, the good lady my neighbour, to whom I told what had been done, was not so well pleased at it as I could have wished. "Ah!" said she, "I should have been much happier to have seen you go to Riom. 'Tis there they make good and holy studies." I begged her to preserve her kindness for me, in case my hopes should be frustrated; and, in my opulence, I went occasionally to see her.

My ecclesiastical habit, the decorum it imposed, and yet more the old desire of personal consideration, that the example of Amalvy had left in my soul, were productive of happy effects; and singularly that of rendering me difficult and reserved in my school acquaintances. I was not hasty in the choice of my friends, and I made but a small number: we were four, and always the same in our parties of pleasure; that is to say, our walks. At our common expense, which was small, we subscribed for our reading at an old bookseller's; and as good books, thank Heaven, are the most common, we read none else. The great orators, the great poets, the best writers of the last century, and some of the present, though of these the bookseller had but few, succeeded from hand to hand; and, in our walks, each recalling what he had collected, almost all our conversations passed in remarks on our reading. In one of our walks to Beauregard, the country-house of the bishoprick, we had the happiness to visit the venerable Masillon. The reception this illustrious old man gave us was so full of kindness, and his presence and the accent of his voice made so lively and tender an impression on me, that the recollection of it is one of the most grateful I retain of what passed in my early years.

At that age, when the affections of the mind and soul have, reciprocally, so sudden a communication, when reason and sentiment act and re-act on each other with so much rapidity, there is no one to whom it has not sometimes happened, on seeing a great man, for ever to remember the features that characterize the soul and genius of such a man. It was thus that, among the wrinkles of that countenance already decayed, and in those eyes that were soon to be extinguished, I thought I could still trace the expression, the impassioned, tender, sublime, and profoundly penetrating eloquence, with which I had just been enchanted in his writing. He permitted us to mention them to him, and to offer him the homage of the religious tears they had made us shed.

After the course of logic was completed, after a year of excessive labour, having had, not to mention my own studies, scholars from three different classes to instruct, morning and evening, I went home to my parents to take a little repose; and, I confess, it was not without some sentiments of pride that I appeared before my father, well dressed, my hands full of little presents for my sisters, and with some money in reserve. My mother wept with joy as she embraced me. My father received me with kindness, though coldly. All the rest of the family were enchanted to see me.

The joy of Mademoiselle B * * * was not so pure; and I myself was very much confused and embarrassed when I had to appear before her in the dress of an abbé. In this change, it is true, I was not faithless to her, but I was inconstant; this was indeed enough; I knew not how to behave to her. I consulted my mother on this delicate point "My dear son," she replied, "she has a just right to testify her vexation, her anger, and even something more poignant, her coldness and disdain. You must bear all; you must, on all occasions, show her the tenderest esteem, and treat with infinite attention a heart you have wounded."

Mademoiselle B * * * was gentle, indulgent, and polite, but reserved and shy; she only carefully avoided any private conversation with me. Thus, in company, we treated each other with as much attention as might make it believed we never had been lovers.

The second year, in which I studied philosophy, was yet more laborious to me than the first. My school was increased; I gave it every care; and, beside, having to dispute publicly on general questions, it was necessary to abridge my sleep very much, in order to prepare for them.

It was on the day that I finished my course of philosophy, by this public exercise, that I heard of the fatal event which plunged myself and family in an abyss of grief.

After my disputation was over, my friends and I, according to the established custom, were partaking of a collation in the professor's room, that should have given joy; and, in the felicitations that were addressed to me, I saw only sadness. As I had solved the difficulties that had been proposed to me tolerably well, I was surprised that my companions, and that the professor himself, did not appear more joyous. "Ah! if I had done well," said I, "you would not all be so sad."—"Alas!" said the professor, "the sadness that surprises you is most deep and sincere; and would to Heaven it had no other source than the brilliancy of the success which you have experienced! I have a much more cruel misfortune to announce to you. You have no longer a father!" I fell under the blow, and was a quarter of an hour without colour and without voice. Restored to life and tears, I would have set off instantly, to go and save my poor mother from despair. But, without a guide, and among the mountains, night would overtake me: I was obliged to wait till day-light. I had twelve long leagues to go on a hired horse; and, though I pressed him as much as possible, I proceeded very slowly. During this melancholy journey, one only thought, one single picture, was present to my mind, and occupied it without ceasing; all the energies of my soul were united to sustain its impression; and soon all my courage must be collected to see it in reality, and to contemplate it in all its mournful horrors.

In the middle of the night I arrived at my mother's door; I knock, I pronounce my name, and instantly I hear a plaintive murmur and a mixture of groaning voices. All the family get up, the door is opened; and, on entering, I am encircled by my weeping friends; mother, children, old helpless women, all almost naked, dishevelled, resembling spectres, and extending their arms to me, with cries that pierce and rend my heart. I know not what force, a force that nature surely reserves for extreme misery, suddenly displayed itself within me. I never felt so superior to myself. I had to raise an enormous weight of grief; I did not sink under it. I opened my arms, my bosom to these wretched creatures; I received them all with the assurance of a man inspired by heaven, and without manifesting weakness, without shedding a tear! I who weep so easily! "Mother, brothers, sisters, we experience," said I, " the greatest of afflictions; let it not overcome us. Children, you lose a father, and you find one; I am he, I will be a father to you; I adopt all his duties; you are no longer orphans." At these words, rivers of tears, but tears much less bitter, flowed from their eyes. "Ah!" cried my mother, as she pressed me to her heart, "my boy! my dear boy! I knew you well!" and my brothers, my sisters, my good aunts, my grandmother, fell on their knees. This touching scene would have lasted through the night, had I been able to support it. I was faint with fatigue; I asked for a bed: "Alas!" said my mother, "there is no other in the house than that of . . . ." Her tears stifled her voice.—" Well! give me that; I will lie in it without reluctance." I did lie there. I did not sleep; my nerves were too much shaken. The whole night long I saw the image of my father as vividly, as strongly impressed upon my soul, as if he had been present. I sometimes thought I really beheld him: it did not alarm me. I extended my arms, I spoke to him. "Ah! why is it not true?" said I. "Why are you not what I seem to see? Why can you not answer me, and at least tell me whether you are satisfied with your son?" After this long watching and this painful disorder of the fancy, which was scarcely a dream, it was grateful to me to see daylight. My mother, who had not slept any more than myself, thought to wait for my waking. At the first noise she heard me make, she came, and was frightened at the revolution which had taken place in me: my skin seemed to have been dyed in saffron.

The physician whom she called in, told her, that this was an effort of great concentrated grief, and that mine might be attended with the most fatal consequences, if it were not removed by some diversion. "A journey, absence, and that as soon as possible, is," said he, "the best remedy that I can indicate to you. But do not propose it to him as a diversion, to that great grief is ever averse: it must be ignorant of the care employed to divert it, and must be deceived in order to be cured." The old curate that had given me lessons during the vacations, had a small parsonage house in the centre of his diocese. He kindly offered to take me thither, and to keep me there till my health should be restored. It was necessary to give a motive to this journey: the intention I had of taking the *tonsure* from the hands of my bishop before I proceeded farther, furnished this motive: for one of my hopes was the happy chance of a simple benefice that I proposed to myself to try and obtain.

"I mean," said my mother to me, "to employ this year in arranging and regulating the affairs of the family. And do you, my son, hasten to enter the career to which God calls you: make yourself known to our holy bishop, and ask his counsel."

The physician was right: there are griefs yet more attaching than pleasure itself. Never, in the happiest times, when the paternal roof was so grateful and smiling to me, did I quit it with so much pain, as when it was in mourning. Of six guineas which I had saved, my mother permitted me to leave three in the family; and, still rich enough, I set off with my old friend for his curacy at St Bonet.

BOOK II.

The tranquillity and silence of the hamlet of Abloville, where I am writing these memoirs, recal to me the calm that the village of St Bonet restored to my soul. It did not offer so smiling or so fertile a landscape. the cherry and the apple-tree did not there shade the ripe corn, with loaded branches; but nature had there too her ornaments and her abundance. The vine arbour formed her porticos, the orchard her saloons, and the green grass her carpets; the cock had there his court of love, the hen her young family; the chesnut-tree majestically displayed its shade and spread its gifts; the fields, the meadows, the woods, the flocks, cultivation, pond-fishing, the grand elements of country scenery, were there sufficiently interesting to occupy a vacant mind. Mine, after the long fatigue of my studies, and that cruel blow, the death of my father, had need of repose.

The curate had some books analogous to his profession; a profession that was soon to be mine. I designed myself for the pulpit; to that he directed my reading: the holy scriptures were begun, and in the fathers of the church he showed me good examples of evangelic eloquence. The spirits of this old man, naturally gay, were only just as much so with me as was necessary daily to efface some tint of my moody melancholy. It subsided insensibly, and I became susceptible of happiness. It was pleasure and friendship that twice a month presided over dinners at which the curates of the neighbourhood used to meet, and which they gave each other in turn. Admitted to these festive parties, it was there that emulation inspired me with a taste for our poetry. Almost all these curates wrote French verses, and used to invite each other in epistles, the gaiety, native ease, and pleasantry of which delighted me. In imitation, I made some attempts, which they deigned to approve. Happy society of poets, where no one was envious or difficult, and where each was content with himself and his companions, as if they had been so many Horaces and Anacreons!

This leisure was not the end of my journey, and I did not forget that I had approached Limoges in order to go thither and take the *tonsure;* but the bishop gave it formally only once a year, and the moment was passed. It was necessary either to wait or to solicit a particular favour. I preferred to submit myself to the common rule, and for this reason the ceremony was every year preceded by a short residence with the Sulpicians, who were supposed to observe the characters, dispositions, qualities, and talents of the candidates, in order to render an account of them to the bishop. I wanted to be recommended, and for that purpose to be perceived, known, and distinguished from the crowd. Inventive necessity counselled me to seize that occasion of making myself known to the Sulpicians and the bishop : but to wait six months, and continue with my poor curate, would have been too burdensome to him. Fortunately, an excellent nobleman, his friend and neighbour, the marquis of Lînars, sent his chaplain to express to me the extreme desire he had that I should dedicate this interval of time to one of his sons, a young knight of the order of Malta, a charming youth, whose education had been neglected. I procured the curate's consent, and accepted the proposal. Nothing can exceed the marks of kindness and esteem with which I was honoured in this distinguished house, which all the nobility of the country frequented. The marchioness herself, daughter of the duke of Mortemart, educated at Paris, and rather of a lofty character, was always kind and gentle to me; because I behaved with simplicity and decorum, and was respectful without affectation; a character that has always made me at my ease in society, and never gave offence.

When the time came for taking the *tonsure*, I went to the seminary, where I found myself under the eyes of three Sulpicians, with twelve other candidates like myself. The reserve of meditation, the silence that reigned among us, and the exercises of piety that occupied us, appeared to me at first but little favourable to my views; but, while I was despairing of being able to make myself known, an opportunity offered itself spontaneously. We had, twice a day, an hour of recreation in a little garden, planted with rows of lime-trees. My companions amused themselves there by playing at *le petit palet*;

and I, who did not like the game, walked by myself. One day, one of our directors came up to me, and inquired why I was thus alone, preferring solitude to the society of the other candidates. I answered that I was the oldest, and that, at my age, I was naturally glad to have a few moments to myself, in order to collect, class, and arrange my ideas; that I was fond of reflecting on my studies and what I had read, and that, having the misfortune to want memory, I could only supply it by the force of meditation. This answer engaged conversation. The Sulpician was desirous of knowing where I had been educated, what questions I had maintained in my public disputations, and for what species of reading I felt most inclination. I answered all this. You may conceive that a director of the seminary at Limoges did not expect to find, in a boy of eighteen, any great fund of knowledge, and that my small store must have appeared to him a little treasure.

I was fully satisfied with the success of my little début, when, in the evening, at the walking hour, instead of one Sulpician, I was accosted by two. It was there that the fruit of my reading at Clermont acquired a real value. I had said that my prevailing taste was oratory, and had rapidly named those of our Christian orators whom I most admired. They kept me to this subject: I had to analyze the authors I spoke of, to mark distinctly their different characters, to quote from each the passages that had most struck me with astonishment, filled me with emotion, or delighted me by the brilliancy and the charm of eloquence. The two men of whom I spoke with the most enthusiasm were, Bourdaloue and Massillon: but I had not time to explain myself. It was not until the next day that I could dilate on their praises. I had all their plans in my head: the extracts I had made from their sermons were present to me; their exordiums, their divisions, their most beautiful traits, even to their texts, recurred to me in multitudes. I may, indeed say, that on that day my memory did me good service: instead of the two Sulpicians of the preceding evening, I had now three for my auditors, and all three, after having listened to me in silence, left me with astonishment. The rest of our conversations (for they quitted me no more during the hours of recreation) fell more vaguely on the most beautiful funeral orations of Bossuet and Fléchier, on some sermons of La Rue, and on the small collection of those of Cheminais, that I knew almost by rote. Afterward, I know not how, poetry became our subject. I acknowledged that I had read some of our poets, and I named the great Corneille. "And the tender Racine," asked one of the Sulpicians; "have you read him?"— "Yes, I confess I have," said I: "but Masillon had read him before me, and from him he learnt to speak to the heart with so much feeling and passion. And do you think," asked I, "that Fenelon, the author of Telemachus, had not read again and again the loves of Dido in the Æneid?"

This question introduced classical literature; and these gentlemen, who knew not how much,—thanks to my misfortune,—I was imbued with this old latinity, were surprised to hear me so full of it. You easily believe that I indulged in all the pleasure of display. I was inexhaustible: verse and prose flowed as from their source; and I had the air of not citing more for fear of wearying them.

I finished by a specimen of the fresh erudition I had amassed at Saint-Bonet. The books of Moses and Solomon presently passed in review; I was at the holy fathers when the day arrived for receiving the *tonsure*. On that day then, after our initiation in the holy profession, we went, conducted by our three directors, to pay our duties to the bishop. He received us all with equal kindness, but just as I was retiring with my companions, he called me back. My heart bounded. "You, sir," said he to me, "are unknown to me. your mother has recommended you to me. She is a most worthy woman, and I esteem her highly. Where do you propose to finish your studies?" I answered, that I was not determined; that I had just had the misfortune to lose my father; that my family, numerous and poor, placed their hopes in me; and that I should endeavour to find some university, where I could procure, during the course of my studies, the means of existence, and of contributing to the support of my mother and our children. "And your children!" replied he, moved at this expression.—"Yes, my lord, I am to them a second father, and if I do not sink under the exertion, I promise myself to fulfil his duties."—"Well," said he, "the archbishop of Bourges, one of our most worthy prelates, is my friend; I can recommend you to him; and if, as I expect, he attends to my recommendation, you will have nothing more to do for yourself and your family but to merit his protection, by using well the talents heaven has granted you." I returned thanks to the bishop for his good intentions; but I asked time to inform and consult my mother, not doubting but that she would be as sensible to them as myself.

The good curate, of whom I went to take leave, was transported with joy on learning what he called an act of heaven in my favour. What would he have said, could he have foreseen that this archbishop of Bourges was soon to be chaplain to the king and minister of the royal benefices, and that the eloquence of the pulpit, to which I intended to devote myself, was to have, under his ministry, the most interesting opportunities of signalizing itself at court? It is true, that, for a young ecclesiastic, who should have united talents to ambition, a charming career was open before me. A vain delicacy, a still vainer illusion, prevented me from entering it. I have had occasion to admire, more than once, how the woof of our destinies is weaved and ravelled, and of how many unconnected and frail threads its web is composed.

On my return to Linars, I wrote to inform my mother that I had taken the *tonsure* under favourable auspices; that I had received from the bishop the most touching marks of kindness; and that, as soon as possible, I would go and communicate them to her. On the same day, I received an express from her, with a letter nearly effaced by her tears. "Is it indeed true," asked she, "that you have had the madness to enlist in the company of the count of Linars, the marquis's brother, and captain of the Enghien regiment? If you have had this misfortune, let me know it; I will sell the little that I have, in order to ransom my son. Oh, God! was this the son you had given me?"

Judge of the despair into which I fell on reading this letter. Mine had made a circuit to arrive at Bort: it would yet be two days before my mother received it, and I saw her disconsolate. I instantly wrote her word that what she had been told was a horrible falsehood; that so culpable a folly had never entered my thoughts; that my heart was rent with the vexation she felt; that I begged her pardon for being its innocent cause; but that she ought to have known me well enough to reject so absurd a calumny; and that I would very soon come and convince her that my conduct was neither that of a libertine nor a madman. The express set off again immediately. But, while I could count the hours that would elapse before my mother would be undeceived, I continued in torture.

As far as I can recollect, Linars was sixteen leagues from Bort, and though I had conjured the express to travel all night, how could I think that he would not take some rest? I could get none, and I had not ceased to bathe my bed with my tears, in thinking of those my mother was shedding for me, when I heard a noise of horses in the court. I got up. It was the count of Linars who arrived. Without giving myself time to dress, I hastened to meet him; but he prevented me, and coming to me with an air of great affliction,—" Ah! sir," said he, " how culpable must a foolish imprudence render me in your eyes, that has spread desolation in your family, and a grief in the heart of your mother which I could not calm! She believes you are enlisted with me. All in tears, she has been throwing herself at my feet, and offering me her gold cross, her ring, her purse, and all she had in the world, to obtain your discharge. In vain did I assure her that this engagement did not exist; my protestations were vain, she only considered them as a refusal to restore you to her. She is still in tears. Set off immediately, go and revive her."— " And who, sir," said I, " can have given birth to this fatal report?"—" I, sir," said he; " it wounds me to the heart; I beg your pardon for it. The necessity of raising new recruits led me to your town. I there found some young men, school-fellows of yours, who were inclined to enlist, but who still hesitated. I saw that there wanted only your example to decide them. I yielded to the temptation of telling them that they would have you for their comrade, that I had enlisted you; and the report of it spread." —" Ah! sir," exclaimed I with indignation, " is it possible that such a falsehood could escape from the mouth of a man like you?"—" Do not spare me," said he, " I merit the bitterest reproaches; but this trick, the consequence of which I so little foresaw, has made me acquainted with such true maternal love as I had never known. Go and console your mother; she has need of you."

The marquis of Linars, to whom his brother avowed his fault and all the ill he had done, furnished me with a horse and guide, and on the following day I set off: but I set off in a fever, for my blood was on fire; and in the evening a paroxysm seized me, at the moment when my guide discovered that, by taking cross roads, he had lost his way. I trembled on my horse, and night was closing upon us in a bleak and desolate country, when I saw a man cross the road. I called to him to know where I was, and whether we were far from the village to which my guide thought we were going. "You are more than three leagues from it," said he, "and are not in the road." But, as he answered, he recognised me: it was a young man from Bort. "Ah, is it you?" said he, calling me by my name; by what accident do I find you at this hour on this heath? You look ill! where are you going to sleep?"—"And where are you going?" said I.—"I?" answered he, "I am going to see my uncle, who lives in a village not far off."—"And do you think," added I, "that your uncle would take care of me for the night? for I very much want rest."—"At his house," said he, "you will be but ill accommodated, but I will ensure you a hearty welcome." He took me there, and I found bread and milk for my guide, hay for my horse, and for myself a good bed of clean straw and some toast and water for my supper. I wanted nothing more, for the fever fit was still on me, and tolerably severe. When I awoke the next morning (for I had slept some hours) I learnt that this village was a parish. It was the day of the Assumption, and though very ill, I would go to mass. A young abbé in the church was an object of attention. The curate perceived me, and after service invited me into the vestry. "Is it possible," said he, after having learnt my adventure, "that, in a village where I am, an ecclesiastic should have slept on straw?" He took me home with him, and never was hospitality more cordially nor more nobly exerted. I was enfeebled by the diet and fatigue of my journey: he was desirous of re-establishing me; and, persuaded that my fever was only in the blood, he affirmed that it should be plentifully diluted by mild and refreshing drink. He was not mistaken. He made me dine with him.

Never did I eat so excellent a soup. It was made by his niece, then eighteen, with a form resembling the virgins of Correggio or Raphael. I never saw a countenance with more sweetness and charms. She was my nurse while the curate was doing the evening duty at church; and, ill as I was, I was not insensible to her cares. "My uncle," said she, "will not suffer you to go in the state you now are: he says Bort is six long leagues from hence; you must recover your strength before you set off. And why be in such a hurry? Are you not very well with us? You shall have a good bed; I'll make it myself. I'll bring you your soups, or, if you prefer it, some warm milk from a goat, that I milk with my own hands: you came hither very pale, and we are determined to send you away as fresh as a rose."—"Ah! Mademoiselle," said I, "happy should I be to wait the recovery of my health with you; but you know not the pain my mother suffers, how impatient she is to see me, and how ardently I desire to find myself in her arms!"—"The more you love her, the more she loves you, and the more you ought," said she, "to spare her the grief of seeing you in this state. A sister has more courage; and I am here like a sister to you."—"It should indeed seem so," said I, "by the tender interest you are kind enough to take in me."—"You certainly interest us," she replied; "and that's very natural; my uncle and I have compassionate hearts for every one; and we very rarely see such sufferers as you." The curate returned from his church. He required of me that I should send back my horse and guide, and insisted on taking upon himself the care of having me conducted home.

In a situation more tranquil, I should have felt myself enchanted at this parsonage, like Rinaldo in the palace of Armida; for my simple Marcelline was an Armida to me; and the more innocent she was, the more I found her dangerous. But though my mother must have been undeceived by my two letters, nothing could have kept me from her beyond the day on which the fit of fever became more feeble, and, my strength improved by two nights tolerably good sleep, I was able to mount on horseback.

My sister (this was the name that Marcelline had given herself, and that I too gave her when we were alone) did not see me at the moment of my departure without a violent emotion of the heart, that she could not dissemble. "Good bye, Mr Abbé," said she, in the presence of her uncle; "take care of your health; do not forget us; and embrace your mother very tenderly for me; tell her I love her dearly." At these words her eyes moistened, and as she retired to conceal her tears, "You see," said the curate, "the name of mother touches her: for it is not long since she lost her own. Good bye, sir; like Marcelline, I beg you not to forget us; we shall often talk of you."

I found my mother entirely recovered from the fears she had felt, but on seeing me, she was alarmed for my health. I calmed her inquietude; and indeed I felt myself much better, thanks to the diet the good curate had prescribed. We both wrote to thank him for his hospitable kindness; and, in returning him his mare on which I had come, we accompanied our letters with some modest presents, among which my mother slipped in a simple ornament for Marcelline, which, though of little value, was elegant and tasteful. After which, as I visibly recovered my health, we both occupied ourselves with the regulation of our affairs.

The bishop's protection, his recommendation, and the prospect that it afforded, appeared to my mother to be all that fortune could grant; and I then thought like her. My stars (and I now say my happy stars) made me change my opinion. This incident obliges me to recur to what is passed.

I have reason to think that, from my examination

by the headmaster at Clermont, the Jesuits had cast their eyes on me. Two of my fellowstudents, and the most distinguished, were already caught in their nets. It was possible that they would wish to entice me; and a somewhat curious fact, which I well remember, persuades me it was in their thoughts.

In the little leisure I had at Clermont, I had amused myself with drawing; and, as I had a taste for it, I was supposed to excel. My eye was accurate and my hand sure; nothing more was requisite for the object that induced the rector of the monastery to send for me. " I am informed," said he, " that you amuse yourself with architectural designs, and I have chosen you to make me a plan of our college: examine the edifice well, and, after having traced the ground plan, draw its elevation. Do it with the utmost care, because it will be submitted to the inspection of the king." Proud of this commission, I hastened to execute it; and, as you may conceive, I gave it the most scrupulous attention. But, desirous of doing it too well, I did it very ill. One of the wings of the building had a first floor, the other wing had none. I found this inequality shocking, and I corrected it by making them equal. " Ah! what have you done here?" said the rector.—" I have made the building regular, father," said I.—" And that is precisely what you should not have done. This plan is destined to show the contrary; first, to the father confessor, and, by his mediation, to the minister, and to the king himself. For we want to obtain a grant from the crown to build the floor that one of the wings wants." I hastened away to correct my mistake; and, when the rector was satisfied, " Will you permit me, father," said I, " to make one observation? This college they have built you is handsome, but it has no church. You are obliged to say mass in a low room. Has the church been forgotten in the plan?" The Jesuit smiled at my simplicity. " Your observation," said he, " is very just; but you may have remarked too that we have no garden."—" That too has surprised me."—" Be not unhappy about either ; we shall have both."—"How ! father ; I see no room."—" What ! you don't see, on the other side of the wall that encloses our college, the church of the Augustins, and that garden in their convent ?"—" Yes, but ———." " Well ! that garden and that church will be ours; and it is providence that seems to have placed them so near us."—" But, father, the Augustins will then have neither church nor garden."—" On the contrary, they will have a much more beautiful church, and a much more extensive garden : God forbid that we should make them suffer ! In removing them we shall take care to recompense them."—" Ah ! you are going to remove the Augustins ?"—" Yes, my son ; and their house will be an infirmary for our old members; for we must have a house for the retreat of our aged." —" Nothing is surely more just ; but I was thinking where you will put the Augustins."—" Let that give you no uneasiness. They are to have the convent, the church, and the garden of the Cordeliers. Will they not be much more comfortable, and much better than where they now are ?"—" Very well! but what will become of the Cordeliers ?"—" I expected this objection, and it is but just that I should answer it : Clermont and Mont-Ferrand were formerly two towns; they now form but one, and Mont-Ferrand is only a suburb of Clermont ; thus we usually say Clermont-Ferrand. Now, you know that the Cordeliers have a superb convent at Mont-Ferrand, and you will readily conceive that it is not necessary for one town to have two convents of Cordeliers. Therefore, in removing those at Clermont to Mont-Ferrand, no one is injured; and so you see, we, without harming any one, shall be possessors of the church, the garden, and convent of these good Augustins, who will be grateful to us for the exchange ; for we must ever act as good neighbours. What I am thus confiding to you is still a secret in our society, but you are not a stranger to it; and from this time I am pleased to consider you as one of us."

Such, as nearly as I can recollect, was this dialogue, in which Blaise Pascal would have found food for ridicule, and which appeared to me so sincere and so simple. What I now infer from it is, that it was not without premeditated design that the professor of rhetoric at Clermont, father Noaillac, in passing through Bort, on his road to Toulouse, came and invited himself to dine with me.

My good mother, who no more suspected his mission than I did, received him in the best manner she could, and during dinner he gratified her by exaggerating my success in the art of teaching. According to him my scholars were distinguished in their classes, and it was easy, on reading their exercises, to recognise those I had instructed. I found in this flattery an excess of politeness, but I did not see its aim. Toward the end of the dinner, my mother, according to the custom of the country, left us alone at table, and my Jesuit was then at his ease. "At present," said he, "let us talk of your projects. What do you intend to do with yourself? and what road do you mean to take?" I confided to him the advances that the bishop had made me, and the intention my mother and I had of profiting by them. He listened to me with a pensive and disdainful air. " I know not," said he at last, " what you can find flattering and seducing in these offers. As for me, I see in them nothing that is worthy of you. First of all, the title of doctor of Bourges is so decried that it is become ridiculous, and, instead of graduating there, you will degrade yourself. Beside . . . . but that is a point too delicate to be touched on There are truths which can only be told to intimate friends, and I have no right to explain myself more freely with you.' This discreet reserve had the effect he expected. "Pray let me hear, father," said I; " and be assured I shall be grateful to you for having spoken to me with an open heart."—" So be it, since it is your wish; and indeed I feel that, in a moment so critical, I should be wrong to conceal from you what I think of a plan in which I see nothing assured to you but disgust."—" And what disgust?" asked I with surprise.—" Your bishop," continued he, "is one of the best men in the world; his intentions are pure, and he wishes you well; of that I am persuaded. But what good does he think of doing you, by placing you under the dependence and at the mercy of this archbishop of Bourges? During your five years of theology, you will be his pensioner, and will live by his bounty; I am willing to suppose, too, that he will aid your family with some charitable donations (these words froze my blood) but are you and your mother made to be on the list of his charities? Are you reduced to that?"—" Certainly not," cried I.—" And yet this it is, and perhaps for a long time, that they propose to you: this is all they induce you to hope."—" It seems to me," said I, "that the church has property, the dispensation of which is committed to the bishops, property of which they have no right to possess themselves, but to dispose of it to others; and this property, these benefices, I thought I could partake of without blushing."—" That is indeed the bait," said he, " with which they excite the ambition of young men. But when, and at what price, do they obtain the benefits they expect? You know not the spirit of domination and of empire that these slow and tardy benefactors exercise over those they protect. They fear lest they should escape; and prolong as much as they can the state of dependence and slavery in which they keep these unhappy expectants. They give easily and liberally to favour and to birth; but if unhappy merit ever obtain any grace, it is very dearly bought!"—" You show me," said I, "an abundance of thorns and briars, where I saw only flowers. But, in my situation, charged with a family that I must maintain, and that wants my support, what do you advise me to do?"—" I advise you," said he, " to put yourself in a position to protect yourself, and not to be protected. I know a profession in which every man that distinguishes himself has credit and powerful friends. That profession is mine. All the avenues of fortune and ambition are interdicted to us personally; but they are all open to the society as a body."—" You advise me then to become a Jesuit?" —" Yes, certainly: and by means that are known to us, your mother will soon be in comfort, her children brought up, the state itself will take care of them, and, when the time comes for providing for them, there are no facilities that our connections do not afford us. It is for this reason that the flower of the youth of our colleges are ambitious of and solicit the advantage of being received into this powerful society; it is for this reason that the chiefs of the greatest houses desire to be affiliated to it."—" I have considered your society," said I, " as a source of knowledge; and for a man who is desirous of instructing himself and of developing his talents, I have said to myself a hundred times that he could not do better than live among you. But in your regulations two things disgust me: the length of the noviciate, and the obligation of beginning by teaching the lower classes."—" As for the noviciate," said he, " two years of probation must be submitted to, the law is invariable. But as to the lower classes, I believe I may answer that you shall be exempt from that." While talking thus, we were drinking a heady wine. The Jesuit was a little elevated; he boasted of the consideration his company enjoyed, and of the lustre it reflected on its members. " Nothing," said he, " can be comparable to the advantages that a Jesuit, a man of merit, enjoys in society; every door is open to him; he is everywhere sure of the most favourable and most flattering reception." His eloquence was so pressing, that he finished by persuading me.

" Well!" said I, " I am now determined to send

the bishop a polite refusal. The rest requires a little more reflection. But I purpose going to Toulouse; and there, if my mother consent, I will follow the counsel you give me."

I communicated to my mother the observations of the Jesuit on the impropriety of going to Bourges to constitute myself the pensioner of the archbishop. She felt the same delicacy and the same pride that I did, and our two letters to the bishop were written in that spirit. It only remained for me to consult her on my design of becoming a Jesuit. That I never had the courage to do. Neither her weakness nor mine could have supported that consultation: to reason coolly on it, it was necessary that we should be at a distance from each other. I reserved myself to write to her; and I went to Toulouse undetermined what course I should take. Shall I say that, as I went, I again missed the road to fortune?

A muleteer from Aurillac, who passed his life in travelling between Clermont and Toulouse, undertook to conduct me. I went on one of his mules, and he, generally on foot, by my side. "Mr Abbé," said he, "we shall be obliged to stop some days at home, for I have business that will detain me there. In God's name, employ this interval of time in curing my daughter of her foolish devotion. I have but her, and were an angel to ask her she would never marry him. Her obstinacy afflicts me." The commission was delicate; I found it comical, and willingly undertook it.

I confess, I had figured to myself as very poor, and humble, the dwelling of a man who was trotting incessantly at the tail of his mules, now exposed to rain, and now to the bleak snow, on the roughest roads. I was therefore not a little surprised, on entering, to find a convenient house, well furnished and of singular neatness, and also a kind of grey-clad sister, young, fresh, well made, who hastened to meet Peter (this was the name of the muleteer) and who embraced him as she uttered the endearing name of father. The supper she ordered for us had no less the air of comfort. The leg of mutton was tender and the wine excellent. The chamber they gave me had, in its simplicity, almost the elegance of luxury. I had never lain in so soft a bed. Before I went to sleep, I reflected on what I had seen. " Is it," said I, " in order to pass a few hours of his life at ease that this man tortures and consumes the rest of it in such painful labour? No, he labours to procure tranquillity and repose for old age, and it is the prospect of this repose that lightens his fatigues. But this only daughter, whom he loves so tenderly, what can have persuaded her, young and beautiful as she is, to wear the habit of a nun? Why does she wear that grey-coloured dress, that unplaited linen, that golden cross on her breast, and that close handkerchief on her bosom? Yet the hair she conceals by a fillet is of an excellent colour. The little that can be seen of her neck is white as ivory. And her arms! they too are of pure ivory and incomparably turned!" I fell asleep on these reflections, and next morning I had the pleasure of breakfasting with this fair devotee. She obligingly inquired whether I had slept well? " I slept very sweetly," said I, " but not tranquilly; I was troubled with dreams. And how did you sleep, mademoiselle?"—" Tolerably well, thank God," said she.—" Did you dream?" She blushed and answered that she very rarely dreamt. " And, when you do dream, it is surely of angels?"—" Sometimes of martyrs," said she, smiling.—" Then it is of the martyrs you make."—" I! I make none, sir."—" I will wager you make more than one; though you forbear to boast. As for me, when in my sleep I see the heavens open, I scarcely ever dream but of virgins. I behold them some in white; others in a waist and petticoat of grey serge; and these simple dresses become them more than the richest ornaments. Nothing, in that modest attire, impairs the native beauty of their hair, or their complexion; nothing obscures the lustre of a pure forehead, or of a rosy cheek; no plait deforms the figure; a straight girdle marks and indicates its roundness. An arm of lilies, and a fair hand with rosy fingers, issue, just as heaven made them, from a plain unadorned sleeve; and what their close handkerchief conceals is easily divined. But, whatever pleasure I may have in thus seeing, as I sleep, all these young virgins in heaven, I confess I am a little afflicted at finding them so ill placed."—" Where then do you find them placed?" inquired she, with some embarrassment.— " Alas! quite in a corner, almost alone, and (what vexes me still more) by the side of the Capuchin monks."—" By the side of the Capuchins!" cried she, contracting her brow.—" Alas! yes; almost forsaken; while the august mothers of families, surrounded by the children they have borne, by the husbands they have already rendered so happy on earth, and by their parents, whose age they consoled and comforted, are placed on a distinguished eminence, in the view of all heaven, and all brilliant with glory."—" And the priests," inquired she, with a malicious air, " where are they put?"—" If there be any," answered I, " they are surely thrust into some corner at a distance from that of the virgins."— " Indeed, I believe it," said she; " that is exceedingly proper, for priests would be to them most dangerous neighbours."

Honest Peter was very much amused at this dispute on our professions. He had never seen his daughter so lively, nor so talkative; for I took care, as Montaigne says, to put into my provocation a sweet sour point of winning flattering gaiety, that while it seemed to displease, was not unwelcome to her. At last her father, the evening before we set off for Toulouse, took me alone into his chamber, and said to me: " I see plainly, Mr Abbé, that without me, you and my daughter will never agree. Let us put an end to this dispute between a nun and an abbé: the means are easy; do you cast off these bands, and let her throw away her collar; and I have some notion that if you be inclined, she would not want much persuasion. As to what regards me, I have for ten years done the commissions of your honest father; I am told by every one that you are like him, and I'll act roundly and cordially with you." He then opened the drawers of his bureau, and showing me piles of crowns: "Look ye," said he, " in business there is but one word necessary. Here is what I have saved, and what I am still hoarding up for my grandchildren, if my daughter should bless me with any; for your children, if you choose, and can persuade her."

I will not say that the sight of this treasure did not at all tempt me. The offer was the more seducing to me as honest Peter made no other condition than that of rendering his daughter happy. "I shall continue," said he, "to drive my mules: at every journey I shall augment this pile of crowns as I pass, and you shall dispose of them; my life is a life of labour and fatigue. I will not quit it while I have health and strength, and when my back shall be bent and my hams stiffened with age, I'll come and finish my days quietly with you."—"Ah! my good friend," said I, "who deserves better than you the gentle repose of a happy and long age! But what are you thinking of, when you propose to marry your daughter to a man who has already five children?"—"You, Mr Abbé! five children at your age!"—"It is indeed true. Have I not two sisters and three brothers? Am not I their only father? It is from my labours, and not from yours, that they must live: it is I who must support them."—"And do you think you can earn as much with your Latin as I with my mules?"—"I hope so," said I; "but I will at least do all that depends on me."—"Then you won't have my little nun? Yet she is very pretty, and particularly so since you have ruffled her a little."

—" Certainly," said I, " she is charming and lovely; and she would tempt me more than your crowns. But, as I have told you, nature has already thrown five children into my arms: marriage would soon bring five others, and, perhaps, more, for your devotees are very prolific, and I should then be too much embarrassed."—" 'Tis a pity," said he: " my daughter will now never marry."—" I think I can assure you," said I, " that she has no longer the same aversion to marriage. I have taught her that, in heaven, good mothers are far above virgins; and, by choosing a husband that pleases her, it will be easy for you to instil into her soul this new species of devotion." My prediction was realized.

Arrived at Toulouse, I called on father Noaillac. " Your affair is going on rapidly," said he: " I have found here several Jesuits who know you, and who have added their good wishes to mine. You are proposed, and accepted; to-morrow you may enter if you please. The provincial expects you." I was a little surprised at his being so urgent; but I made no complaint, and suffered him to conduct me to the provincial. I found him fully disposed to receive me as soon as I should think fit, provided my vocation was sincere and decided. I answered that, on leaving my mother, I had not the courage to declare my intention to her; but that I would go no farther without consulting her, and asking her consent; and I requested time to write to her, and to receive her answer. The provincial thought all this very proper, and on leaving him I wrote.

The answer arrived very quickly; and, great God! what an answer! what language and what eloquence! Not one of the illusions, with which father Noaillac had filled my head, had made the smallest impression on the mind of my mother. She had seen only the absolute dependence, the profound submission, the blind obedience, to which her son was going to devote himself, by taking the habit of a Jesuit. "And how can I think," said she, "that you will still be mine?" You will no longer be your own. What hope can I found for my children in him who will himself have no existence but that of which a stranger may dispose at his will? I am told, I am assured, that, if, by the caprice of your superiors, you be nominated to go to India, China, or Japan, and the general send you there, you cannot hesitate; and that, without resistance and without reply, you must go. What, my son! ha nots God made you an independent being; has he not given you a sound reason, a kind heart, a feeling soul; has he endowed you with a will so naturally upright and just, and with inclinations so eminently virtuous, only to reduce you to the state of an obedient machine? Oh! believe me; leave those vows, those inflexible rules, to souls that feel the necessity of such chains. I dare assure you, I, who know you well, that yours delights in freedom, and that the more independent it is, the more forcibly will it stimulate you to all that is honourable and praise-worthy. Ah! my dear boy! recall that fatal moment, yet dear to my memory, though it rend my heart to recollect it, that moment when, in the midst of your afflicted family, heaven gave you strength to revive its hopes by declaring yourself its support And can the heart that nature has made capable of these emotions be rendered better by slavery? When it shall have renounced the liberty of indulging them, when you shall retain nothing of yourself, what will become of those virtuous resolutions of never abandoning your brothers, your sisters, or your mother? Ah! you are lost to them: they expect nothing more from you. My children! your second father is dead to the world and to nature. Weep over him. And I, hopeless mother, I will weep too over you, whom he has forsaken. Great God! was it this you secretly meditated at home with that perfidious Jesuit? Did he come to steal a son from an unhappy widow, and a father from five orphan children! cruel, pitiless man! and with that deceitful gentleness he flattered me! That, they say is their genius and their character. But you, my son, you who never before had a secret from your mother, you too deceived me! Has he then taught you dissimulation? and your first essay has been to entrap your mother! The noble and generous motive for refusing the aid of the bishop was but a vain pretext to divert me, and disguise your designs! No, all this cannot come from you. I love rather to think that some sorcery has fascinated your mind. I will not cease to esteem and to love my son: these are two sentiments to which I am more attached than to life. 'Tis some ambitious hope that has intoxicated him. He believed he was sacrificing himself for me, and for my children. His head has erred, but his heart is pure. He will not read this letter bathed with his mother's tears, without detesting the perfidious counsels that had for a moment perverted him."

Ah! my mother indeed was right: it was impossible for me to finish reading her letter without being suffocated with tears and sobs. From that moment, the idea of becoming a Jesuit was discarded, and I hastened to go and tell the provincial that I declined it. Without disapproving my respect for the authority of my mother, he expressed some regret that was personal to me, and said that the company would always think kindly of my good intentions. Indeed, I found the masters of the college favourably disposed to give me, as at Clermont, scholars from the different classes. But my ambition then was to procure a school of philosophy, and about this I was occupied.

My age was always the first obstacle to my views. In beginning my degrees by philosophy, I thought myself at least capable of teaching its elements; but scarcely one of my scholars would be younger than myself. On this great difficulty I consulted an old private tutor, whose name was Morin, the most distinguished in the university. He conversed with me a long time, and found me sufficiently advanced. But which way persuade these young men to be my pupils! However, an idea struck him that fixed his attention. "That would be excellent," said he, laughing in his sleeve. "Never mind, I'll try; may succeed." I was curious to know what this idea was. "The Bernardins," said he, "have here a kind of seminary, to which they send their young men from all parts to complete their studies. The professor of philosophy whom they expected is taken ill, and they have applied to me to supply his place till he arrives. As I am too much occupied to be his substitute, they beg me to recommend one, and I will propose you."

They accepted me on his word. But when he took me there next day, I distinctly saw how ridiculous they thought the contrast between my functions and my age. Almost all the college had beards, and the master had none. To the contemptuous smile that my presence excited, I opposed a cool, modest, and dignified air; and, while Morin conversed with the superiors, I enquired of the young men what were the regulations of the college for the time of study and the hours of lectures; I spoke to them of some books with which they must provide themselves, in order to suit their lectures to their studies; and, in all I said, I was careful that there should be nothing either too young or too familiar; so much so, that, toward the end of the conversation, I perceived, on their part, a serious attention had taken place of the light tone and jeering air by which it had begun.

The result of the consultation that Morin had just had with the superiors was, that I should give my first lecture on the following morning.

I was nettled at the insulting smile I had experienced on presenting myself to these monks. I wished to revenge myself, and I did it thus. On beginning the philosophical lectures, it was customary to dictate a kind of prelude, that should serve as the vestibule to that temple of wisdom into which the tutor introduces his pupils, and in which therefore somewhat of elegance and majesty ought to combine.

I composed this piece with care; I learned it by heart; I traced, and learned at the same time, the plan that the various divisions of this edifice ought to present when united; and, with my head full of my subject, I gravely and proudly mounted the desk. My young Bernardins seated themselves around me, and their superiors stood leaning on the backs of their chairs, impatient to hear me. I ask whether they are ready to write as I dictate. They answer "Yes." Then, folding my arms, without book or paper before me, speaking as from abundant knowledge, I dictate my preamble first, and next my distribution of this course of philosophy, in which I mark, as I pass, the most distinguished points, and most prominent views.

I cannot, without smiling, recollect the astonished air of the Bernardins, and with what profound esteem they received me when I descended. This first trick had too well succeeded not to induce me to continue and support the part I acted. I every day studied the lecture I was to give, and, in dictating it from my memory, I had the air of arranging and composing without needing reflection. Some time afterward, Morin called on them, and they spoke to him of me with as much astonishment as of a prodigy. They showed him my lectures; and, when he himself expressed to me his surprise at my having dictated them without notes I answered in the language of Horace, that "eloquence is the natural offspring of a clear and accurate conception." Thus, among Gascons, I began by a gasconade; but it was necessary to my success. And, when the Bernardine professor came to resume his place, Morin, who had more pupils than he could himself attend to, gave me as many of them as I wished. Fortune too smiled on me from another quarter.

There was at Toulouse a kind of college, founded for students from the province of Limosin. In this college, called Saint Catherine, the scholars had their lodging gratis, and eight guineas a-year during the five years of graduation. When one of these places became vacant, the scholars themselves elected a successor by ballot: a good and sage institution. It was on one of these vacancies that my young countrymen had the kindness to think of me. In this college, where liberty was regulated only by decency, each lived as he pleased: the porter and the cook were paid at a common expense. Thus, by any economy, I could aid my family with the greater part of the fruit of my labour; and these savings, that increased every year with the number of my pupils, became so considerable as to begin to make my mother comfortable. But, while fortune was providing me with the greatest enjoyments, nature was preparing the most afflicting grief. However, I had yet some time of prosperity.

In looking over, by accident, a collection of prize poems, given at the academy of Floral Games, I was struck with the richness of the prizes it distributed: they were flowers of gold and silver. I was not equally astonished at the beauty of the pieces that had borne the prizes, and it appeared to me easy enough to make better. I thought of the pleasure of sending my mother these gold and silver bunches of flowers, and of the pleasure she herself would feel on receiving them from my hand. Hence I conceived the idea and desire of being a poet. I had never studied the rules of our poetry. I went quickly and bought a small book that taught these rules, and, by the advice of the bookseller, I purchased at the same time a copy of the odes of Rousseau. I meditated and reflected on both, and was soon occupied with the search of some good subject for an ode. I fixed on "the invention of gunpowder." I recollect it began thus :

"Kneaded by some infernal fury's bloody hands."

I could not recover from my astonishment at having written so fine an ode. I recited it with all the intoxication of enthusiasm and self-love; and, when I sent it to the academy, I had no doubt but that it must bear away the prize. It did not succeed; it did not even obtain the consolation of honourable mention. I was enraged; and, in my indignation, I wrote to Voltaire, sent him my poem, and cried to him for vengeance: all the world knows with what kindness Voltaire received all young men who announced any talent for poetry: the French Parnassus was an empire whose sceptre he would have yielded to no one on earth, but whose subjects he delighted to see multiply. He sent me one of those answers that he could turn with so much grace, and of which he was so liberal. The praises he bestowed on my poem amply consoled me for what I called the injustice of the academy, whose judgment, as I said, did not weigh one single grain in the balance against such a suffrage as that of Voltaire. But that which flattered me still more than his letter, was the present he sent me of a copy of his works, corrected by his own hand. I was mad with pride and joy, and ran about the town and the colleges with his present in my hands. Thus began my correspondence with that illustrious man, and that intimate friendship that lasted without change for five and thirty years, dissolved only by his death.

I continued to write for the Floral Games, and obtained prizes every year. But the last of these little literary triumphs had a more rational and more sensible interest for me than that of vanity, and it is for that reason that this scene deserves a place in the memoirs I transmit to my children.

As in the estimation of mankind all is appreciated by comparison, and as at Toulouse there was nothing more brilliant in literature than success in the lists of the Floral Games, the public assembly of this academy for distributing the prizes had the pomp and crowd of a great solemnity. Here three deputies from the parliament presided The chief magistrates and all the corporation of the city attended in their robes. The whole hall, in the form of an amphitheatre, was filled with the principal inhabitants of the town, and the most beautiful women. The brilliant youth of the university occupied the space round the academic circle: the hall, which was very spacious, was decorated with festoons of flowers and laurel, and the trumpets of the city, as each prize was given, made the capital resound with the signal of victory.

I had that year sent five pieces to the academy; one ode, two poems, and two idyls. The ode failed; the prize was not given. The two poems were supposed to have equal merit: one of them obtained the prize for epic poetry, and the other a prose prize that happened to be vacant. One of the two idyls obtained the prize of pastoral poetry, and the other an inferior honour. Thus the three prizes, and the only three the academy were going to distribute, were adjudged to me: it was I who was to receive them all. I walked to the hall with such consummate vanity that I could never recollect it since without confusion, nor without pity for my youth. It was still much worse when I was loaded with my flowers and my crowns. But where is the poet of twenty whose head would not have turned with such honours?

An attentive silence reigns in the hall, and after the eulogy of Clémence Isaure, foundress of the Floral Games, a eulogy inexhaustible, and pronounced every year with becoming devotion at the foot of her statue, comes the distribution of the prizes. The judges announce, that the prize for the ode is reserved. It was well known that I had sent an ode to the academy; it was known too, that I was the author of an idyl that had not been crowned: I was pitied, and I smiled at their pity. The poem is then named aloud to which the prize is adjudged; and at these words, "Let the author advance," I rise, approach, and receive the prize. I am applauded as usual, and I hear whispered around me: "He has lost two; but he gains the third; he has more than one string to his bow, and more than one arrow to shoot." I retire to seat myself modestly, amid the sound of the trumpets. But soon the second poem is announced, to which the academy, they say, has thought proper to adjudge the prize of eloquence, rather than to reserve it. The author is called, and again it is I who rise. The applauses redouble, and the reading of this poem is listened to with the same favour and indulgence as that of the first. I had again taken my place, when the idyl was proclaimed, and the author invited to come and receive the prize. I rise for the third time. Then, if I had written Cinna, Athalie, and Zaïre, I could not have been more applauded. The interest I excited was extreme. The men bore me through the crowd on their arms; the women embraced me. Light vapour of vain glory! Who knows it better than I? since, of these essays that were thought so brilliant, there is not a single one that forty years afterward, though read even with indulgence, has appeared to me worthy of a place in the collection of my works! But what still sensibly touches me in the recollection of that day, so flattering for me, is what I am going to relate.

Amid the tumult and noise of the captivated crowd, two long black arms are raised and extended to me. I look, I recognise my master of the third class, the good father Malosse, whom I had not seen for eight years, and who happened to be present at this ceremony. I instantly rush forward, cut my way through the crowd, and, throwing myself into his arms, with my three prizes: "Here father,"

said I, "they are yours, it is to you I owe them."
The good Jesuit raised his eyes to heaven, and they
were filled with tears of joy: and I may say I more
sensibly felt the pleasure I gave him than the brilliancy of my triumph. Ah! my children, that
which interests the heart is always grateful: it
delights to the end of life. That which has only
flattered the pride of genius recurs but as a vain
dream, the error of which we blush to have so madly
cherished.

These literary amusements, although very seducing
to me, did not trench on my more solid occupations.
I gave to poetry my hours of recreation and leisure;
but at the same time I applied assiduously to my
studies, and to those of my school. In my second
year of philosophy, not being able to engage my
Jesuit professor to teach us the Newtonian system, I
determined to go and study it at the school of the
Doctrinaires. Their college, called the Esquilée,
had, for professors in philosophy, two men of distinguished merit; but one of the two, and he was
mine, with much information and talent, inclined too
much, either by disposition or feebleness of constitution, to indolence and repose. He found it convenient to have in me a pupil, who, having already
studied philosophy, might from time to time spare
him the fatigue and weariness of lecturing.

"Mount," would he say to me, "mount the pulpit, and render that easy to them, which you so
easily understand." This eulogy well repaid the
pains I gave myself; for it ensured me the confidence
of the scholars, and made the pensioners of the college desirous of having me for their private tutor;
an excellent and solid provision for me.

To please my professor, I consented, against my
inclination, to engage in public disputations. He
attached a vast importance to the numbering me
among those of his pupils who were soon to appear
in public: and, as he was a member of the academy

of sciences at Toulouse, he would have my thesis dedicated to that company. "A thesis thus honoured," said he, "will be equally new and striking." It was by this exhibition that he wished to terminate his philosophic career; and he conceived the project of adding to the pomp of this spectacle a signal testimony in my favour, which, though very honourable to me, should completely astonish me. He succeeded but too well; and my astonishment was such that it had nearly made me mad, or foolish, for the rest of my life.

In these public exercises, it was the constant custom for the professor to be in his pulpit, and his scholars before him, in what is called a desk, a kind of tribune below the pulpit. When all the company were seated, and the illustrious academy arranged before the tribune, notice was given me, and I appeared. You may well conceive that I had prepared a compliment for the academy, and in this little speech I had employed all the art and talent I possessed. I knew it by heart, I had repeated it twenty times without any hesitation, and was so sure of my memory that I had neglected to take with me the manuscript. I appeared, and, instead of finding my professor in his pulpit, I perceived him seated with the academicians. I respectfully invited him by my looks to come and take his place. "Mount, sir," said he aloud, with his air of indolence and security; "mount the pulpit, or the desk, just as you please; you have no need of me." This splendid testimony excited in the assembly a murmur of surprise, and, I think, of approbation: but its effect on me was that of freezing my senses and disordering my brain. Amazed, trembling, I ascend the steps of the tribune, and kneel, as was usual, as if to implore the light of the Holy Spirit. But when I want to recollect the beginning of my compliment before I rise, I cannot: memory is lost; the clue has escaped; I search for it in vain, and only find a thick impenetrable cloud. I make incredible efforts to recover the first word of my speech; but not a word, not one idea recurs. In this state of anguish, I remain for some minutes in a feverish stupor, and almost ready to burst the veins and nerves of my head by the frightful contention into which this labour had put them, when suddenly, and as by miracle, the cloud that enveloped my mind is dissipated; my thoughts are freed, my ideas revive, I seize the thread of my eulogium, and much fatigued, but tranquil and reassured, it is pronounced. I say nothing of the success it had; praise is rarely ill received, and I had seasoned this as delicately as I could. Neither do I boast of the favour that supported me in all this exercise. In leading me to the most brilliant questions in physics, the academicians who deigned to contend with me studied to make my answers shine. They were true Mæcenases, full of indulgence and kindness. But what was most remarkable, and most affecting to me, was the noble conduct of the Jesuit professor, whom I had too hastily quitted to go to the Esquille, and who, at this moment, came to make me feel my error: he disputed with me last on the system of gravitation, and, with the appearance of attacking me with all his force, he contrived to offer me every means of developing my knowledge. I fortunately gave him to understand by my answers that, in the manner he contended with me, it was easy to recognise the superiority of the master, who would exercise the powers of his scholar, but was careful not to crush them. When I descended, the president of the academy, in congratulating me, said that the academy could not mark its satisfaction better than by offering to number me among its associates, as there was then a vacancy. I accepted this offer with humble gratitude, and received the prize of my combat amid the plaudits of the assembly.

But the solid benefit I derived from these youthful

successes, was the number of pupils that increased my school, and enabled me to send additional aid to my mother. Rich enough, by my industry, to provide for the education of the eldest of my brothers, I now lent him a helping hand and brought him to Toulouse. He was fourteen, and did not know a word of Latin; but he had a very lively conception, an excellent memory, and a passionate desire of profiting by my lessons. I simplified the rules, and abridged the method; in six months he had surmounted all the difficulties of syntax; and a year more well employed enabled him to proceed without a master. That was his ambition; for he saw me overloaded with employment, and was gratified when he could lighten it. Poor brother! The sentiment he felt for me was not friendship only, it was idolatry. The name of brother had, in his mouth, a character of sanctity. He expressed to me his desire of dedicating himself to the church, and of this I was glad: for this same desire began to cool in me for more than one reason, and particularly on account of the forbidding difficulties that were thrown in my way.

The college of Saint Catherine, where I had a place, had for its inspector and spiritual guard one of the archbishop's proctors, whose name was Goutelongue, an intriguing, haughty, confident man, and, as was said, somewhat of a knave, who wanted to lead the college at his will, and dispose of the scholarships as his caprice directed. He vaunted of his intimacy with the archbishop, rang the changes on his lordship's authority, and being himself a proctor, so far intimidated some and seduced others, that he had formed a party among our comrades, subjugated by fear and hope. But there was one Pujalou in the college, of a frank, independent, and firm character, who, wearied of such sovereignty, dared to oppose him, and gave the signal for rebellion against his usurped authority. "What right, my friends," said be to his young companions and countrymen, " what right has this man to intrigue in our assemblies, and influence our elections ? The founder of this college, in leaving to ourselves the liberty of nominating and electing to the vacant scholarships, has wisely judged that youth is the age at which there is most natural equity, most rectitude, and most integrity. Why should we suffer any one to corrupt the equity that animates us? Among us, the vacant scholarships are destined to the most worthy, and not to the most patronized. If Goutelongue want creatures, let him obtain favours for them from the archbishop, and not come to gratify them at our expense. To conduct us in our choice, we have our conscience, which is at least equivalent to that of the proctor. I who know him, declare that I confide less in his probity than in that of a horse-jockey." This last stroke, though not of noble eloquence, was that which carried the day: the proctor ever afterwards retained the epithet of the jockey, and his intrigues were likened to the honest dealings of that profession.

I arrived in these circumstances, and Pujalou had no difficulty to engage me in his party. From that moment I was noted in the tablets of the proctor; but I was soon signalized there by a mark that was personal to me. There was a scholarship vacant in the college. The contest between the two parties was doubtful, and, in case of equality, it was the archbishop who decided the election. Our party consulted its forces, and thought itself sure of carrying it, but by a single vote. In the evening before the election, this vote was withdrawn from us. One of our fellow-students, an honest and good youth, but timid, had disappeared. We learnt that, in a village three leagues from Toulouse, he had an uncle, a clergyman, and that this uncle had come and taken him away to pass the Christmas holidays at his house. We had no doubt but that this was a stratagem of Goutelongue. We knew the name of the village, and the road to it; but it was already dark, the rain that fell was mixed with snow and hail, and it was a folly to think that in such weather the clergyman would consent to let his nephew come, particularly as he had taken him away at the request of the proctor. "Never mind," said I suddenly, "I'll go and fetch him, and will bring him back to you behind me; give me but a good horse." The horse was provided in an instant, and, muffled up in Pujalou's long cloke, I arrived in two hours at the door of the parsonage, just as the rector, his nephew, and his maid, were going to bed. My fellow-student came to me when he saw me alight; and, as I embraced him, "Behave with courage, my friend," said I, " or you are dishonoured." The rector, to whom I announced myself as coming from the college of Saint Catherine, inquired the object of my journey. "I come," said I, "in the sacred name of Christ, the universal father of the poor, to conjure you not to be the accomplice of the despoiler of the poor, of that unjust and cruel man, who steals from them their substance to lavish it at his caprice." I then developed to him the arts of Goutelongue, to usurp over us the right of nominating to the vacant places, and consign them to intrigue. "To-morrow," said I, "we have either to elect a scholar whom he protects, and who has no need of the place that is vacant, or a poor student who deserves and expects it. Which of the two would you wish to suceeed?" He answered that the choice would not be difficult if it depended on him. "And it does depend on you," said I: "the party of the poor youth want but one vote; that vote was assured to him; and, at the solicitation, at the instance of Goutelongue, you have brought your nephew here to deprive him of it. Restore it to him: restore him the bread of which you have robbed him." Amazed and confused, he again answered that his nephew was free, that he had brought him to pass the holidays with him, and that he had used no compulsion. "If he be free," replied I, "let him come with me; let him come and fulfil his duty; let him come and save his honour; for his honour is lost, if it be believed that he is sold to Goutelongue." Then looking at the young man, and seeing him disposed to follow me, "Come," said I, "embrace your uncle, and come and prove to the college that you are neither of you the slave of the proctor." In an instant we were both on horseback, and far from the village.

Our fellow-students were not gone to bed. We found them at supper, and with what transports of joy did they see us arrive together! I thought that Pujalou would have smothered me with embraces: we were wet to the very bones. They began by drying us; and then the ham, the sausage, and the wine, were lavished on us. But, prudent amid so much intoxication, I required that the subject of our joy might be kept secret from the opposite party till the moment of election; and indeed the sudden appearance of the fugitive was a death-blow to our adversaries. We carried the vacant place at the point of the sword; and Goutelongue, who knew the cause of it, never forgave me.

Thus, when I presented myself to the archbishop, to beg him to obtain from the bishop of my diocese a permission to be ordained by him, I found him quite prejudiced against me: "I was only a gallant abbé, wholly occupied with poetry, paying my court to the ladies, and writing songs and idyls for them, nay sometimes, in the dusk of the evening, taking my walk with pretty girls."..... This archbishop was La Roche-Aymond, a man of little delicacy in his political morality; but, affecting rigour for vices that were not his own, he wanted to make me do penance to the most dirty and most bigoted of all seminaries. I recognised the good offices of Goutelongue, and my disgust for the seminary of Calvet revealed to me, as a secret I had concealed from myself, how much my inclination for the church was cooled.

My correspondence with Voltaire, to whom I sometimes wrote as I sent him my poetry, and who had the kindness to answer me, had not a little contributed to change my fancy for this profession.

Voltaire, in encouraging me to hope for success in the career of poetry, pressed me to go to Paris, the only school of taste where talent can form itself. I answered him, that Paris was too vast a theatre for me; that I should there be lost in the crowd; that, beside, being born without fortune, I should want the means of existence; that at Toulouse I had created myself a comfortable and honourable livelihood, and that, unless Paris could offer me one nearly equal, I should still have the fortitude to resist my desire of going to render my homage to the great man who deigned to invite me.

However, it soon became necessary to decide. Literature at Paris, the bar at Toulouse, or the seminary at Limoges: these were what offered themselves, and in each I beheld only uncertainty and delay. In this irresolution, I felt the necessity of consulting my mother. I had no idea she was ill; but I knew she was feeble: I hoped that my presence would restore her to health: I went to see her. How charming, how delightful would this journey have been to me, had it corresponded to so dear a hope!

I leave my brother at Toulouse; and, on a little horse I had bought, I set off: I arrive at the farm, at the hamlet of Saint Thomas. It was a holiday. My eldest sister, and the daughter of my aunt d'Albois, had come thither for a walk. There I rest myself, and change my clothes; for I carried in a bundle, in my cloke-bag, all the dress of an abbé. From Saint Thomas to Bort, by fording the river, there is but one meadow to cross. I take the two girls across the river on my horse, and I arrive at the town by that charming walk. Pardon these details: I repeat it again, it is for my children that I write.

As I passed by the church, the people were at vespers; one of my old school-fellows, Odde, the same that afterward married my sister, met me as he was going there, and he soon spread the news of my arrival in the church. My friends first steal out, then our neighbours, and insensibly the whole congregation: the church is empty, and my house is soon filled and surrounded by this crowd, who come to see me. Alas! I was at that moment severely afflicted! I had just embraced my mother; and in her thinness, in her cough, in the burning red that coloured her cheek, I thought I recognised the same disorder of which my father died. It was but too true; my mother was attacked by it before the age of forty. That fatal consumption was contagious in my family, and made most cruel ravages. I did all that was possible to conceal from my mother the grief that seized me. She, who knew her disorder, forgot it, or at least appeared to forget it, on seeing me, and spoke only of her joy. I afterwards learnt that she had engaged the physician and my aunts to flatter me on the state of her health, and not suffer me to indulge my inquietude. They all united with her to deceive me, and my soul caught eagerly at the gentle hope. I return to the inhabitants.

My mother was enchanted at my academic successes, and the enchantment had spread itself around her. The flowers of silver that I sent her, and with which she every year adorned the altar on the *Fête-Dieu*, had given such an idea of me in the town as is not to be defined. The people there, who have since perhaps changed their nature like so many others, were then kindness itself. Each was emulous of loading me with all that friendship can dictate. The good mothers were pleased to call to mind my infancy; the men listened to me as if my words were

to have been collected and preserved. Yet I only
uttered the simple feeling language that my heart
prompted in its emotion. As everybody came to
congratulate my mother, Miss B*** came too with
her sisters, and, according to custom, she was obliged
to permit the new comer to embrace her. The others
gently leaned to the innocent kiss I gave them, but
she withdrew her cheek and shunned it. I felt this
difference, and was hurt.

Of the three weeks that I passed with my mother,
it was impossible not to steal some moments from
nature, in order to give them to grateful friendship.
My mother desired it; and, that she might not
deprive my friends of the pleasure of my visits, she
herself went to the little treats they gave me. These
treats were dinners that each friend gave in his turn.
There, continually occupied and continually moved
by what was said to her son, and by what her son
answered, observing my very looks, anxious at every
moment how I should reply to the attentions that
besieged me on every side, my mother felt these long
dinners a fatigue to her mind, and a painful effort for
her frail organs. Our private conversations, by creating a livelier interest, fatigued her yet much more.
I endeavoured to spare her feeble voice, either by my
long recitals, or by my diligence in interrupting the
dialogue to interpose my reflections. But, no less
animated while she listened than while she spoke,
attention was not less hurtful to her health than
speaking, and I could not see, without the most
afflicting emotion, that fire sparkle in her eyes which
was consuming her blood.

I at last spoke to her of the diminished ardour I felt
for the profession of the church, and of my irresolution about the choice of a new one. It was then
that she appeared calm, and spoke to me coolly.

"The profession of the church," said she, "essentially imposes two duties; that of being pious, and
that of being chaste: it is impossible to be a good

priest but at this price, and on these two points it belongs to you to examine yourself. As to the bar, if you enter there, I must require from you the most inviolable promise that you will never affirm what you do not believe to be true, nor ever defend what you believe is not just. With regard to the career that M. de Voltaire invites you to pursue, I think it a prudent precaution to assure to yourself at Paris a situation that may leave you time to instruct yourself, and to acquire more talent; for you must not flatter yourself; what you have already done is but little. If M. de Voltaire can procure you some honourable, liberal, and sure employment, go, my dear son, go, enter the lists of fame and fortune; I consent: but never forget that the most honourable and most dignified companion of genius is virtue." Thus spoke this astonishing woman, who had no other education than that of the little convent at Bort.

Her physician thought it necessary to inform me that my presence was hurtful to her. "Her disorder," said he, "is a blood too vivid and too highly inflamed; I calm it as much as I can, and you involuntarily, nay necessarily, agitate it again; and every evening I find her pulse more full and quick. If you wish her health to be re-established, sir, you must leave her; and, above all, be careful that your parting be not too affecting for her." It was a cruel parting; and, in that moment, my mother's courage was superior to mine; for she flattered herself no longer, though I continued to hope. At the first word I said to her of the necessity of returning to my pupils, "Yes, my son," said she, "you must go. I have seen you. Our hearts have spoken. We have nothing more to say to each other but a tender farewell, for I have no need to recommend——" She interrupted herself; and, as her eyes filled with tears, "I am thinking," said she, "of that good mother I have lost, and who loved you so. She died like a saint; her joy would have been great to have seen you once again. But let us try to die as like a saint as herself: we shall meet again before God." She afterwards changed the subject, and talked to me of Voltaire. I had sent her the handsome present he had made me of a copy of his works: it was a corrected edition: she had read them, and was reading them again. "If you see him," said she, "thank him for the gentle moments he has made your mother pass; tell him that she knew by heart the second act of Zaire, that she wept over Merope, and that these verses of the Henriade on Hope, have never left her memory nor her heart."

>...........that which heaven sends inspires
> No empty pleasures, nor no vain desires;
> It brings God's promise, his defence and aid,
> Pure, immutable, as the heaven he made.

This allusion to herself, speaking as of one who would soon cease to exist, rent my very heart. But, as I was advised carefully to avoid all that might affect her too sensibly, I dissembled what I presaged: and the next day, both mutually studying to conceal the affliction of parting, we only granted to our farewell what it was impossible we should refuse to nature.

From the moment I was separated from her, I resigned myself to deep sorrow, and all the recollections that occurred to me on my journey united to torture me. Yet a little while and she will be no longer mine; this mother who, from my birth, has breathed only for me; this adored mother, whose displeasure I feared as that of heaven, and, if I dare say it, yet more than heaven itself; for I thought of her much oftener than of God; and when I had some temptation to subdue, or some passion to repress, it was always my mother that I fancied present. What would she say if she knew what passes in me? What would be her confusion, what would be her grief?

Such were the reflections with which I combated my affliction; and reason then resumed its empire, seconded by nature, who always did what she pleased with my heart. Those who, like me, have known this tender filial love, need not be told what was the sadness and despondency of my soul. Yet I still held by a frail hope; a hope too dear to be wholly relinquished until the last moment.

I went to complete the course of my studies; and, as I had providentially entered myself at the school for canon law, it is probable that my final decision would have been in favour of the bar. But, toward the end of this year, a little note from Voltaire came and determined me to set off for Paris. "Come," said he in his note, "and come without inquietude. M. Orri, whom I have spoken to, undertakes to provide for you. Signed VOLTAIRE." Who was M. Orri? I knew not. I went to ask my good friends at Toulouse, and showed them my note. "M. Orri!" exclaimed they; "why, 'tis the comptroller-general of finance! My dear friend, your fortune is made; you will be a farmer-general. Remember us in your glory. Protected by the minister, it will be easy for you to gain his esteem and confidence. You will be at the fountain-head of favour. Dear Marmontel, make some of its rivulets flow down to us. A little streamlet of Pactolus will content our ambition." One would be receiver-general, another would be satisfied with an humbler place in the finance, or with some other employment of two or three hundred a-year; and this depended on me.

I had forgotten to say, that among us young students, and in order to rival the academy of Floral Games, we had formed a literary society, formerly celebrated under the name of The Little Academy. It was there that all vied to exalt my hopes: and I soon became eager to set off. But, as my future opulence did not supersede the necessity of present economy, I was inquiring how I could make the journey at the least expense, when a president of the parliament, M. de Puget, sent for me, and proposed to me, in obliging terms, to travel to Paris with his son, in a litter, at our joint expense. I told the president that the litter appeared to me very slow and tedious, but that the pleasure of being in good company would compensate for the inconvenience; that, as to the expense of the journey, I had already calculated the amount; it would cost me but five guineas by the courier, and I was determined not to exceed that sum. The president, after having tried in vain to draw something more from me, thought proper to accept what I offered: and, indeed, as he must otherwise have paid the whole expense of the litter, my little share was all gain to him.

I left my brother at Toulouse; and my scholarship at St Catherine's would have been secure to him, had he been in the class of philosophy; but these places could be held only during the five years of graduation. He was therefore obliged to renounce this advantage for the present, and I gave him an asylum in the Irish seminary. I paid one year of his schooling in advance, and, when I bade him farewell, left him all the rest of my money, having only one half-crown for myself when I set off from Toulouse. But in passing through Montauban I was to find a fresh supply.

Montauban, as well as Toulouse, had a literary academy, that every year gave a prize. I had gained it this year, and had not taken it away. It was a silver lyre, of the value of twelve guineas. On my arrival, I went and took my lyre, and instantly sold it. Thus, after paying the muleteer in advance the expenses of my journey, and after treating my friends handsomely, who accompanied me in cavalcade as far as Montauban, I had still more than six guineas in my pocket. Was not this an ample provision for one whom fortune awaited at Paris? Never did any one go more slowly to meet her. Yet this journey in the litter was not so tiresome as I should have thought it. I was fortunate in finding an honest muleteer. He gave us most excellent cheer. I have never eaten better red-legged partridges, nor more juicy turkeys, nor better tasted truffles. I was ashamed at being so well fed for my five guineas, and determined to recompense this honest man as soon as I should be in a situation to be more liberal.

It is true, that my fellow traveller paid him better than I: and he was willing enough to take advantage of it; but he did not find me disposed to entire acquiescence. The first day, I gave him the back seat, and, notwithstanding the sickness which the balancing of the carriage and the motion backward occasioned me, I suffered the inconvenience. I even dissembled my fatigue at hearing the most stupid of all spoiled children eternally displaying, with a puerile emphasis, his noble origin, his immense fortune, and the dignity of president with which his father was invested. I let him boast of the beauty of his large blue eyes, and the charms of his face, with which, he innocently told me, all the women were in love. He talked to me of their lures, their caresses, and the kisses they gave his fine eyes; I listened patiently and said to myself: " How ridiculous is vanity !"

The next day, he got into the carriage first, and seated himself on the back seat. " Softly, marquis," said I, " in front if you please. To-day it is my turn to be at my ease." He answered that it was his place, and that his father had understood that he should occupy the back seat. I replied that, if his father had understood that in his bargain, I had not understood it in mine; and that had he proposed it to me, I should not have cased myself up like a fool in that jolting carriage; that I should now have been, for the same money, in the open air, upon a good horse, enjoying the scenery around me; that I had already been duped enough for having employed my five guineas so ill, and that I would not be so much so as to give him constantly the best place. He persisted in keeping it; but though he was as tall as I, I entreated him not to oblige me to force him from it, and to leave him in the road. He listened to this argument, and took the front seat. He was in ill humour till dinner time. However, he contented himself with depriving me of his conversation, but at dinner his superiority recurred to him. They brought us a red-legged partridge. He thought himself an excellent carver: *quo gestu lepores, et quo gallina secetur.* And, indeed, this exercise had made a part of his education. He took the partridge on his plate, cut off very judiciously the two wings and the two legs, kept the two wings for himself, and left me the legs and the back-bone. "What!" said I, "you like the wings of a partridge?"—"Yes," said he, "very well." —"And I too," said I; and smiling, without discomposing myself, made an equal division. "You make very free," said he, "to take a wing from my plate!" —"You are much more so," answered I in a firm tone, "for having taken two from the dish." He was red with anger; but it subsided, and we dined peaceably.

The next day: "It is your turn," said I, "to take the back seat of the carriage." He seated himself there, saying: "You do me a great favour:" and our tête-à-tête was going to be as silent as on the evening before, when an incident gave it life. The marquis took snuff, I took it too, thanks to a young and pretty girl, who gave me a taste for it; in his sullen mood he opened his fine snuff-box, and I, who was not in ill humour, extended my hand and took a pinch, as if we had been the best friends in the world. He did not refuse, and, after a few minutes reflection, "I must tell you," said he, "a circumstance that happened to M. de Maniban, first president of the parliament at Toulouse." I foresaw it was something impertinent, and listened. "M. de Maniban," continued he, "once gave audience in his cabinet, to a quidam, who had a cause, and who came to solicit his favour. The magistrate, as he listened, opened his snuff-box: the quidam took a pinch: the president did not discompose himself, but rang for his servant, and throwing away the snuff that the quidam had touched, he sent him for more." I avoided any appearance of applying this story to myself, and some little time afterward, when the coxcomb again displayed his box, I again took of his snuff as tranquilly as before. He looked surprised; and I, smiling, said: "Why don't you ring, marquis?"—"Here is no bell."—"You are very fortunate that there is not," said I; "for the quidam would have drubbed you soundly for having rung." You may guess the astonishment that my reply created. He chose to be angry, and I was angry in my turn. "Be quiet," said I, "or I'll trample on you. I see that I have gotten a young fop to correct, and, from this moment, I will submit to no impertinence. Recollect that we are going to a city where the son of a provincial president is nothing, and begin from this time to be simple, polite, and modest, if you can: for, in the world, self-sufficiency, foppery, and foolish pride, will expose you to much more bitter vexations." While I spoke, he concealed his eyes, and I saw he wept. I pitied him, and assumed the tone of a sincere friend: I made him reflect on his ridiculous boasting, his puerile vanity, and his foolish pretensions; and I thought I perceived that his head became gradually less inflated with the vapours that filled it. "What can I do?" he asked: "I have been brought up thus." To various marks of my kindness, I added the politeness of almost always giving him the best place in the carriage, for I was more accustomed than he to the inconvenience of riding backward, and this complaisance completely reconciled us. However, as our conversation was often interrupted by long and continued silence, I had time to translate into verse the poem of 'The

K

Rape of the Lock;' an amusement that was soon to prove of such utility to me.

In my meditations, I had likewise two abundant sources of agreeable illusions. One was the hope of fortune, and, if heaven preserved my mother, the hope of enjoying her society at Paris: the other was the superb and fantastic picture I made myself of that capital, where that which I supposed least magnificent could not but have all the elegance of proportion, and all the beauty of simplicity One of these illusions was destroyed on my getting to Paris: the other did not flatter me long. On my arrival, I lodged at the Julian-baths, and the next morning I I was at the levee of Voltaire.

BOOK III.

THOSE young men who, born with some genius and love for the arts, have been introduced into the presence of the most celebrated men in the art that forms their own study and delight, have felt like me the confusion, the oppression of heart, the kind of religious fear, that I experienced on appearing before Voltaire.

Persuaded that I should have to speak first, I had turned in twenty ways the phrase with which I should address him, and was satisfied with none. He relieved me from this difficulty. On hearing my name he came to me, and extending his arms, " My good friend," said he, " I am very glad to see you. Yet I have bad news to tell you; M. Orri had undertaken to provide for you; M. Orri is no longer in favour."

I could scarcely have received a more severe, more sudden, or more unexpected blow; but I was not stunned by it. I have always been astonished at the courage I have felt on great occasions, for my heart is naturally feeble. "Well, sir," said I, "then I must contend with adversity; I have long known, and long struggled with it."—" I am glad to find you have confidence in your own powers. Yes, my good friend, the true and most worthy resource of a man of letters is in himself and in his genius. But, till yours shall have procured you something to exist on, I speak to you candidly as a friend, I must provide for you. I have not invited you hither to abandon you. If even at this moment you be in want of money, tell me so: I will not suffer you to have any other creditor than Voltaire." I returned him thanks for his kindness, assuring him that, for some time at least, I should not want to profit by it, and that, when I should, I would confidently have recourse to him. "You promise me," said he, "and I depend on you. In the mean time, let's hear what you think of applying to?"—"I really don't know; you must decide for me."—"The stage, my friend, the stage is the most enchanting of all careers; it is there that in one day you may obtain glory and fortune. One successful piece renders a man at the same time rich and celebrated; and if you take pains you will succeed."—"I do not want ardour," replied I, "but what should I do for the stage?"—"Write a good comedy," said he, in a firm tone.—"Alas! sir, how should I draw portraits? I do not know faces." He smiled at this answer. "Well then, write a tragedy." I answered that I was not quite so ignorant of the passions and the heart, and that I would willingly make the attempt. Thus passed my first interview with this illustrious man.

On leaving him, I went and took a lodging at three half-crowns a month, near the Sorbonne, at a cook's house in Mason-street, where I had a tolerably good dinner for nine-pence. I used to reserve a part of it for my supper, and I lived well. However, my six guineas would not have gone very far. But I found an honest bookseller, who offered to buy the manuscript of my translation of 'The Rape of the Lock,' and who gave me twelve guineas for it, but in promissory notes, and these notes were at long dates. A Gascon, whose acquaintance I had made at a coffee-house, discovered for me, in the street of St Andreé-des-Arts, a grocer, who consented to take my notes in payment, provided I would purchase goods of him to that amount. I bought twelve guineas' worth of sugar of him; and after having paid him, I entreated him to resell it for me. I lost but little by it; and with my six guineas of Montauban, and my eleven pounds fifteen shillings of my sugar, I was enabled to go on till the harvest of academic prizes, without borrowing of any one. Eight months of my lodging and my eating would only amount together to eleven guineas and a half. I had therefore near six guineas left for my other expenses. This was quite enough; for, by keeping in bed, I should burn less wood in winter. I might therefore go on with my literary labours till Midsummer, without inquietude; and, if I gained the prize at the academy, which was twenty guineas, I should get through the year. This calculation kept me in spirits.

I began by studying the art of play-writing. Voltaire furnished me with books. Aristotle's Art of Poetry, P. Corneille's Discourses on the Unities, his Reflections, the Greek tragedians, our modern tragedies, were all eagerly and rapidly devoured. I longed to try my strength; and the first subject that my impatience seized on was the Portuguese revolution. On this I lost some precious time; the political interest of this event was too feeble for the stage; and still more feeble was the manner in which I hastily conceived and executed my project. However, some scenes that I showed to an intelligent player, made him augur well of me. But he said that the art of play-writing must be studied at the theatre, and he advised me to engage Voltaire to ask for a free admission for me. "Roselli is right," said Voltaire; "the theatre is the school for us all; it must be open to you; and I ought to have thought of it sooner." My free admission to the French theatre was liberally granted me: and I afterwards never failed to go and take my lesson there. I cannot express how much this assiduous study hastened the developement and progress of my ideas, and of the little talent I might have. I never returned from the representation of a tragedy without some reflections on the nature of the art, nor without some new degree of warmth in my imagination, my heart, and my style.

To draw beautiful tragic subjects from the same sources, it would have been necessary to become a student of history; and I should have had the courage to do this, but I had not time. I looked hastily over ancient history, and, the subject of Dionysius the Tyrant having struck my fancy, I could not rest till the plan of it was formed, and all the incidents of the fable invented and arranged; but I said nothing of it to Voltaire, both that I might proceed alone, and without a guide, and that I might show him my first effort with all the advantage of a finished work.

It was at this time that I met at his house the man whose society has, of all others, most charmed and delighted me, the good, the wise, the virtuous Vauvenargue. In his person, he had been cruelly treated by nature, but his mind was one of her rarest works. I used to think I beheld in him Fénélon, infirm and suffering. He showed me much kindness, and I easily obtained the permission to go and see him. I should make a good book of his conversations, if I were able to recollect them. Some traces may be seen of them in the collection he has left of his thoughts and meditations. But, eloquent and feeling as he is in his writings, it seems to me that he was still more so in his conversations with us. I say *with us*, because I generally found with him a man who was wholly devoted to him, and who for that reason soon gained my confidence and esteem. This man was Beauvin, the same who has since given to the stage the tragedy of the Cheruscians, a man of sense and taste, but of an indolent disposition; devoted to pleasure, though almost as poor as myself.

As our sentiments for the marquis of Vauvenargue so perfectly accorded, they established between us a kind of sympathy. We used to meet every evening after the play, at the Procope coffee-house, the tribunal of criticism, and the school for young poets, to study the humour and taste of the public. There we always conversed together; and, when there was no play, we passed our evenings in retired walks. Thus we became every day more necessary to each other, and every day felt more regret at separating. "And why should we separate?" said he at last: "why not live together? The green-grocer, at whose house I lodge, has a chamber to let: and, by living at a common expense, we shall spend less." I answered that this arrangement would please me exceedingly; but that for the moment I could not think of it: he insisted and pressed me so strongly that I was obliged to tell him why I refused. "In the house where I now live," said I, "the punctuality with which I have hitherto paid has necessarily gained me a degree of credit which I should not find elsewhere, and of which I may perhaps soon have occasion to make use." Beauvin, who had twelve or fifteen guineas, bade me be under no anxiety; that he could advance me money, and that he had a plan in his head to enrich us both. On my part I displayed to him my hopes and resources; I showed him the piece I had written for the prize of the academy; he thought it a bar of gold. I told him the plan, and read to him the first scenes of my tragedy: he answered for its success; and this was a mine of silver. The marquis of Vauvenargue lived at the Hotel de Tours, Petite rue du Paon, and opposite this hotel was the house of Beauvin's green-grocer. Here then I came to lodge. His project of publishing between us a periodical review was not so good a thing as he expected: we had neither gall nor venom: and as this review was neither a faithless unjust criticism on good works, nor a bitter biting satire on good authors, it had but little sale However, by means of these little profits, and the academical prize which I had the good fortune to obtain, we went on till autumn, I ruminating tragic verses, and he meditating on his intrigues.

He was ugly, bandy-legged, and advanced in years, yet he was the favoured lover of a young Artésienne, of whom he talked to me every day with the most tender regret; for he suffered the torment of absence, and I was the echo that answered to his sighs. Although much younger than he, I had other cares in my head. The keenest of my sorrows was the repugnance the cook had already shown to trust us. The baker and the green-grocer consented to furnish us still, the one with bread, and the other with cheese: and these were our suppers. But from day to day, we ran the risk of being without a dinner. I had one hope left me. Voltaire, who suspected that I was more proud than opulent, had desired that the little poem crowned by the academy might be printed for my benefit, and he had engaged a bookseller to reckon with me for it after deducting the expense of printing. But, whether it be that the bookseller had gained but little by it, or that he loved his own profit better than mine, he said that I had nothing to receive, and that at least half the edition was still left. "Well," said Voltaire, "give me what you have left, I'll dispose of it." He left Paris for Fontainbleau, where the court then was; and there, as the subject proposed by the academy was a panegyric on the king, Voltaire took upon himself to distribute this panegyric, appreciating the author's benefit at his will. It was on this sale that I depended, though not to any great amount; but Voltaire did not return.

At length such was our situation, that one evening Beauvin said, sighing, "My dear friend, all our resources are exhausted; we have not even enough left to pay the man who brings us water." I saw he was dejected; but I was not. "The baker and the green-grocer," asked I, "do they refuse us credit?" —"No, not yet," said he.—"Well then," replied I, "we are but where we were; it is very easy to manage without this man."—"How so?"—"How! why by going ourselves to fetch water from the fountain."—"Will you have the courage to do that?"— "Most certainly I will. And a fine courage it is! It is now quite dark; and were it light, where is the dishonour of serving one's self?" I then took the pitcher, and went boldly to fill it at the neighbouring fountain. On returning, my pitcher in my hand, I beheld Beauvin coming to me with open arms, in an extasy of joy: "Look there, my dear friend, 'tis she! she's come! friends, relations, family, she has quitted all for me! Is this love?" Motionless with surprise, my pitcher still in my hand, I look and behold a fine, tall, fresh girl, well made, pretty, though her nose is rather flat, and who curtsies to me without any embarrassment. The contrast between this romantic incident and our situation made me suddenly burst into such a mad fit of laughter that they were both dumb with astonishment. "You are heartily welcome, mademoiselle; you could not," said I, "have chosen a happier moment, nor arrive more opportunely." After the first compliments were over, I went down to my green-grocer. "Madam," said I, gravely, "this is an extraordinary day, a day of joy and festivity; and you, if you please, must aid us to do the honours of the house, and enlarge a little the acute angle of cheese that you usually give us for supper."—"And what's this woman come to do here?" enquired she.—"Ah! Madam," said I, "'tis a miracle worked by love; and miracles are never explained. All that you and I should know of it is, that we shall want this evening one-third more of your excellent Brie cheese, for which we will very soon pay you, please heaven."—"Yes," said she, "please heaven! But when one has neither money nor credit, it is scarcely the time to think of love."

Voltaire, on his return from Fontainbleau a few days afterwards, filled my hat with crowns, saying that they were the produce of the sale of my poem. Although in my distress I should have been pardonable had I accepted aid, yet I took the liberty of representing to him that he had sold my little work too much above its value. But he made me understand that those who had so nobly paid, were persons from whom neither he nor I could refuse anything. Some of Voltaire's enemies wanted to persuade me that this incident ought to separate us. I was not of that opinion: and with these crowns, which it would have been more unbecoming to refuse than to accept, I went and paid all my debts.

Beauvin had received some money from his family; I had nothing to receive from mine, and was again advancing to the end of my finances. It was therefore neither just nor possible, on account of his new way of living, that we should continue any longer together at a common expense.

In this conjuncture, one of the cruellest in my life, and in which, bathing my pillow every night with my tears, I regretted the comfort and tranquillity I had enjoyed at Toulouse, I know not by what happy influence of fortune or of the good opinion Voltaire gave of me, a lady whose memory I revere was desirous that I should undertake to complete the education of her grandson. Ah! in every way, the remembrance of this event should be dear to my heart! What inestimable pleasures of society and friendship has it diffused over my life; and how many years of happiness has it made me enjoy.

A director of the India Company, whose name was Gilly, engaged in a commercial speculation that at first enriched and afterward ruined him, was left a widower with two children, a son and daughter; and of these children his mother-in-law, Madame Harenc, had kindly taken charge. It is impossible to imagine a woman advanced in age more amiable than Madame Harenc; and to this amiability she joined the most enlightened mind, the rarest prudence, and the most solid virtue. Her ugliness was, at first sight, repulsive; but all the charms of her wit and heart shone through this deformity, and made it, not forgotten, but beloved. Madame Harenc had an only son, as ugly as herself, and as amiable. This son is M. de Presle, who, I believe, is still living, and who has long been distinguished by his taste and judgment among the lovers of the arts. Their society, perfectly well chosen, was remarkable for its intimacy, its security, its peaceful serenity mixed with mirth, and the most perfect harmony of sentiment, taste, and opinion. A few ladies, always the same, and tenderly united, were its ornament. There was the beautiful Desfourniels; the regularity, the delicacy, the exquisite softness of whose features the most skilful painters despaired of imitating; and to whom nature seemed to have delighted to give a soul suited to so divine a form: there was her sister, Madame de Valdec, as amiable, though less beautiful than the thrice happy mother of that unfortunate de Lessart, whom we have seen murdered at Versailles, with the other Orleans prisoners. There was the young Desfourniels, since Countess of Chabrillant, who, without having either the beauty or the heart of her mother, mixed with a little bitterness so much engaging wit, that her vivacity was easily pardoned when it indulged in too keen a satire. Mademoiselle Lacome, a maiden lady, the intimate friend of Madame Harenc, had, among these characters, a tone of sound and gentle reason that was conciliating to all. M. de Presle, curious about all literary novelties, made a choice collection of them, and gave us the first reading. M. de Lantage, in whose country house I have just been living, in this valley, and his elder brother, a man of talents, a passionate admirer of Rabelais, brought with them there the good taste of ancient gaiety. I will not forget, in speaking of this charming society, the good M. l'Osilière, the most truly philosophic man I have ever known after M. de Vauvenargue, and who, by the contrast between the wisdom of his mind and the simple candour of his soul and language, used to bring to our minds la Fontaine.

To this house then I was invited, and soon was cherished as one of the family. Judge of my happiness, when to so many comforts was added that of having for my pupil a young man perfectly well bred, of the purest innocence, of most excellent docility, and with intelligence and memory enough to lose nothing of what I taught him. He died before the age of manhood, and in him nature has destroyed one of her most charming works. He was as beautiful as Apollo, which I never perceived that he suspected. It was while I was with him, and without stealing from him any of the time or care I owed to his studies, that I completed my tragedy. I again obtained the prize of poetry that year, and I should reckon it among the most happy of my life, were it not for the grief into which I was plunged by the death of my mother. Every relief and consolation of which so deep a sorrow was susceptible were offered me by Madame Harenc. I left her when my pupil's father, choosing another kind of education for him, called him back to his home. But afterward, and till the death of that respectable woman, she loved me tenderly, and her house was mine.

My tragedy was finished. It was time to submit it to the correction of Voltaire; but Voltaire was at Cirey. The wisest plan would have been to wait his return to Paris, and I felt it strongly. What advantage should I not have reaped from the observations, the criticism, the counsel of such a master! But, the more the work would have been improved by his review, the less would it have been my work. Perhaps too, by requiring more of me than my abilities could effect, he might have discouraged me. These reflections induced me to form my determination, and I went and asked the players to hear my piece read.

This reading was listened to with much kindness. The three first acts and the fifth were fully approved. But they did not hesitate to decide that the fourth was too feeble. I had at first conceived an idea for this fourth act, which afterwards appeared to me too hazardous, and which I had given up. I discovered at this moment that, in wishing to be prudent, I had become cold, and found my boldness return. I requested three days to correct my error, and a second hearing for the fourth day. I slept little in the interval; but I was well paid for this long watching by the success that my new act obtained at the reading, and by the opinion that this prompt and happy composition gave of my talents. It was then that the vexations of an author began; and the first arose from the distribution of the parts.

When the performers had granted me a free admission to the theatre, Mademoiselle Gaussin had been the most eager to solicit in my favour. It was she who played the parts of princesses: she excelled particularly in all tender parts, and such as required only the simple expression of love and grief. Beautiful, and of the most touching kind of beauty, with a tone of voice that went to the heart, and a look that when in tears had an inexpressible charm, her simplicity, when well placed, defied criticism; and this verse, which Orosmane addresses to Zaïre,

"Art is not made for thee, thou need'st it not,"

had been inspired by her. Hence it may be well conceived how dear she was to the public, and how secure of favour. But in characters where majesty, force, and tragic passion were requisite, her powers were too feeble; and that voluptuous softness, which accorded so well with tender parts, was quite contrary to the vigour which that of my heroine demanded. Yet Mademoiselle Gaussin had not dissembled her desire to play the part, which she expressed in the most flattering and seducing manner, by affecting, at the two readings, a very lively interest both for the piece and for its author.

At that time, new tragedies were rare, and still more rare were the parts that were favourable to the success of the performer; but the most interesting motive with her was that of taking this part from an actress who every day stole one from her. Never did the jealousy of talent inspire more hatred than the beautiful Gaussin bore the young Clairon. The latter had not the same charm in her face; but, in her, the features, the voice, the look, the action, and above all the dignity, the energy of character, all accorded to express violent passion and elevated sentiment. Since she had taken possession of the parts of Camille, Didon, Ariane, Roxane, Hermione, and Alzire, it had become necessary to resign them to her. Her acting was not yet so accurate nor so sage as it afterward became: but it had already all the sap and vigour of great talent. In a character of force, dignity, and enthusiasm, such as that of Arétie, I could not hesitate between her and her rival; and, in spite of my repugnance to disoblige the one, I determined to offer it to the other. The indignation of Mademoiselle Gaussin could not contain itself. She said

" that it was very well known by what species of seduction Mademoiselle Clairon had won this preference. She certainly was very wrong. But Mademoiselle Clairon became angry in her turn, and obliged me to follow her into the box of her rival; and there, without having told me what she was going to do: " Here, Mademoiselle," said she, " I bring him to you, and to let you see whether I have seduced him, whether I have even solicited the preference he has given me, I declare to you, and I declare to him, that, if I accept the part, it shall only be from your hand." With these words she threw the manuscript on the toilet-table in the box, and left me there.

I was then twenty-four, and I found myself tête-à-tête with the most beautiful woman in the world. Her trembling hands clasped mine, and I may say that her fine eyes were fixed like suppliants on mine. " What then have I done to you," said she, with her gentle voice, " to deserve the humiliation and the grief you cause me? When M. de Voltaire requested for you a free admission to this theatre, it was I who spoke for you. When you read your tragedy, no one was more alive to its beauties than I I listened attentively to the part of Arétie; and I was too much affected by it not to flatter myself that I should play it as I felt it. Why then deprive me of it? it belongs to me by the right of seniority, and perhaps by some other title. You do me an injury by giving it to any other; and I doubt whether you benefit yourself. Believe me, it is not the noise of laboured declamation that suits this character. Reflect well on it. My own success is dear to me, but yours is not less so, and it would be a grateful pleasure to me to have contributed to it."

I confess that the effort I made over myself was painful. My eyes, my ears, my heart, were exposed without defence to the gentlest of enchantments. Charmed by all my senses, moved to the bottom of my heart, I was in immediate danger of falling at the knees of her who seemed disposed to receive me kindly. But the fate of my work depended on it, my only hope, and the well-being of my poor children: and the alternative of failure or complete success was so vividly present to my mind, that this interest prevailed over all the emotions with which I was agitated.

"Mademoiselle," said I, "were I so happy as to have written such a part as that of Andromaque, Iphigenie, Zaïre, or Inis, I should be at your feet to pray you to give it still greater effect. No one feels better than I the charm that you add to the expression of touching sorrow, or of timid and tender love. But, unfortunately, the fable of my play is not suited to such a character: and, though the powers that this requires are less rare, less precious than the engaging simplicity which you possess, you will yourself allow that they are quite different: I shall one day perhaps have an occasion to employ with advantage the gentle accents of your voice, those enchanting looks, those eloquent tears, that divine beauty, in a part that is worthy of you. Leave the perils and risks of my first effort to her who is willing to run them; and, by reserving to yourself the honour of having resigned the character to her, avoid the dangers, which in playing it, you would yourself share with me."—"You have said enough," said she, disguising her displeasure. "It is you who request it; I give up the part." Then, taking the manuscript from her toilet-table, she went down with me, and, finding Mademoiselle Clairon in the green-room, "I restore to you," said she with an ironical smile, "and I restore to you without regret, the part from which you expect such success and glory. I am of your opinion that it suits you better than me." Mademoiselle Clairon received it with modest dignity; and I in silence, without daring to look up, waited the close of the scene. But in the evening, at supper, tête-à-tête with my actress, I breathed free from the embarrassment into which she had plunged me. She was not a little sensible of the constancy with which I had sustained this trial; and it was this incident that gave birth to that lasting friendship which has grown old with us.

This was not the only part that vexed me. The performer to whom I destined that of Dionysius the father, Grandval, refused it, and would play only that of young Dionysius. I was therefore obliged to give the first to another performer, whose name was Ribou, much younger than Grandval. Ribou was handsome and well made, and, in his action, he did not want dignity; but he wanted intelligence and instruction to such a degree, that it was necessary to explain his part to him in vulgar language, and to teach it him word by word as to a child. However, by dint of pains and lessons, I made him play it passably, and, with a little disguise in dress, he looked the character well enough not to destroy all theatrical illusion by his youth.

Now came the rehearsals. It was there the connoisseurs began to judge me. I have mentioned my fourth act, which I had at first thought too bold; it was this that awakened all the energy of the performers. The critical moment was that in which young Dionysius retains his mistress as a hostage in the palace of his father, in order to disarm the factions. Mademoiselle Clairon had heard it said that this was the rock on which the piece would strike, and that it would go no farther. She proposed to me to assemble a few men of taste at her house, whom she herself was in the habit of consulting, to read my piece to them, and, without telling them our fears, to see what they would think of it; I submitted, as you may believe, and the council was assembled It consisted of that D'Argental, the vile tool of Voltaire, and the enemy of all talent that seemed likely to succeed; of the abbé de Chauvelin, the denouncer of the Jesuits, and to whom that odious part gave some celebrity; it was him of whom it was asked—

> What is that grotesque uniformly thing?
> Is it a man? Is it a monkey?
> It speaks, &c.

of the count de Praslin, who, like D'Argental, lived but in the green-room, till the duke de Choiseul, his cousin, gave the importance of an embassy to his inutility; and of that despicable marquis of Thibouville, distinguished among the infamous by the impudence with which he practised the dirtiest of vices, and by the refinements of luxury, the effeminacy and vanity of which inspired disgust. The only merit of this man, thus deep in shame, was that of reciting verses in a broken half-extinguished voice, and with an affectation that suited his morals.

How could such men have credit and authority at the theatre? By courting Voltaire, who did not enough despise the homage of those who were vilely devoted to him; and by persuading the little duke d'Aumont that he could not conduct the government of the French theatre better than by following the advice of Voltaire's friends. My young actress had suffered herself to be imposed on by the air of consequence and wisdom that these gentlemen gave themselves, and I was struck with her respect for their talents. I read them my work; and they listened with the gravest silence: and, after the reading, Mademoiselle Clairon, having assured them of my docility, begged them to give their opinion freely. They begged D'Argental to speak first: the way in which he used to pronounce sentence is notorious; a word and a pause, sentences half suppressed, indecisive phrases, vagueness and obscurity, were all that I could draw from him: and, gaping like a fish, he at length pronounced that we must see how it would be received. After him, M. de Praslin said that, indeed, there were many things in this piece that deserved reflection, and in a sententious tone he advised me . . . . to think on them. The abbé de Chauvelin sitting perched on an arm chair, and dangling his little legs, assured me that they were sadly deceived, who thought a tragedy was a thing so easy; that to combine and compose the plan, the intrigue, the manners, the characters, the diction, was no child's play; that, for his own part, without judging my piece with rigour, he recognised in it the work of a young man; and that, for the rest, he referred to the opinion of M. D'Argental. Thibouville spoke in his turn, and stroking his chin that we might admire the brilliancy of his ring, said that he believed he knew something of tragic poetry : " He had recited so much, he himself had written so much, that he ought to be some judge. But how enter into such details after one single reading? He would only refer me to the models of the art : by naming them, he should clearly express what he wished me to understand; and that, by reading Racine and M. de Voltaire, it was easy to see in what style they had written."

Having listened with all possible attention, and heard nothing clear and precise on my work, it struck me that delicacy might have induced them to assume, in my presence, this insignificant language. " I leave you with these gentlemen," whispered I to my actress; " they will explain themselves better when I am gone." On seeing her again in the evening: " Well," said I, " did they speak more clearly of me in my absence than when I was present?"—" Indeed," said she, laughing, " they spoke quite at their ease."—" And what did they say?"— " They said it was possible that this piece might succeed ; but it was possible also that it might fail. And, all things duly considered, one will answer for nothing, and another dares not be too confident."— " But did they make no particular observation? . . . .

On the subject for example?" . . . . . —" Ah! the subject; that is the critical point. Yet, who can say? The public are so fickle!"—" And the action, what did they think of that?"—" As for the action, Praslin does not know what to say of it, D'Argental does not know what to think of it, and the two others are of opinion that it must be judged of upon the stage."—" Did they say nothing of the characters?"—" They said that mine would be fine enough, if . . . . . ; that of Dionysius would also be well enough, but" . . . . —" Well! *if, but!* and what followed?"—" They looked at each other, and said nothing more."—" And the fourth act, what thought they of that?"—" Oh! as for the fourth act, its fate is decided; it will either fall or be applauded to the skies."—" Well!" cried I with vivacity, " I accept the presage; and it depends upon you, mademoiselle, to determine the prediction in my favour."—" How so?"—" Thus. At the moment when young Dionysius opposes your deliverance, if you see the public rising against this effort of virtue, do not leave them to murmur, but, pressing the reply, pronounce boldly the verses beginning thus :

" Va, ne crains rien," &c.

The actress understood me, and it will soon be seen that she surpassed my hopes.

During the rehearsals of my piece, I met with an adventure which I have told my children, but which I have an inclination again to relate. I had left Toulouse more than two years, and had paid but one year of my brother's schooling at the Irish seminary. I now owed a whole year, and with great economy I had reserved my twelve guineas to pay it. But I wanted to send them to their place of destination securely and without expense. Boubée, an attorney at Toulouse, and an academician of the Floral Games, was then at Paris : I called on him, and, in the presence of a man decorated with the red ribbon, whom I did not know, I asked him if he had any safe mode of conveying my money. He told me he had none. "Ah! bless me!" cried the other, whom I took for an officer, and who was but a sharper, "is it not Mr Marmontel that I have the pleasure to meet? He does not recollect his Toulouse friends." I confessed with confusion that I did not know to whom I had the honour of speaking. "What, not the chevalier d'Ambelot, who used to applaud you so heartily when you received the academic prizes? Well! notwithstanding this ingratitude, I'll render you the little service of transmitting your twelve guineas to the Irish seminary. Give me your address. You shall receive from me to-morrow morning a draft for that sum, payable at sight; and, when the superior informs you that he has received the money, you shall remit it to me here at your leisure." Nothing could be more obliging: and I thanked him heartily for his readiness to serve me.

The conversation then turning gaily on Toulouse, and I praising the engaging originality of mind that marks the people; "I am sorry," said Boubée, "that you who frequent the courts were not present when I pleaded the cause of the town-hall painter. You know Cammas, who is so ugly and so foolish, and who every year daubs at the capitol the portraits of the new magistrates. A strumpet of the neighbourhood accused him of having seduced her. She was with child, and demanded that he should marry her, or that he should pay the damages of her innocence which she had publicly resigned fifteen years ago. The poor devil was miserable. He came and related his misfortune to me. He swore it was she who had corrupted him; he even wanted to explain to the judges how she had done it, and offered to draw a picture of it, which he would expose at the trial. ' Hold your tongue,' said I, ' with that great nose of yours, it becomes you well to play the young lad who has been seduced! I'll plead your cause, and gain it, if you promise to sit quietly by me at the trial, and not interrupt me, whatever I may say; you understand me? otherwise you will be cast.' He promised me all I desired. The day came, and the cause being called over, I suffered my adversary to declaim amply on the modesty, the weakness, and the frailty of the fair sex, and on the artifices and snares that were contrived to entrap them. After which I began my reply: 'I plead,' said I, 'for an ugly man, I plead for a poor man, I plead for a fool. (He would fain have murmured, but I bad him be silent.) For an ugly man, gentlemen, look at him: for a man worth nothing, gentlemen, he is a painter, and what is worse, the town painter: for a fool, let the court have the goodness to interrogate him. These three great truths once established, I reason thus: One can only seduce by money, wit, or beauty. Now my client could not seduce by money, since he is worth nothing; neither by wit, since he is a fool; nor by beauty, since he is one of the ugliest of men: whence I conclude that he is falsely accused.'—My conclusions were admitted, and I gained my cause with few words."

I promised Boubée not to forget a word of so fine a specimen of pleading, and, when I went away, again thanked the chevalier d'Ambelot for the service he was going to render me. The next day, a tall footman, his hat bordered with broad Spanish lace, brought me the draft, which I instantly sent off.

Three days afterward, in passing along *la rue de la Comédie Française*, I heard some one call me from a second floor. It was a Languedocian, Favier, a man since well known, who from his window invited me up to his room. I ascend, and find there five or six Gascons round a table covered with oysters. "My dear friend," said he, "a slight indisposition obliges me to keep my room. These gentlemen have the kindness to bear me company; we are breakfasting together, breakfast with us." His slight indisposition was an order of the court for his arrest. Favier was over head and ears in debt; but, as on that day he had still credit with his wine-merchant, his baker, and his oyster-woman, he gave us oysters and champagne as amply and as gaily as if he had been in opulence. The negligence of a savage and a most complete dissolution of manners formed the character of this man, who in other respects was engaging, full of wit and information, eloquent in a high degree, and with such a talent for business, that, with less indolence and less profligacy, he would have been capable of filling the greatest offices. I saw him rarely, but he interested me by his frankness, his gaiety, his natural eloquence, and, if I must own it, by that love of pleasure that in him, as in Horace, had a dangerous charm.

My knight of the red ribbon was one of the guests at breakfast. I again renewed thanks for the draft: "Don't mention it," said he, "that is the least service that we fellow-townsmen can render each other; for you may say what you will, you are a Toulousian; we are determined that you must and shall be so." And, seeing me ready to go away, "I am going too," said he; "I have my carriage below: where shall I set you down?" I refused; he insisted and made me get in. "Just permit me," said he, "to pass by the door of one of my friends in Dove-house street. I have but one word to say to him, and will be with you again in an instant. You have just seen," continued the sharper, "that good fellow, Favier; he is a fine-spirited, generous creature; but no order, no conduct. He has been rich, and is now ruined; but he is not the less prodigal. At this moment, he is in distress; I am going to relieve him if I can; for who can see his friend in need and not aid him?"

Arrived at the hotel where he said he had business, he alighted from his carriage, and a moment afterward he returned out of humour, murmuring to himself. I saw he was agitated, and I asked the reason. "My good friend," said he, "you are young, and new in the world; be careful whom you trust, for there are very few honest men! This man, for instance, whom I would have trusted with my whole fortune, the marquis of Montgaillard".....—"I know him. What has he done to offend you?"—"Yesterday evening—but I tell you this as a secret · mention it to no one; I do not wish to injure him—yesterday evening, at a gaming-house, he had the madness to sit down to play. I, who never play, wanted to dissuade him from it. He did not listen to me. He punts, he loses: he doubles and redoubles his bets, till he loses all his money. He comes to me and begs me to lend him what I have. I had but twelve guineas, and I had given my word to this good Favier to bring them to him this morning to pay an urgent debt. I expose to Montgaillard the want I have of them, without telling him for what purpose. He gives me his word of honour to return them to me this morning. I lend them to him: he stakes and loses them; and when I come hither, thinking to receive them, the marquis is out, or chooses not to be at home, and poor Favier, who expects them, will think I have broken the promise I made him, I who never broke a promise in my life! Indeed it is enough to make me angry. Have I not reason to be so? You, sir, who understand what's equitable and right, tell me, is this honest?"—"Sir," said I, "your draft has left Paris these three days. I am already your debtor, and this debt I will instantly discharge."—"Oh! no," said he, "no, I would borrow rather."—"Indeed," said I, "that is what I will not suffer. The money would lie useless in my hands, and since you want it, it is justly yours. Allow me instantly to remit it to you." He made a very handsome defence; but on my part, I persisted so strongly that he was obliged to yield, and take my twelve guineas.

Some days afterward, a letter from the superior of the seminary was a thunder-stroke to me. In this letter, he reproached me with having trifled with him by sending him a strip of paper worth nothing. "The man," said he in his letter, "on whom your adventurer has had the impudence to draw, does not owe him a farthing. I have had the draft protested, and I return it to you." Judge of my indignation. It was, in my estimation, a great crime to have cheated me out of my twelve guineas; but it was a much more horrible treason to have made me pass, if not for a dishonest man, at least for an inconsiderate one. "Great God!" cried I, "and in what light is my brother now looked on?" Mad with grief and rage, and with my sword by my side (for in devoting myself to the stage I had changed my profession) I hasten to d'Ambelot's lodgings, and enquire for him. "Ah! the scoundrel!" answered the porter of the hotel, "he is at Fort l'Evêque. He has cheated us all of the little money we had." I did not pursue him to his prison; but I soon afterward heard that he died there, and I felt not the least afflicted.

On the day of my misfortune, I went and poured my afflictions into the bosom of madame Harenc. "This is indeed a sacrilege," said she. "But pray come and sup with me?"—"Yes, madame."—"Permit me to leave you for a moment." She very soon returned. "I am thinking," said she, "of your poor brother; it is, perhaps, on him that the anger of this Irish priest now falls. To-morrow, my dear friend, you must send him a better draft."—"Yes, madame," said I, "that is my intention, only tell me of a banker." "You shall have one. Now let's talk of your rehearsals. Do they go on well? Are you satisfied with them?" I confided to her my anxiety on the obscurity of the oracles pronounced at mademoiselle Clairon's. She laughed heartily. "Do you know," said she, "what will be the consequence of them? If your piece succeed, they will have foretold it; if it fall, they will have announced it. But, whether it succeed or fall, remember that on that evening you sup with me and my friends; for we will either rejoice or grieve with you."

As she was talking to me thus kindly, her steward came in to say a word to her; and when he was gone, "Here," said she, "here is a draft payable at sight, which I trust is worth more than that of your chevalier:" and when I talked of returning her the money, "Dionysius," said she, "is the debtor; I'll engage he will discharge it."

I was now only anxious about the fate of my tragedy, and that was quite enough. It was an event of such importance to me, that I hope I shall be pardoned the moments of weakness with which I am going to accuse myself. At that time, the author of a new piece had for himself and his friends a little grated box in the third circle over the stage, the seat of which, I may truly say, was a cushion full of thorns. Thither I went about half an hour before the curtain drew up, and till then I preserved power enough to support my anxiety: but, at the noise the curtain made as it rose, my blood froze within my veins. Spirits were applied in vain to restore me, I could not recover. It was not till the end of the first monologue, amid long reiterated plaudits, that I began to revive. From that moment all went well, gradually gaining on the public favour, till the scene in the fourth act, with which I had been so much threatened. But, as this moment approached, I was seized with such a trembling that, without exaggerating, my teeth chattered in my mouth. Were the great revolutions that pass in the soul and in the senses mortal, I should have died under what I suffered when the sublime

Clairon, so happily catching the feelings of the spectators, pronounced these verses:

" Va, ne crains rien," &c.

The whole theatre resounded with redoubled plaudits. Never did any one pass from more lively apprehensions, to more sudden and sensible joy; and, during the rest of the play, this last sentiment agitated my heart and soul with such violence, that when I breathed I did but sob.

As the curtain fell, when amidst the plaudits and acclamations of the pit, that loudly called for me, my friends came to tell me that I must go down and show myself on the stage, it was impossible for me to crawl thither alone; my knees bent under me; I was obliged to be supported.

Merope had been the first piece at which the author had been called for, and Dionysius was the second. What is since become so common, and so little flattering, was then honourable, and at the three first representations this honour was granted me; but this extravagant success arose from circumstances that raised excessively the merit of my tragedy. Crébillon was old, Voltaire was declining; no young man offered to replace them. I seemed to fall from the clouds: this first effort of a country youth of Limosin, then but twenty-four, appeared to promise wonders; and in pleasures the public always delight to exaggerate its hopes. But woe to him who deceives them. Reflection soon taught me this, of which the critics were eager to warn me. However, I had some days of pure and calm happiness, such as that I enjoyed most gratefully at madame Harenc's supper. M. de Presle took me there after the play. His good mother, who expected me, received me in her arms; and when she heard of my success, bathed me with her tears. So tender a reception recalled my mother to memory; and instantly a tide of bitterness mixing with my joy. "Ah! madame," said I, melting into tears, "why is not my tender mother, of whom you remind me, why is she not still living? She too would embrace me, and what would be her happiness!" Our friends arrived, thinking they had only to congratulate me. "Come," said madame Harenc to them, "console this poor youth. See, he is lamenting his mother, who, he says, would have been so happy at this moment!"

This return of grief was only transient; and the friendship that was shown me soon possessed all my soul. Ah! if in adversity it be a comfort to communicate our pains, it is in prosperity a most vivid and exquisite delight to find hearts that share our pleasures! I have always found it more easy to bear grief in solitude than joy. When my heart is sad, it loves to be alone. It is to share my happiness that I want my friends.

When the fate of my piece was decided, I sent it to Voltaire, and begged him, at the same time, to permit me to dedicate it to him. It may be seen in the collection of his letters with what satisfaction he learnt my success, and with what kindness he accepted my homage.

The same year in which I had the misfortune to lose my mother, Vauvenargue died; I wanted to relieve the sorrows that oppressed me, and in my epistle to Voltaire it was a gentle pleasure to express them. This epistle was written with more rapidity than any of my works. Verse seemed to flow spontaneously: I finished it in one evening: and it has not been altered since.

Voltaire's prediction was verified. In one day, almost in one instant, I found myself rich and celebrated. I made a worthy use of my riches: but it was not so with my celebrity. My fame became the origin of my dissipation, and the source of my errors. Till then, my life had been obscure and retired. I lodged in Mathurin's street, with two studious men,

Lavirote and the abbé de Prades; one occupied in translating the mathematical works of Maclaurin, and the other Huet's theology. There also lived two Gascon abbés, charming idlers, and of inexhaustible gaiety, who ran about in pursuit of pleasure while we were occupied with our studies, and returned of an evening to amuse us with the news they had collected, or the tales they had invented. The houses that I used to frequent were those of madame Harenc and madame Desfourniels her friend, where I was always welcome; that of Voltaire, where I enjoyed with rapture the conversation of my illustrious master; and that of madame Denis his niece, most amiable in her ugliness, and whose natural and facile mind had so caught the tint of that of her uncle, of his taste, his gaiety, and his exquisite politeness, as to make her society sought and admired. All these intimacies contributed to fill my soul and mind with courage and emulation, and to infuse more warmth and genius into my works.

Above all, what a school for me had that been, where every day for two years, the friendship of the two most enlightened men of their age had permitted me to go and instruct myself! The conversation of Voltaire and Vauvenargue presented such richness and fertility as can never be excelled. Voltaire, with an inexhaustible mine of interesting facts and strokes of genius; Vauvenargue, with an eloquence full of amenity, grace, and wisdom. Never were debates distinguished by so much talent, gentleness, and good faith: and what charmed me yet more was, on one side, the respect of Vauvenargue for the genius of Voltaire, and, on the other, the tender veneration of Voltaire for the virtue of Vauvenargue: both, without flattering each other by vain adulation or faint complaisance, honoured themselves, in my estimation, by a freedom of thought which never troubled the harmony and accord of their mutual sentiments. But, at the moment of which I am speaking one of these two illustrious friends was no more, and the other was absent. I was too much abandoned to myself.

After the success of 'Dionysius,' an infinity of curious, seducing, and frivolous people seized on me, and I saw myself borne away in the vortex of Paris. It was a kind of fashion to invite and show the author of the new piece; and I, flattered by this lively interest, could not refuse. Every day invited to dinners and suppers where the master and his company were equally new to me, I suffered myself to be carried from one party to another without knowing, very often, whither I was going, or where I had been. So fatigued was I, with the perpetual mobility of this ceremony, that in my leisure moments I had no power to apply to anything; yet this variety, this change of scene, pleased me, I confess: and my friends themselves, while they recommended prudence and modesty, thought that I ought to yield to this first desire of seeing me. "If not friendship," said they, "you will acquire favour and personal esteem. You want to know the manners, the taste, the tone and usages of the world; it is only by seeing it near that it can be well studied; and you are happy in being so favourably and so early introduced."

Ah! my friends were right, had I prudently known how to profit by this advantage; but an extreme facility was the fault of my youth; and, when opportunity and pleasure united, I never could resist them.

During this time of dissipation and folly, a Mr Monet called on me, who has since been director of the comic opera, and whom I did not know. "Sir," said he, "I am charged with a commission to you that, I think, will not displease you. You have surely heard of mademoiselle Navarre?" I answered that the name was new to me. "She is," continued Monet "the prodigy of our age for wit and beauty. She comes from Brussels, where she has been the delight and ornament of the court of marshal Saxe: she has seen

'Dionysius the Tyrant;' she is ardently desirous of knowing its author, and sends me to invite you to dine with her to-day." I easily engaged myself.

I never have been so dazzled as I was on seeing her. She had still more brilliancy than beauty. She was in a Polish dress, most graceful and genteel, two long tresses fell on her shoulders, and on her head jonquil flowers, mixed with her hair, heightened marvellously the lustre of her fine clear brown complexion, which was animated by the fire of two sparkling eyes. The reception she gave me redoubled the danger of being in the presence of so many charms, and her language soon confirmed the eulogy that had been made of her wit. Ah, my children! if I could have foreseen all the vexation that this day was to cause me, with what horror should I have started back and saved myself from the danger I was about to run! These are no fables: 'tis the example of your father teaching you to dread the most seducing of the passions.

Among the company that my enchantress had invited on that day, I found men of taste and talent. The dinner was brilliant. Gallantry and gaiety were freely indulged, but not abused. Mademoiselle Navarre knew how to hold with a light hand the reins of liberty. She knew too, how to measure her attentions; and till the dinner was nearly over, no one could complain; but they were insensibly fixed on me in so marked a manner, and when we were walking in the garden, she so clearly showed her inclination to be alone with me, that the whole company, one by one, stole silently away. While they were thus slipping from us, her dancing-master came. I saw her take her lesson. The dance she danced was then known by the name of "The lovely conqueror." She displayed in it all the graces of an elegant figure, with gestures, steps, and attitudes, now dignified, and now full of softness and voluptuousness. The lesson scarcely occupied a quarter of an hour, and Lany was dismissed. Then, humming the air she had danced, mademoiselle Navarre asked me if I knew the words of it? I knew them; they began thus:—

"Lovely conqueror!
Tyrant love!
Gentle's thy sway!" &c.

"And if I did not know the words," said I, "I should invent them; so happily is this moment suited to inspire them." A conversation that began thus, could not soon end. We passed the evening together, and in some tranquil moments she enquired about what new work I was occupied. I told her the subject and explained the plan, but complained of the involuntary dissipation into which I was forced. "Do you wish," said she, "to study in peace, at your ease, and without distraction? Come and pass a few months with me in Champagne, at the village of Avenay, where my father has a house and some vineyards. He is at Brussels, at the head of a mercantile house that he cannot quit, and I am come to transact some business for him. I set off to-morrow for Avenay; I shall be alone there till after the vintage: as soon as I shall have prepared everything to receive you, come and join me there. It will be hard indeed, if, with me and excellent champagne, you cannot make charming verses." What reason, what prudence, what force, could I oppose to the irresistible charm of such an invitation? I promised to set off at the first signal she should give. She required my most sacred promise to have no confidant. She had the strongest reasons, she said, for concealing our acquaintance.

From the time of her departure to mine for Avenay, there was an interval of two months; and, though it was filled by a diligent and very animated correspondence, all that in absence could most strongly interest the mind and heart, that did not save me from anxious weariness. The letters I received, inspired by a lively and brilliant imagination, while they exalted mine by the sweetest illusions, only made me desire more ardently to see her again, who even in absence caused me such extacy. I employed this time in dissolving a great number of the acquaintances I had formed: telling some that my new work required retirement, and pretending to others that I was going to visit my native province. Without explaining myself to madame Harenc and mademoiselle Clairon, I prevented their anxiety: but, fearing the curiosity and penetration of madame Denis, I was totally silent to her on my project of evasion. It was wrong, I confess. Her friendship for me had not waited my success to declare itself. Unknown in the world, I was received at her house as cordially as at her uncle's. Nothing was neglected that could render my visits agreeable to me. My friends were received there: they were become hers. My old friend, the abbé Raynal, recollects with me the entertaining suppers we there enjoyed. The abbé Mignot, her brother, the good Cideville, and my two Gascon abbés of Mathurins street, brought with them a frank gaiety; and I may say, that I, then young and jovial, used at these suppers to be the hero of the table. My spirits had there the extravagance of madness. The lady and her company were scarcely more prudent or less merry than myself; and, when Voltaire could escape from the bonds of his marchioness de Châtelet and from his suppers with the great, he was too happy to come and heartily join in the laugh. Ah! why did this gentle, peaceful, equal, and unalterable happiness, not satisfy my desires? What other relief could I want, after a long day of labour and study? And what could I expect to find in that dangerous Avenay?

The letter so desired, so impatiently expected, the letter that should call me from Paris, at length arrived. I had then lodgings by myself, near the

Louvre. No longer obliged to limit so strictly the expenses of my table, I separated from the companions with whom I lived, and kept an old woman at five shillings a month, and a barber at the same price. To the latter I confided the care of finding me a courier from the letter office, who would take me and my portmanteau as far as Rheims in his cariole. The bargain was made, the place fixed, and I sat off: from Rheims to Avenay I went on a posthorse, and though it be said that love has wings, he really had none for me. I found myself shaken to pieces when I arrived.

Here, my children, I throw a veil over my deplorable folly. Although the time is distant, and though I was then very young, I will not appear before you in a state of intoxication and madness.

But what you ought to know is, that the faithless caresses with which I was loaded were mixed with most frightful ills; that the most seducing of women was at the same time the most capricious; that, among her enchantments, her coquetry incessantly invented some new means of exercising her empire over me; that at every moment her will changed, and at every moment mine was forced to submit; that she seemed to delight to make me by turns the happiest lover and the most unhappy slave: were we alone, she had the art of troubling our solitude by unforeseen incidents. The mobility of her nerves, the singular vivacity of her spirits, made her subject to hysterics, which alone would have been my torment: when she was most brilliant in gaiety and health, these fits would seize her with bursts of involuntary laughter; to this laughter succeeded a torsion of her members, trembling, and convulsive motions, that terminated in tears. These attacks were more painful to me than herself; but they made her yet more dear and more interesting to me; happy, if her caprices had not occupied her gayer intervals! Tête-à-tête, surrounded by the vineyards of Champagne, what means did she not invent to afflict and torture me? That was her study, that was her talent. Every day she imagined some new trial for my soul: it was a romance that she composed in action, and whose scenes she introduced.

The nuns of the village refused to admit her into their garden; this to her was an odious and insupportable privation; every other walk was to her insipid. I had to scale with her the walls of the forbidden garden: the guard came with his gun to beg us to go out; she did not mind him: he levelled his piece at me; she observed my countenance: I went up to him, and boldly slipped half-a-crown into his hand, but without her perceiving it, for she would have taken it for a mark of weakness. She at last thought it better to comply, and we retired without noise, but in good order, and with slow steps.

Another time, she came with an air of inquietude, holding in her hand the letter, true or fabricated, of an unfortunate lover, jealous and frantic at my happiness, who threatened to revenge on me the contempt with which she treated him. As she showed me this letter, she looked to see whether I read it coolly, for she esteemed nothing so much as courage; and had I appeared agitated, I should have been lost in her opinion.

As soon as I was escaped from one trial she invented others, and left me no time to breathe: but the most critical situation into which she threw me was this. Her father having learnt that she had a young man with her, had written a letter of reproach. She exaggerated his indignation: she represented herself as wholly lost, and her father as hastening to drive us from our retreat; she said there was but one way of appeasing him, and that this depended on me; but that she would die rather than indicate it: my affection for her must dictate the measure. I understood her perfectly; but though, with her, love made me forget the world, I had not forgotten myself. I adored her as a mistress, but had no inclination to make her my wife. I wrote to M. Navarre: my letter was filled with praise of his daughter, and expressed for her the purest esteem and most innocent friendship. I went no further. The good man answered, that, if my intentions were honourable (as she had apparently made him understand) there was no sacrifice that he was not disposed to make for our happiness. I replied by repeating my esteem, my friendship, and the praises of his daughter. I glanced lightly over the rest. I have reason to think she was dissatisfied with it; and, either to revenge herself for my refusal of her hand, or to know what would be the character of my love in a fit of jealousy, she chose to pierce my heart with the most keen and most pointed dart. In one of those moments when I could not but think her wholly occupied with thoughts of me as I with her, the name she pronounced was the name of my rival, of that rival with whose jealousy she had threatened me. I heard from her mouth: "Ah! my dear * * * !" Figure to yourself, if possible, the transport of passion that seized me; I went out desperate, and, calling loudly for her servants, ordered post-horses instantly. But I had scarcely locked myself in my room to prepare for my departure, when she came dishevelled, and knocking at my door, with piercing cries and fearful violence, till she forced me to open it. Assuredly, if she only wished to behold in me a distracted wretch, she must have triumphed; but alarmed at the state in which she saw me, I beheld her, in turn disconsolate and dismayed, throw herself at my feet, and ask my pardon for an error of which, she said, her tongue only was guilty, and to which neither her fancy nor her heart had consented. How this scene was acted! It seems incredible, and I was then very far from suspecting the truth. But, the more I have reflected since on the inconceivable singularity of this romantic character, the more I have found it possible that she was desirous of seeing me in this new situation, and that afterwards, touched with the violence of my grief, she wished to assuage it. At least it is true, that I never saw her so sensible nor so beautiful as in this horrible moment. Thus, after remaining some time inexorable, I suffered myself at last to be persuaded, and yielded to her. But, a few days afterwards, her father having recalled her to Brussels, we were forced to separate. Our parting words were promises to love each other for ever, and with the hope of seeing her soon again, I left her and returned to Paris.

The cause of my flight was no longer a mystery: a ballad-making poet, the abbé de Lattaignant, canon of Rheims, where he then was, having learned this adventure, had made it the subject of an epistle to mademoiselle Navarre, and this epistle was handed about Paris. I returned then with the reputation of a man of intrigue, which I should have been well contented not to have had, for it excited jealousy, and made me enemies.

The day after my arrival, my two Gascon abbés of Mathurins street called on me, and gave me a kind of serious comic admonition. "Where do you come from?" said the abbé Forest. "A pretty conduct this! You run away like a thief, without saying a parting word to your best friends! You fly down into Champagne! Every corner is hunted, and hunted in vain! Where is he? no one knows. And that interesting feeling woman, whom you abandon; leaving her in affright and tears! What cruelty! Oh! you are a sad libertine, you don't deserve the love she bears you!"—"Who," said I, "is this Ariadne in tears? Who are you talking of?"—"Who?" replied the abbé Debon; "why that disconsolate woman who has supposed you drowned, who has searched for you even in the nets of Saint Cloud, and who has since discovered that you had betrayed her—of madame Denis, in short."—"Gentlemen," said I in a firm tone, and with a serious air, "Madame Denis is my friend, and nothing more. She has not the right to complain of my conduct. I made a mystery of it to her, as well as to you, because I was bound so to do."—" Yes, a pretty mystery !" replied Forest, " for a mademoiselle Navarre, a— !"—I interrupted him; " Softly, sir, "said I : " I believe you have no intention to offend me, and you will offend me if you proceed farther in that tone. I never took the liberty of reproving you, and I beg you will not think of chiding me."—" This is all very well," said Forest, " you talk of it very much at your ease! You steal away cleverly into Champagne to drink the best wine in the world with a charming girl; and we, forsooth, must suffer here. We are accused of being your confidants, your approvers, your accomplices : madame Denis herself looks on us with a suspicious eye, and receives us coldly; in short, if you must know, there are no more suppers at her house : the poor woman is in mourning."—" Ah! I understand you : this, then," said I, " is the great crime of my absence. I assure you, I am no longer surprised at your being so angry. No more suppers! Well, they shall be renewed. Tomorrow you shall be invited."—Joy smiled on their faces.—" Do you expect to be pardoned then?" said one.—" Oh! yes," said the other, " she is so good a woman; he will soon make his peace."—" The peace of friendship," I replied, " is never difficult to make : it is not the same with that of love ; and, to prove that love has no concern in this dispute, to-morrow there shall be no trace of it left. I must leave you, I am going to madame Denis."

She received me with a little ill-humour, and complained of the inquietude that my flight had caused her, as well as all my friends. I bore her reproof, and confessed that at my age one was not exempt from weakness and folly. As to the secrecy of my journey, it had been enjoined me; I could not betray it. "Let me entreat you, madame," said I, "not to appear offended; you will be thought jealous, and that's a report that should be contradicted rather than authorized."—"Contradicted!" said she; "Is it possible that the report has been spread?"—"Not yet," said I; "but those who used to assemble here, and who are now dispersed, may soon make it current. I have just seen two of them this morning, who have loaded me with reproaches; and who, because your suppers are interrupted, believe you are in despair." I told her what had passed: she laughed with me, and felt that it would be better to invite them immediately, in order to destroy the idea of Ariadne in tears. "This," said I, "is friendship: facile, indulgent, and peaceful, it suffers no change, it affords content, joy, and concord through life: whereas love—"—"Love!" cried she; "heaven guard me from it! Love is only good in tragedy, and it is comedy that suits me. You, sir, who should know how to express the torments, the fury, the transports of tragic love, may well want some lessons to aid the fancy; and I am told that for that purpose you could not have made a better choice. I congratulate you."

Alas! yes, I then knew by fatal experience how truly the passion of love, even when it is thought happy, is a state of vexation and violence. But till then I had known only its lightest pains; it reserved for me a much longer and more cruel torment!

The first letter I received from mademoiselle Navarre was lively and tender. The second was still tender, but less lively. The third made me wait, and showed but the pale embers of a dying fire. I complained, and my complaint was answered by light excuses: "Balls, plays, parties," were the causes alledged for this neglect and coldness. "I ought to know women: amusement and dissipation had such charms for them, that they must be permitted, at least in absence, to indulge in them." Then it was that I began to feel the real torments of love. To three burning heart-rending letters no answer. I at first thought this silence so incomprehensible, that, after the postman had passed and had uttered the afflicting words, "there is nothing for you," I went to the post myself, to see whether some letter directed to me had not been left in the office; and, after having been once there, returned again. In this continual expectation, every day deceived, I wasted and pined away; I consumed myself with grief.

I have forgotten to say, that, on my arrival at Paris, in passing by the cloister Saint-Germain-l'Auxerrois, an old picture of Cleopatra having struck me with its resemblance to mademoiselle Navarre, I had instantly bought it, and carried it home. It was my only consolation. I shut myself up alone with this picture, and, addressing my sighs to it, demanded, for pity's sake, one line to restore me to life. Senseless madman! How could this image hear me? She, whom it resembled, did not deign to listen. This excess of rigour and contempt was not natural. I fancied her sick, or confined by her father and kept a close prisoner like a criminal. All seemed to me possible and probable, except the frightful truth.

I had not been able to conceal my grief so effectually from mademoiselle Clairon as to elude her inquiries. I confessed to her its cause, and she did all she could imagine to flatter and allay it. One evening, when we were in the green-room at the theatre, she heard the marquis of Brancas-Cerest tell some one that he had just arrived from Brussels. "Marquis," said she, "may I ask if you saw mademoiselle Navarre there?"—"Yes," answered he, "I saw her more beautiful and brilliant than ever, leading, chained to her ear, the chevalier de Mirabeau, with whom she is in love, and who worships her." I was present; I heard his answer. Struck to the heart, I staggered home like a sacrificed victim. Ah! my children, what madness was it to believe in the fidelity of a woman already celebrated for her frailty, and for whom the fascination of pleasure was such that modesty was forgotten!

However, less libertine than romantic, she appeared to have changed her manners in her amours with the chevalier de Mirabeau. But the romance did not long continue, and it finished wretchedly.

The fever, that seized me the same evening I learned my misfortune, still confined me, when I one morning saw a handsome young man, unknown to me, enter my room, and who announced himself as the chevalier de Mirabeau. "Sir," said he, "I have the honour to present myself to you in two characters: first, as the intimate friend of your friend, the late marquis de Vauvenargue, my ancient comrade in the king's regiment: I should be proud to deserve the place he occupied in your heart, which I wish to obtain. My other character is not so favourable to me: it is that of your successor in the good graces of mademoiselle Navarre. I can and ought to testify that she has the tenderest esteem for you. I have myself often been jealous of the manner in which she spoke of you, and the thing she most expressly recommended to me, when I left Brussels, was to call on you, and entreat your friendship."

"Sir," said I, "you see me sick; it is you who have made me so; and I confess I do not feel disposed so suddenly to regard the man who has done me such an injury as my friend. But, the noble, loyal, and frank manner in which you announce yourself, commands my esteem; and, since I am sacrificed, it is at least a consolation to me to be so to a man like you. Have the kindness to take a chair. We'll talk of our friend M. de Vauvenargue; we'll talk too of mademoiselle Navarre, and I shall speak only in praise of both."

After this conversation, which was long and interesting: "Sir," said he. "I flatter myself, that you will not be offended to learn that mademoiselle Navarre has shown me your letters. Here they are; they do no less honour to your heart than to your mind. In returning them on her part, I am commissioned to receive hers."—" Sir," asked I, " has she had the kindness to write one word to authorise me to remit them to you?"—" No," said he, " she thought, with me, that you would not refuse to believe me on my honour."—" Excuse me," answered I," for what concerns myself, I may give my confidence; I then dispose only of what is mine; but the secret of another I do not dispose of in the same way. Yet, there is a method of conciliating all, and you will be satisfied." Then taking from my writing desk the packet of mademoiselle Navarre's letters, " You recognise her hand-writing, and you see," said I, " that I take nothing away from this collection; you shall witness to her that these letters have been burnt." I instantly threw them into the fire with mine, and, while they were burning, " My duty is fulfilled," added I; " my sacrifice is consummated." He approved my delicacy, and retired satisfied.

The fever did not leave me; I was melancholy; I would no longer see any one. I felt the necessity of breathing a purer air than in the neighbourhood of the Louvre; I thought a solitary walk might contribute to my recovery, and went and lodged near the Luxembourg.

It was there that, still sick in my bed, in the absence of the Savoyard who waited on me, I one morning heard some one enter my chamber. "Who's there?" I hear no answer; my curtains are half opened, and in the dark I find myself embraced by a woman whose face, leaning over mine, bathes me with her tears. "Who are you?" asked I again; and without answering me, her embraces, her sighs, and her tears, are redoubled. At length she rises, and I behold mademoiselle Navarre, in a morning undress, more beautiful than ever in her grief and tears. "Is it you, mademoiselle?" exclaimed I: "Alas! who brings you here? will you tear me from the little hold I have on life?" As I said this, I perceived behind her the chevalier de Mirabeau, mute and motionless. I thought it the dream of madness; but she, turning to him with a tragic air, "Look, sir," said she, "see what I sacrifice to you: the most passionate lover, the most faithful, the tenderest and best friend I had in the world; see to what a state my love for you has reduced him, and how culpable would you be if ever you rendered yourself unworthy of such a sacrifice." The chevalier was petrified with astonishment and admiration. "Are you able to get up?" said she.—"Yes," answered I.—"Well, get up then, and give us breakfast; for we wish you to be our adviser, and we have things of great importance to communicate to you."

I rose, and as soon as my Savoyard came, I sent for some coffee. When we were left alone: "My dear friend," said she, "the chevalier and I are going to consecrate our love at the foot of the altar: we mean to marry, not in France, where we should have many difficulties to conquer, but in Holland, where we shall be free. Marshal Saxe is furious with jealousy. Here is the letter he wrote to me. The chevalier is treated contemptuously in it; but he knows how to act justly and like himself." I represented to her that a jealous rival was not obliged to be just toward his rival, and that it would be scarcely prudent or possible to attack marshal Saxe. "What do you call attacking?" replied she; "in duel! with the sword? 'Tis not that; I have not made myself understood. M. le chevalier, after his marriage, engages in the service of some foreign power: he is known, and can choose. With his name, his valour, his talents, and that face, he will make a rapid progress: he will soon be at the head of the armies, and it is on the field of battle that he will contend with the marshal."—" Very well, mademoiselle," exclaimed I; "this now is what I approve, and I recognise you both in so generous a project." I saw them indeed as proud and as pleased with their resolution as if it had been to be executed on the next day. I learnt afterwards that, after having been married in Holland, they had gone to Avignon; that the brother of the chevalier, the pretended friend of mankind, and the enemy of his brother, had had sufficient influence to have him pursued even into the states of the pope; that at the moment when the sbirri, by order of the vice-legate, came to arrest him, his wife was in child-bed; and that on seeing them enter her room, she was seized with such terror that it created a sudden revolution in her frame, and terminated in her death.

I wept over her memory; and from that time, this friend of mankind, whom I have known for a hypocrite in morality, and an intriguer at court, full of hatred, haughty, and malicious, has been the object of my aversion. I cannot express the sudden change that took place in me when I had learnt that the chevalier de Mirabeau loved mademoiselle Navarre so much as to make her his wife. Cured of my love, and above all of my jealousy, I thought the preference she gave him was just, and, far from being humiliated, I applauded myself for having resigned her. I here recognised how much the sentiment of self-love and wounded vanity embittered the vexations and the pains of love.

Still there was left at the bottom of my heart a discomfort, an inquietude, a weary inactivity, that governed me. This picture of Cleopatra, that was still before my eyes, had lost its resemblance; it no longer touched, but importuned me, and I got rid of it. What redoubled my sadness was the loss of my talents. Among the charms and torments of Avenay, I had some hours of poetic fancy to give to study: to this, mademoiselle Navarre herself encouraged me.

In fearful storms, as she was afraid of thunder, we had to dine or sup in her cellars (which were those of the marshal), and, amid fifty thousand bottles of champagne, it was difficult not to warm the imagination. It is most true that on those days my verses were vapid; but reflection dissipated these vapours. As I advanced, I read my new scenes to her. To judge them, she used to seat herself on what she called her throne: it was a little grass mount at the top of the vineyards, surrounded by bramble-bushes; and the description of this throne, that she said awaited us, should be seen in her letters: that of Armida had nothing more enchanting. It was there that I read my verses at her feet, and, when she approved, I thought them incomparable. But, when the charm was broken, I saw myself alone in the world; instead of flowers with which the paths of poetry were strewed for me, I perceived only thorns. I was abandoned by the genius that inspired me! My mind and soul fell faint and languishing, like the sails of a vessel that suddenly lose the wind that filled them.

Mademoiselle Clairon, who saw the languor into which I had fallen, was eager to find a remedy. "My dear friend," said she, "your heart has need of love, and this weary anxiety is but want of love: this heart must be occupied, must be filled. Is there then but one woman in the world who can be lovely in your eyes?"—" I know but one only," said I, " who could console me, if she were inclined; could she but be so generous as to feel this inclination?" —" This is what we must know," replied she with a smile. " Is she of my acquaintance? I'll aid you if I can."—" Yes, you know her, and have much influence over her."—" Well! name her; I'll speak for you. I'll tell her that you love from the heart; that you are capable of all the constancy and fidelity she can wish for, and that she is sure of being happy in loving you."—" Do you then believe all this of me?"—" Yes, I am fully persuaded of it."—" Then have the kindness to tell it to yourself."—" To myself, my dear friend?"—" To yourself."—" Ah! if it depend on me, you shall be consoled, and the glory shall be mine."

Thus was this new connection formed, which, as may well be foreseen, was not of long duration: but it had for me the inestimable advantage of re-animating me to study. Never were love and the love of glory more happily united than in my heart.

'Dionysius' was revived; and it had now the same success as in its novelty. The part of Arétie sensibly increased in interest by the exertions of her to whom nothing was dearer than my glory. She was more sublime, more enchanting in it than ever; and you may imagine with what pleasure the applauded actress and applauded author retired home to sup together.

My enthusiasm for the talents of mademoiselle Clairon was too lively, too exalted a sentiment, to allow me to distinguish accurately how much of my passion was love. But, independently of the charms of the actress, she was, in my eyes, a most desirable mistress; for she had the brilliant vivacity of youth, gaiety, and all the attraction of a lovely temper, unmixed with caprice, and delighting in the sole desire of rendering her lover happy by the most delicate attentions. While she loved, no one loved more tenderly, more passionately, nor more faithfully. As sure of her as of myself, my head at liberty, and my heart at peace, I gave a part of the day to study, and reserved the rest for her. I left her charming; charming and yet more charming I found her on my return. What pity that so seducing a character should be so fickle, and that, with so much sincerity, nay fidelity in her attachments, she should have so little constancy!

She had a friend with whom we sometimes supped. One day she said to me, " Don't go there this evening; you would be uncomfortable: the Bailli de Fleury will sup there, and is to bring me back."—" I know him," answered I most simply, " he'll bring me back too."—" No," said she, " he will be only in a vis-à-vis." This was a ray of light; and, as she saw I was struck by it, " Well, my dear friend," said she, " 'tis a whim of mine, which you must pardon."— " Is it indeed true," said I, " do you speak seriously?" —" Yes, I am sometimes foolish, mad, but you will never find me false."—" I thank you for your candour," said I, " and resign the place to M. le Bailli." For once I felt courage and reason; and what happened to me the day after, taught me how much more congenial and grateful to my heart was an honourable sentiment than a frivolous and passing inclination.

An attorney of my native town, Rigal, called upon me and said : " Mademoiselle B * * * has promised you never to marry, without the consent of your mother. Your mother is no more : mademoiselle B * * * is not less faithful to her word : she has received an advantageous offer, and she will accept none without your consent." At these words, I felt revive in me not the love I once had for her, but an inclination so gentle, so lively, and so tender, that I could not have resisted it, if my fortune and situation in life had any stability. " Alas !" answered I, " would I were in a state to make an offer of myself to my dear B * * * ! But unhappily the lot I could propose to her is too vague, and too uncertain. The hazards with which my life will be chequered are such as hers should not be exposed to. She merits a solid happiness; and I can only envy him who is able to secure it to her."

A few days afterwards I received a note from mademoiselle Clairon in these words: " Your friendship is in this moment necessary to me. I know you too well not to depend on it. Come and see me, I expect you." I went to her house. She had company. " I want to speak to you," said she, on seeing me. I followed her into her cabinet. " You tell me, mademoiselle," said I, " that my friendship can be of use to you. I come to know in what way, and to assure you of my zeal."—" 'Tis neither your zeal nor your friendship alone that I reclaim," said she ; " it is your love : you must restore it to me." Then, with an ingenuousness that to any other than to me would have been diverting, she told me how little that puppet, the Bailli de Fleury, had deserved to excite my jealousy. After this humble confession, she employed, but in vain, all the most seducing arts that a lovely coquette can employ to regain a heart in which reflection had extinguished love.

" You have not deceived me," said I to her ; " I will be as sincere with you ; it is my duty. We are made to be friends, and we will be so all our lives, if you incline ; but we can never be lovers." I abridge a dialogue of which this was the invariable conclusion. I left her in sadness and in grief : but I felt that I was a little too severely revenged.

'Aristomène' was finished ; I read it to the performers. Mademoiselle Clairon was present at this reading, and listened with cold dignity. They knew we were no longer intimate : I was the more applauded. It was a problem among the players, whether I should give her the part of the wife of Aristomène. She was uneasy about it, particularly when she heard that the other parts were distributed She received hers ; and a quarter of an hour afterwards she came to me with one of her friends. "Here, sir," said she to me (coming in with that air that marked her on the stage, and throwing the manuscript on my table) " I will not accept the part without its author : the one belongs to me by as good a title as the other."— " My dear friend," said I, embracing her, " in this character I am yours ; do not ask more of me. Another sentiment would render us miserable."—" He is right," said she to her companion ; " my giddy head would be his torment and my own. Come then, my friend, come and dine with your good friend."

From that moment the most perfect intimacy was established between us; it has lasted thirty years the same; and though separated from each other by my new way of life, nothing has changed the integrity of our mutual sentiments.

I recollect a feature of that frank and sincere friendship that reigned between us, which ought not to escape me.

Mademoiselle Clairon was neither rich nor economical. She often wanted money. She said to me one day, "I want twelve louis: have you them?"—"No, indeed I have not."—"Try and get them for me, and bring them to me this evening into my box at the theatre." I instantly began my search. I knew many rich people, but I did not choose to address myself to them. I went to my Gascon abbés, and to some others of that class: I found them dry. I went sorrowfully into mademoiselle Clairon's box; she was tête-à-tête with the duke de Duras. "You come very late," said she.—"I have been in quest of some money that is due to me," said I; "but I have lost my walk." Mademoiselle Clairon understood me, and I retired. As I was going to take my place in the amphitheatre, I heard some one call me by my name from the end of the corridor. I turn, and see the duke de Duras coming up to me: "I have just heard you say," said he, "that you are in want of money; how much do you want?" At these words he drew out his purse. I thanked him, assuring him that my wants were not so urgent. "That is no answer," replied he; "what is the sum you expected to receive?"—"Twelve louis," answered I at last.—"Here they are," said he; "but on condition that, whenever you want money, you will address yourself to me." And, when I returned them to him and pressed him to take them again, "You insist on it?" said he, "therefore I take them; but remember that this purse, in which I put them, is yours." I made no use of this credit, but from that moment there was no kindness which he did not show me. We had been together at the French academy; and on every occasion he is entitled to my praise. He took pleasure in seizing opportunities of doing me kind offices. When I dined at his house, he always gave me his best champagne: and even in his fits of the gout he expressed pleasure at seeing me. He has been called capricious; he certainly never was so with me. Let us return to 'Aristomène.'

Voltaire was then in Paris: he had expressed his inclination to see my piece before it was completed, and I had read to him four acts, with which he was pleased. But the act I had still to write gave him some inquietude; and not without reason. In the four acts he had heard, the action appeared complete, and uninterrupted. "What!" said he, after the reading, "do you pretend, in your second tragedy, to supersede a general rule? When I wrote the 'Death of Cæsar' in three acts, it was for a school, and my excuse was the constraint I was under to introduce only men. But you, on the great theatre, and on a subject where nothing could confine you, give a mutilated piece, in four acts, for which unsightly form you have no example! This, at your age, is an unfortunate licence, that I cannot excuse."—"And, indeed," said I, "this is a licence I have no intention of taking. In my own imagination, my tragedy is in five acts, which I hope to complete."—"And how?" inquired he. "I have just heard the last act; all is perfectly coherent, and you surely do not think of beginning the action earlier?"—"No," answered I, "the action will begin and finish as you have seen; the rest is my secret. What I meditate is perhaps folly. But however perilous the step may be, I must take it; and if you damp my courage all my labour will be lost."—"Cheerly then, my good friend, go on: risk, venture, 'tis always a good sign. In our profession, as in war, there are fortunate temerities;

and the greatest beauties frequently burst forth under the most desperate difficulties."

At the first representation, he insisted on placing himself behind me in my box; and, I owe him this testimony, that he was almost as agitated and as trembling as myself. " Now," said he, " before the curtain is drawn up, tell me from what incident you have drawn the act that was wanting." I made him recollect, that at the end of the second act it was said, that the wife and son of Aristomène were going to be tried, and that at the commencement of the third it appeared they had been condemned. " Well," said I, " this trial that was then supposed to take place between the acts I have introduced on the stage." —" What! a criminal court on the stage!" exclaimed he; " you make me tremble."—" Yes," said I, " it is a dangerous sand, but it was inevitable; it is Clairon that must save me."

'Aristomène' had no less success than 'Dionysius.' Voltaire at every burst of applause pressed me in his arms. But what astonished him, and made him leap for joy, was the effect of the third act. When he behead Léonide, loaded with irons like a criminal, appear before her judges, command them by her dignity and magnanimity, get full possession of the stage and of the souls of the spectators, turn her defence into accusation, and, distinguishing among the senators the virtuous friends of Aristomène from his faithless enemies, attack, overwhelm, and convict them of perfidy, amid the applauses she received, " *Brava, Clairon!*" cried Voltaire; " *macte animo, generose puer!*"

Certainly, no one feels more intimately than I do how little worthy I was, in point of talent, to excite his envy; but my success was enough to have made him jealous, had he been subject to that weakness. No: Voltaire was too sensible of his own superiority to fear vulgar talents. Perhaps a new Corneille, or a new Racine, might have vexed him; but it was not so easy as was supposed to disquiet the author of Zaire, Alzire, Merope, and Mahomet.

At this first representation of Aristomène, I was again obliged to show myself on the stage; but at the subsequent representations my friends encouraged me to conceal myself from the acclamations of the public.

An accident interrupted my good fortune, and troubled my joy. Roselli, the actor whom I have already mentioned, played the part of Arcire, the friend of Aristomène, and played it with as much warmth as intelligence. He was neither handsome nor well made; he had even a very sensible lisp in his pronunciation. But his defects were thrown into shade by the correctness of his action, and an expressive countenance full of soul and intelligence. To him I attributed the success of the dénouement of my tragedy; which he ensured by the following means. In the last scene, speaking of the decree by which the senate had completed the measure of its atrocities, when he said

Théonis le défend, et s'en nomme l'auteur;

he perceived the public were rising with indignation; and, instantly advancing to the edge of the stage, with the liveliest action, he cried to the pit, as it were to appease them:

Je m' èlance, et lui plonge un poignard dans le cœur.

At the attitude and gesture that accompanied these words, they thought they beheld Théonis expiring, and the whole theatre resounded with transport.

But, after the sixth representation of my piece, and in the height of success, I was informed that Roselli was attacked with an inflammation in the lungs; and, to supply his place, they proposed an incapable performer. It was a very great prejudice to me to interrupt this concourse of the public: but it would have been a yet more serious evil to have degraded my work. I required that the representations should be suspended, till the health of Roselli should be re-established; and it was not till the following winter that 'Aristomène' was revived.

At the first representation of the revival, the public emotion was so strong that the author was again called for. I refused to appear on the stage, but I was behind some friends in a box. Some one perceived me from the pit, and cried, "There he is!" The box was towards the amphitheatre; the whole pit faced about, I was obliged to advance, and answer by an humble salutation to this new favour.

The man, who took me in his arms from an obscure part of his box to present me to the public, will occupy a considerable place in these memoirs, on account of the harm he did in seeking to benefit me, and of the attracting and dangerous charms I found in his society. It was M. de la Poplinière. Ever since the success of 'Dionysius the Tyrant,' he had invited me to his house. But, at the time of which I am speaking, the courage he had to offer me a retreat in his country-house, at the risk of displeasing the all-powerful man I had offended, strongly attached me to so generous a friend. The danger from which he drew me arose from one of those youthful adventures in which my imprudence engaged me, and which will teach my children to be more sage than I was.

BOOK IV.

While I lived near the Luxembourg, an actress, who had formerly performed at the comic opera, La Darimat, the friend of mademoiselle Clairon and the wife of Durancy, a comedian in a provincial company, being brought to bed at Paris, had engaged another actress to be godmother to her child, and I was chosen for its godfather. It happened, in consequence of this christening, that madame Durancy, who had sometimes heard me talk on the art of acting at mademoiselle Clairon's, said to me one day, " Would you like that I should give you a young and pretty actress to form? She is ambitious of excelling in tragedy, and it is well worth your while to instruct her. 'Tis mademoiselle Verrière, a young lady, who is protected by marshal Saxe. She is your neighbour, is prudent, and lives very decently with her mother and sister. The marshal, as you know, is gone to see the king of Prussia, and we wish, at his return, to give him the pleasure of finding his ward playing Zaire and Iphigénie better than mademoiselle Gaussin. If you will undertake to teach her, I'll introduce you tomorrow, we'll dine together at her house."

My adventure with mademoiselle Navarre had not at all offended marshal Saxe; he had even shown me some kindness; and, before 'Aristomène' was given to the theatre, he had sent to invite me to go and read it to him. This reading, tête-à-tête, had interested him; he was moved by the part of Aristomène; he thought that of Léonide theatrical: " But, zounds!" said he, " that's a most desperate woman! I would not have her for the world." This was his only criticism. He appeared pleased, and expressed his satisfaction with that noble and manly frankness which marked the hero.

I was enchanted, therefore, at having an opportunity of doing what might be agreeable to him, and very innocently, but very imprudently, accepted the above proposal.

This girl, whom the marshal protected, was one of his mistresses. She had been given to him at the age of seventeen. He had had a daughter by her, since acknowledged and married under the name of Aurore de Saxe. At the birth of this child, he had settled an annuity on her of one hundred pounds: he gave her, besides, five hundred pounds a-year for her expenses He loved her tenderly, as a friend; but, as to his pleasures, she was no longer admitted to them. The gentleness, the ingenuousness, the timidity of her character had nothing sufficiently inviting for him. It is notorious, that, with much nobleness and dignity of soul, the marshal was fond of mirth and jollity. By taste, as well as by system, he loved merriment in his armies, saying that the French never did so well as when they were led on gaily, and that what they most feared, in war, was weary inactivity. He had always a comic opera in his camp. It was at the theatre that he gave the order of battle; and on those days the principal actress used to come forward and say, "Gentlemen, tomorrow there will be no play, on account of the battle the marshal gives; after to-morrow, the Cock of the Village, with the Merry Intrigues," &c.

Two actresses of this theatre, Chantilly and Beaumenard, were his two favourite mistresses, and their rivalship, jealousy, and caprices, gave him, as he said, "more torment than the hussars of the queen of Hungary." I have seen these words in one of his letters. It was for these women that mademoiselle Navarre had been neglected. He thought her too haughty, with too little complaisance, and too much delicacy. Mademoiselle Verrière, with infinitely less artifice, had no ambition to dispute the preference with her rivals: she seemed to repose on her beauty for the care of pleasing, without contributing to it otherwise than by the quality of an amiable temper, and by the indolence with which she suffered herself to be loved.

The first scenes that we rehearsed together were those of Zaire with Orosmane. Her face, her voice, the melting of her eye, and her air of modest candour, perfectly accorded with her part; and I did but express mine with too much vehemence and warmth. At our second lesson, these words, "Zaire, you weep!" were the rock on which my prudence struck.

The docility of my pupil made me assiduous. This assiduity was maliciously interpreted. The marshal, who was then in Prussia, being informed of our acquaintance, fell into a transport of anger that was little worthy so great a man. The fifty pounds that mademoiselle Verrière received every month were stopped, and he declared that so long as he lived he never would again see either the mother or her child. He kept his word, and it was not till after his death, and partly by my mediation, that Aurore was acknowledged and educated in a convent as the daughter of this hero.

The situation of my Zaire, thus forsaken and abandoned, overwhelmed us both with grief. I had forty pounds left of the produce of my new tragedy; I prayed her to accept them. Mademoiselle Clairon, and all our friends, advised us not to see each other, at least for some time. It cost us a flood of tears, but we followed their advice.

The marshal returned; I was told by every person that he was furious against me. I have since learned, from marshal Leowendal and two other of his friends, that they had found great difficulty in moderating his anger. He went about saying in every society, at court, and to the king himself, that a little insolent poet had robbed him of all his mistresses (yet I had only those he had abandoned). He showed a letter of mine, that a faithless servant had stolen from my Zaire. Fortunately in this letter, speaking of the tragedy of 'Cléopâtre,' which I was then writing, it was said that Antony was a hero in love as well as in battle. "Aye; this Antony!" said the marshal; "you see well enough who he means." This allusion, which I never thought of, flattered, and, by flattering, calmed him.

Yet my torments were the more cruel, because I was resolved, at the peril of my life, to revenge myself, if he had dared to insult me. In this situation, one of the most painful in which I have ever been, M. de la Poplinière proposed to me to retire to his country-house; and, on the other side, the prince of Turenne alleviated the sorrow I felt at leaving my Zaire in misfortune.

This prince, meeting me one evening in the green-room at the French theatre, came to me, and said, "It is on your account that marshal Saxe has quitted mademoiselle Verrière; will you give me your word never to see her again? Her misfortune shall be repaired." This explained to me the mysterious rendezvous she had given the evening before in the wood of Boulogne, and the tears she had shed on bidding me farewell. "Yes, prince," answered I, "I give you the promise you ask. May mademoiselle Verrière be happy with you! I consent to see her no more." He took her, and I was faithful to my word.

Retired, almost solitary, in this country-house, then very different from what it had been, and from what it since was, I had full time to indulge in reflections on myself. I turned my eyes to the abyss, on the border of which I had just passed. The hero of Fontenoy, the idol of the army and of all France, the man before whom the first nobility of the kingdom bowed with respect, and whom the king himself received with all the distinction that could flatter a great man, was he whom I had offended, without even having for my excuse the distraction of imperious love. This imprudent and frail girl had not concealed from me that she was still bound to the marshal, by his favours, and as the father of her child. I was so well persuaded, so convinced of the dreadful risk we both ran, that, when at undue hours I stole to her house, it was never without trembling. I used to find her and leave her still more trembling than myself. There was no pleasure that would not have been too dearly paid by our being surprised and denounced. And if the marshal, informed of my temerity, disdaining to take my life, had only bribed one of his servants to insult me, I could only oppose this fear by a resolution which I cannot think of without shuddering. Ah! shudder like me, my children, at the dangers that a too ardent youth has made me run, for a fortuitous and transient connection, without any other inducement than that of pleasure and opportunity. I have thought it right to mark to you this shoal, in order to preserve you from shipwreck.

A little time after, the marshal died. He had finished by showing himself magnanimous towards me, like the lion towards the mouse in the fable. At the first representation of ' Cléopâtre,' finding himself face to face with me in the corridor as he came out of his box (a meeting that made me turn pale) he had the kindness to express his approbation in these words: " Well done, sir, well done!" I sincerely regretted in him the defender of my country, and the generous man who had pardoned me; and to honour his memory as much as I could, I made on him this epitaph :—

Fabius at Courtnay, Hannibal at Brussels,
Condé on the Meuse, Turenne on the Rhine,
'Twas he inspir'd with awe the savage leopard !
'Twas he that clipt the rapid eagle's wing !

The retreat in which I had sought to take refuge, from the temptations of Paris, soon offered me new ones: but at that instant it only afforded me serious lessons on moral conduct. To make you acquainted with the cause of the silent and gloomy sadness that then reigned, where pleasures seemed to have fixed their seat, I must recur a little to what is past, and tell you how this enchantment was formed and destroyed.

M. de la Poplinière was not the richest financier of his time, but he was the most sumptuous. He began by taking for his mistress, and afterwards for his wife, the daughter of an actress. He had no intention to marry her, but she obliged him to do so: and by the following means. The famous madame de Tencin, after having raised her brother to the dignity of cardinal, and introduced him to the council of state, had through him an obscure but powerful interest with the old cardinal Fleury. Mademoiselle Daucour contrived to be presented to her, and, as a young innocent creature that had been seduced, she complained that M. de la Poplinière, after having flattered her with the hopes of becoming his wife, thought no longer of marriage. "I'll undertake he shall marry you," said madame de Tencin. "Conceal from him that you have seen me, and take no notice of what has passed."

The critical moment approached for renewing the leases for farming the king's revenues, and, among the old farmers-general, it was who should remain on the list. It was hinted to cardinal Fleury that this was the moment to put an end to a scandal that afflicted all honest men. Mademoiselle Daucour was represented to him as an interesting victim of seduction, and la Poplinière as one of those men who trifle with innocence, after having surprised its frailty and good faith.

The act of keeping publicly a mistress was a luxury yet unauthorized among financiers, and the cardinal pretended to make a point of maintaining good morals. When la Poplinière went to solicit his favour for the new lease, the cardinal asked him who mademoiselle Daucour was. "She is a young lady, that I have taken under my care," answered la Poplinière; and he spoke in praise of her wit, accomplishments, and good breeding. "I am very glad," replied the cardinal, "to hear you speak so highly of her. Everybody says the same, and it is the king's intention to give your place to him who will marry her. It is at least equitable that, after having seduced her, you should leave to her, as her marriage portion, that situation in life which she had a right to expect from you and from the promises you made her." La Poplinière wanted to deny ever having made such an engagement. "You have abused her," insisted the minister, "and without you she would still have had her innocence. It is a wrong that you ought to repair. This is the advice I give you, and don't hesitate to follow it, otherwise I can do nothing for you." Lose his place or marry! The alternative was painful. La Poplinière chose the least evil of the two; but he wanted to give the appearance of free-will to his forced resolution, and the next day, as mademoiselle Daucour awoke, "Get up," said he, "and come with your mother, where I am going to lead you." She obeyed. He took them to his attorney's. "Now," said he, "listen to the act that we are going to sign." It was the marriage contract. The scene seemed to produce its effect. The daughter pretended to faint, the mother embraced the knees of him who completed his own kindness and their vows. He enjoyed to the full their feigned gratitude, and, as long as he could indulge the delusion of a husband who thinks himself beloved, he saw his house embellished by the enchantments of his brilliant wife. The first nobility partook of his suppers and balls; but jealous inquietude and suspicion soon troubled his repose. His wife had taken wing. Borne away by the crowd, through which he could not follow her, she was invited to suppers where he was not present, and his enemies took a malicious pleasure in telling him in anonymous letters that he was the fable and mockery of that brilliant court with which she was surrounded. It was at this time that he invited me to his house; but I was at first only admitted to his private society. There I met the celebrated Rameau-Latour, the most ingenious painter in pastel that we have had; Vaucanson, that wonderful mechanician; Carle-Vanloo, the great designer and colourist; and his wife, who with the voice of a nightingale, first taught us Italian singing.

Madame de la Poplinière showed me some attention. She wished me to read 'Aristomène' to her, and of all the critics I had consulted, she was, in my opinion, the best. After having heard my piece, she analyzed it with a clearness and precision that were surprising; she retraced to me scene by scene the course of the action, remarked the passages that had appeared to her beautiful, as well as those which she had thought feeble; and in all the corrections she proposed, her observations struck me as so many rays of light. A view so lively, so rapid, and yet so just, astonished the whole company; and at this reading, though I was abundantly applauded, I must say that her success eclipsed mine. Her husband sat amazed and sad. His admiration for this happy facility of memory and intelligence, for this vein of eloquence that seemed like inspiration, in short, for this union of talent and taste that astonished him as well as us in his wife, was clouded by a fund of grief and melancholy of which he only knew the cause. He had wanted to withdraw her from the circles of fashion into which she had been hurried; but she had treated the constraint he would have imposed on her as a capricious tyranny, and humiliating slavery; and hence arose the violent disputes that took place between them in private.

La Poplinière alleviated his cares in our company, and particularly in mine, by satires on this splendid crowd, with which he said he was fatigued, and from which he would gladly remove. He had persuaded me to live near him. My simplicity and frankness pleased him. "Let us live together," said he; "we are formed to love each other, and leave, I entreat you, this gay society that has seduced you as it had once seduced me. What can you expect from it?"—"Protectors," replied I, "and the means of fortune."—"Protectors! Ah! if you knew how all those creatures protect!.... Fortune! and have I then not enough for us both? I have no child, and, thank heaven! I never shall have one. Stay tranquilly with me, and let us not separate; for I feel every day that you are more necessary to me."

In spite of his repugnance to see me escape from him, he could not refuse madame de Tencin, to whom he was respectful by policy, when she requested that he would take me to her house to read my tragedy. The piece was 'Aristomène.' The audience was respectable. I there saw assembled Montesquieu, Fontenelle, Mairan, Marivaux, the young Helvetius, Astruc, and others, all men of letters or science, and in the midst of them a woman of excellent talents and profound judgment, but who, enveloped in her exterior of plainness and simplicity, had rather the air of the housekeeper than the mistress. This was madame de Tencin. I had occasion for all my lungs to make myself heard by Fontenelle; and, though very near his ear, I was obliged to pronounce every word very loudly and forcibly. But he listened to me with so much kindness, that he made the efforts of this painful reading pleasing. It was, as you may well conceive, extremely monotonous, without inflexion or colour: yet I was honoured with the suffrages of the assembly; I had even the honour of dining with madame de Tencin, and from that day I should have been inscribed on her list of dinner visitors; but M. de la Poplinière had no difficulty in persuading me that there was too much wit there for me; and, indeed, I soon perceived that each guest arrived ready to play his part, and that the desire of exhibiting did not always leave conversation the liberty of following its facile and natural course. It was, who should most quickly seize the moment as it flew to place his epigram, his story, his anecdote, his maxim, or his light and pointed satire, and to make or find this opportunity the circuit they took was often unnatural.

P

In Marivaux, impatience to give proof of acuteness and sagacity was visibly betrayed. Montesquieu, with more calm, waited till the ball came to him, but he expected his turn. Mairan watched opportunity. Astruc did not deign to wait. Fontenelle alone let it come without seeking; and he used so soberly the attention with which he was listened to, that his acute remarks and charming stories never occupied but a moment. Helvetius, attentive and discreet, sat collecting for a future day. His was an example that I should not have had the constancy to follow: and therefore to me this society had but little attraction.

It was not the same with that of a lady to whom my happy star had introduced me at madame de Tencin's, and who from that time had the kindness to invite me to go and see her. This lady, who was then beginning to choose and compose her literary society, was madame Geoffrin. I answered her invitation too late, and it was again M. de la Poplinière who prevented me from going to her house. "What should you do there?" said he; "it is but another rendezvous of fine wits."

It was thus that he held me captive when my adventure happend with marshal Saxe. But what attached me more intimately to him was, to see' him so wretched, and perceive the want he had of me. Anonymous letters did not cease to torment him. He was assured that at Passy itself a happy rival continually saw his wife. He observed her; he had her watched night and day; she was told of it, and only looked on him as her jailor.

It was there that I learnt what a family is, when on one side jealousy, and on the other hatred, steal into it like two serpents. A delightful house, which arts, talents, and all rational pleasures seemed to have made their residence, but where luxury, affluence, abundance of all that is estimable, were all corrupted by mistrust and fear, by sad, suspicious, and cruel vexation! You should have seen this couple opposite each other at table; the melancholy taciturnity of the husband, the proud and cold indignation of the wife, the care their eyes took to avoid each other, and the terrible and gloomy air with which they met, particularly before their servants; the effort they made to address a few words to each other, and the dry unfeeling tone in which they answered. It is difficult to conceive how two beings so strongly alienated could live together; but she was determined not to quit his house, and he, in the eyes of the world and in justice, had not the right to drive her away.

I, who at last knew the cause of this misunderstanding, neglected nothing to mitigate the sorrows of him whose heart seemed to lean on mine. A wretch whom I disdain to name, because he is dead, has accused me of having been the devoted slave of la Poplinière. I begin by declaring that I never received from him the slightest favour. After this, I acknowledge without blushing, that, from a sentiment no less ingenuous than sincere, I studied to please him. Equally distant from adulation and neglect, I did not flatter, but I consoled him: I rendered him the good office that Horace attributed to the muses, "vos lene consilium et datis, et dato gaudetis almæ." And would to heaven that he had not been more indulgent to my vanity than I was to his! The spirit of self-love which exaggerates in our eyes the value of all that interests us, had so cheated his fancy about the young poet he had adopted, that whatever flowed from my pen appeared to him beautiful; and, instead of the severe friend I wanted, I found in him only a very facile approver. This was one of the causes to which I attribute that faintness of exertion which marks everything I wrote while I lived with him.

Towards the end of autumn he became weary of the melancholy of his country house, which he quitted. A short time afterwards happened the adventure that separated him from his wife.. One day, when marshal Saxe treated the public with a review of his Hullands, in the *plaine des Sablons*, la Poplinière, more tormented than ever by anonymous letters, which repeated to him that his wife received marshal Richelieu every night in her chamber, chose the time she was passing at the review to examine her apartment, and try to discover how a man could be introduced there in spite of the vigilance of a porter of whom he was sure. He had with him, to aid him in his search, Vaucanson and Balot; the latter was a little attorney, of an acute and penetrating mind, but a strange grotesque personage, as well for the singularity of his language, which was trivial and hyperbolic, as of his character, which was a mixture of meanness and arrogance; he being proud and lofty by starts, and servile by habit. It was he that used to praise M. de la Poplinière for the delicacy of his skin, and who said of him, in a moment of ill humour,—" He is drunk with gold, let him sleep it off." As for Vaucanson, all his mind was in his peculiar talent; and out of mechanics, no one could be more ignorant or more stupid.

In examining the apartment of madame de la Poplinière, Balot remarked that, in the cabinet where her harpsichord stood, a carpet had been laid, and that in the chimney there was neither wood, ashes, nor fire-irons, although the weather was already cold, and there were fires in every other room. By induction, he took it into his head to strike the plate that formed the back of the chimney with his cane; the plate sounded hollow. Then Vaucanson coming up, perceived that it was mounted on hinges, and so perfectly united to the lining on each side that the juncture was almost imperceptible. "Oh! sir," cried he, turning to M. de la Poplinière; "what a beautiful piece of workmanship is this! and what an excellent workman was he who made it! This plate is moveable, it opens; but its hinges are of such delicacy!..... No. sir; no snuff-box can be more highly finished. An excellent mechanic!"—"What, sir!" said la Poplinière, turning pale, "you are sure that this plate opens?"—"Certainly, I'm sure of it, I see it," said Vaucanson in an extacy of admiration; "nothing can be more wonderful."—"What have I to do with your wonder? we are not here to admire."—"Ah! sir, such workmen are very rare! I surely have very good ones, but I have not one who ...."—"Think no more of your workmen," interrupted la Poplinière; "but let me send for one who can force this plate."—"'Tis pity," said Vaucanson, "to destroy so exquisite a piece of workmanship as that."

Behind the plate, an opening made in the partition wall was closed by a pane of wainscot, which, covered by a looking-glass in the adjoining house, could be opened at will, and afford the clandestine occupier of the neighbouring room a free passage into the cabinet of madame de la Poplinière. The unhappy husband, who only sought, I believe, some legal means of getting rid of his wife, sent for a police officer, and had his discovery and his misfortune formally confirmed by a written declaration.

His wife was still at the review when she was told what was passing at home. That she might at all events be admitted on her return, she entreated marshal Loewendal to accompany her; but the door was shut, and the marshal would not take on himself to force it. She then addressed herself to marshal Saxe; "Let me but enter my house," said she to him, "and let me speak to my husband, 'tis all I ask; you will have saved me." The marshal desired her to get into his carriage, and when he arrived at the door got out and rapped himself. The faithful porter, half opening the door, was telling him he could not enter.—"And don't you know me?" said the marshal; "I will teach you that no door is shut to me. Come in, madame, enter your house." He took her by the hand, and walked up with her.

La Poplinière, affrighted, came to meet him. "Why, what's all this, my good friend?" said the marshal; "a disturbance, a dispute, a scandalous public exhibition? You can gain nothing by all this but ridicule. Don't you perceive that your enemies are seeking to separate you, and that they employ every artifice to succeed? Do not be the dupe of them. Listen to your wife, who will fully justify herself in your eyes, and who only asks to live suitably with you." La Poplinière kept a respectful silence, and the marshal retired, recommending decency and peace.

Alone with her husband, madame de la Poplinière armed herself with all her courage, and with all her eloquence. She asked him on what new suspicion, what new accusation, he had shut his door against her? And when he mentioned the plate at the back of the chimney, she was indignant that he should think her the accomplice of so culpable an invention. Was it not rather into his apartment than into hers that its contrivers wished to penetrate? And, to form clandestinely this passage from one house to the other, what more was necessary than to bribe a servant and a workman? But how could he doubt the cause of a stratagem so visibly invented to ruin her in his opinion? "I was too happy with you," said she, " and it is my happiness that has excited envy. 'Tis envy that dictated those anonymous letters; but, not satisfied without adding proof to accusation, this envy in her rage has imagined that detestable machine. What do I say? Ever since she has persisted to persecute me, could you not see what was the crime that irritated her? Is there another woman in Paris whose repose and honour have been so violently attacked? Ah! because there is not another who has offended envy so much as myself, as I should still offend her if you were more just. I contributed to the happiness of a man, whose understanding, accomplishments, consideration, and honourable existence are the torments of the envious. It is you whom they wish to make wretched and ridiculous. Yes, this is the motive of those anonymous libels you every day receive ; and this the success they hope for from this palpable snare they have laid for you." Then throwing herself at his feet; "Ah! sir, restore me to your esteem, to your confidence, and, if I dare ask it, to your tenderness; and my love shall revenge you, while it revenges myself for the wrong our common enemies have done us."

Unhappily, too strongly convinced, la Poplinière was inflexible. "Madame," said he, "all the artifice of your language cannot make me change my resolution. We can live no longer together. If you retire modestly, without disturbance, I will provide for you. If you oblige me to have recourse to rigorous measures, to force you away, I will employ them; and every sentiment of indulgence and kindness for you will be stifled in my bosom." He allowed her, I believe, eight hundred pounds a-year, with which she went to live, or rather die, in an obscure retreat, forsaken by the splendid society that had so often flattered her, and that despised her when she was in misfortune. A slight swelling that she had in her breast was the germ of a corrosive humour that slowly devoured her. Marshal Richelieu, who sought elsewhere for new pastime and new pleasures, while she was consuming in the most cruel torture, did not neglect to pay her the duties of civility as he passed; and hence it was said, after her decease, "Indeed, M. de Richelieu has behaved most admirably to her! He did not cease to see her till her last moment."

It was to be loved thus that this woman, who at her own house, had her conduct been correct, would have enjoyed the public esteem, and all the comforts of an honoured and enviable life, sacrificed her repose, her fortune, and all her pleasures. That which renders this delirium of vanity still more frightful, is, that neither her heart nor her understanding had any considerable share in it. Madame de la Poplinière, with a lively imagination, was of extreme coldness: but an intriguing duke had appeared to her, as to many others, a glorious conquest: this it was that ruined her.

La Poplinière, separated from his wife, thought only of living as an independent opulent man. His house at Passy again became a most enchanting but most dangerous residence for me. He had in his pay the best concert of music that was known at that time. The performers lived at his house, and rehearsed together in a morning, with marvellous accord, the symphonies they were to play in the evening. The first comedians, and particularly the female singers and dancers of the opera, came and embellished his suppers. At these suppers, after brilliant voices had charmed the ear, the company were agreeably surprised to see Lany, his sister, and the young Puvigné, quit the table during the concert, and dance in the same room to the airs of the symphony. All the great musicians that came from Italy, violin players and singers of both sexes, were received, lodged, and boarded in the house; and each was emulous of excelling in these concerts. Rameau there composed his operas; and, on festivals, at mass in the private chapel, he gave us on the organ specimens of astonishing genius. Never did a private man live more like a prince, and princes came and partook of his pleasures.

At his theatre, for he had one, they played comedies of his own writing only, and the performers were chosen from his own society. These comedies, though indifferent, were at least so well written, and showed so much taste, that it did not require any excessive complaisance to applaud them. Their success was the more infallible as the play was followed by a splendid supper, to which the most select spectators, the ambassadors from the different courts of Europe, the first nobility, and the most beautiful women in Paris, were invited.

La Poplinière did the honour of his supper like a man to whom fashionable society had taught a just sense of propriety, whose air, tone, and manners, had nothing that was not perfectly decorous, whose pride even had learnt to envelop itself in politeness and modesty, and who, even in the attentions he showed the great, always preserved a certain air of freedom and simple civility, that well became him, because it was natural. No man, when he wished to please, was more amiable than himself. He had wit, gallantry, and, without any study or much cultivation, a considerable talent for versification. Away from his house, those who came to enjoy his luxury and expense, did not fail to ridicule the life he led: but at home he heard only congratulation and praise, and, with more or less complaisance, each paid him in flattery the pleasures he bestowed. He was indeed, as has been said of him, an old spoiled child of fortune; but I, who saw him habitually and near, and who sometimes was afflicted at finding him a little too vain, am now astonished that he was not more so.

A defect in him, much more deplorable than this vanity of wealth and state, was the thirst of Tantalus for a species of enjoyment of which he was no longer, or scarcely capable. La Fontaine's financier complained that, at market, no one sold sleep as well as meat and drink. As for la Poplinière, it was not sleep for which he would have paid so dearly.

Pleasures courted him; but while fortune brought them to him in crowds, nature prescribed him a humiliating abstinence, and this alternative of continual privation was a torment. He could not imagine that the defect was in himself. He never failed to accuse the object that was present; and, whenever some new object appeared to him to have more charm, he became gallant and gay, as if expanded by this gentle ray of hope. It was then that he was cheerful and pleasant. He told us merry stories, sang songs of his own composing, and in a style sometimes free, sometimes delicate, according to the object by which he was animated. But the next morning his mirth and gaiety were gone: he was sad and dissatisfied.

I, too, who was here courted by opportunity, was far from infallible. I felt that indulgence hurt me, and that, to avoid it, I must remove from temptation; but I had not the courage. The corridor, in which I lodged, was generally inhabited by girls from the theatre. In such a neighbourhood it was difficult to be economical, either of my hours of sleep or of study. The pleasures of the table likewise contributed to obscure my mental faculties. I never suspected that temperance was the nurse of genius, and yet nothing is more true. I awoke with my head troubled, and my ideas heavy with the vapours of an ample supper. I was astonished that my spirits were not as pure and as free as in Mathurin or in Mason street. Ah! 'tis that the labour of the imagination will not be disordered by that of other organs. The muses, it has been said, are chaste; it should have been added, that they are temperate; and both these maxims were totally forgotten by me.

I had carelessly finished my tragedy of 'Cléopâtre;' and this piece, which, in the collection of my works, is that on which I have employed the most labour, then savoured, as I have said elsewhere, of the precipitation with which we write, at an age when we have not yet felt how difficult it is to write well. It needed all the indulgence of the public to obtain the very moderate success of eleven representations. I had introduced upon the stage the dénouement with which history furnished me, and Vaucanson had undertaken to contrive for me an automaton aspic, that, at the moment when Cléopâtre pressed it to her bosom to excite its bite, should imitate, almost to nature, the motion of the living aspic. But the surprise, created by this ingenious piece of mechanism, diverted the spectators from the true interest of the moment. I have since preferred a dénouement more simple. Beside, I ought to acknowledge that I had presumed too much on my own powers, when I hoped to persuade my audience to pardon Antony's excessive error. The example it affords is terrible; but the extreme difficulty was to make it affecting.

I looked for a subject more pathetic, and I thought I had found it in the story of the Héraclides. It had some resemblance to that of 'Iphigenie en Aulide;' but the two subjects were so different in the characters and incidents of the action, that the same Greek poet, Euripides, had written a tragedy on each. However, scarcely had my piece been received and given for rehearsal, before the report everywhere was current that, on a subject similar to that of Racine, I wanted to contend with him for the laurel.

This report was spread with such an affectation of marked malevolence, that I perceived I had enemies; I soon learned I had a cloud of them. I inquired the reason, of which I was then ignorant; but since, I have known it well. At the theatre, the gentle but perfidious Gaussin had alienated from me all her party, and her party was numerous; for it was formed first of her own friends, and then of the enemies of mademoiselle Clairon, to whom were added the zealous partisans of mademoiselle Duménil. Clairon, by her excellence, perpetually bore away some part from each of these actresses, and I, her faithful poet, was the object of their enmity. Among the frequenters and intriguers of the green-room, I had against me all the enemies of Voltaire; and, beside those, all his enthusiasts, who, less generous than himself, could not even tolerate merit below his own. Several societies, which I had neglected after having been received into them, were offended that I had not made a suitable return to their offers of kindness; and the friendship that M. de la Poplinière had for me made the hatred of those who envied him rebound on me. Add to these, that crowd of people, who are naturally disposed to cry down those who are rising, and to enjoy the misfortunes of those they have seen prosper, and you will conceive how, without having injured, without having even offended any one, I was already oppressed by so many enemies. I had even some among the young men, who, having heard my frivolous adventures mentioned in society, supposed that in gallantry I had all the pretensions of their foppery, and who would not pardon me for rivalling them; which proves by the bye, that the old maxim, "conceal thy actions," suits no one better than a man of letters, and that it is only by his writings that he should be celebrated.

But a more terrible enemy to me than all these was the Procope coffee-house. I had at first frequented this coffee-house, the rendezvous of the frequenters and arbiters of the pit, and was very well received there. But after the success of 'Dionysius' and 'Aristomène,' I had been imprudently advised not to go there; and this advice I had followed. So sudden and so abrupt a desertion, attributed to my vanity, did me the greatest harm; and the favour which this tribunal had before shown me was now turned into enmity. It is a warning to you, my children, to be reserved in the connections you form while young; for it is difficult to dissolve those in which we are once engaged without leaving bitter resentments and cruel enmities. Instead of withdrawing insensibly, I quitted mine abruptly; this was a very great fault.

Finally, too much sincerity, perhaps too much roughness, which was in my character, never permitted me to dissemble the aversion and contempt with which I was filled for those wretched journalists, who, as Voltaire said, "attack every day that which is best, and praise that which is worst; and who convert the noble profession of letters into a trade as base and as despicable as themselves." From the moment my successes began, I found myself assailed by them as by a swarm of wasps; and, from Fréron to the abbé Aubert, there was not one of those vile writers who did not revenge my contempt by an outrageous invective against all my works.

Such were the dispositions of a part of the public when I brought out the 'Héraclides.' It was the most feebly written of all my theatrical works, but it was the most pathetic; and at the rehearsals I cannot express the impression it had made. Mademoiselle Duménil played in it the part of Déjanire; mademoiselle Clairon that of Olimpie; and in their scenes, the expression of the love and grief of the mother was so heart-rending, that she who played the daughter was so affected by it as to be unable to speak. The audience melted into tears. M. de la Poplinière, as well as all who were present, answered for its full success.

I have mentioned elsewhere by what event all the effect of those pathetic scenes were destroyed, at the first representation. But what I have not chosen to explain in a preface, I may state clearly in these private memoirs. Mademoiselle Duménil loved wine. It was her custom to drink a tumbler between the acts, but so weakened with water as not to intoxicate her. Unfortunately, on that day her servant brought it her pure, without her knowledge. In the first act she had just been sublime, and applauded with transport. Heated with exertion, she drank the wine, and it flew to her head. In this state of intoxication and insensibility she played the rest of her part, or rather stammered it out with so wild, so insane an air, that the pathetic became laughable; and, you know, when the pit once begin to take the serious as raillery, nothing touches them any longer, and, like cold parodists, they seek only to ridicule.

As the public knew not what had passed behind the scenes, they did not fail to attribute to the part the extravagance of the actress; and the report through Paris was, that the tone of my piece was that of a familiarity so extravagant, and so comical, that the spectators had burst with laughter.

Although I was no favourite with mademoiselle Duménil, yet, as she attributed to herself at least a part of my misfortune, she thought it her duty to exert herself to repair it. The piece was given again, in spite of me; it was played by the two actresses as well as possible: the few people who saw it shed gentle tears; but, the contrary prejudice once established, the blow was struck. It rose no more; and at the sixth representation I desired that it might not be played again.

My children will have read the recital I have made elsewhere of the fête that awaited me at Passy on the day of the first representation of the 'Héraclides,' and the unseasonableness of which would have completed my humiliation, if I had not had the presence of mind to place on the head of mademoiselle Clairon the crown of laurel that was so untimely offered me. I only mention here this incident to show with what assurance M. de la Poplinière had reckoned on the success of my work. He persisted in the opinion he had had of it, and the warmth of his friendship was redoubled to rouse me from the melancholy dejection that preyed on my spirits.

My mind, as it rose from this depression, assumed a more masculine character, and even some tint of philosophy; thanks to adversity, and thanks too, perhaps, to the connections I had formed. My enchantment at Passy was not so extravagant as to make me forget Paris. I made little excursions there, oftener than la Poplinière could have wished. At my good madame Harenc's, whom I never neglected, I made the acquaintance of d'Alembert, and the young mademoiselle l'Espinasse, who both accompanied madame du Défand whenever she came to sup there. In this place I only name these very interesting people. I shall afterward speak of them at leisure.

Another society into which I was introduced, I do not recollect how, was that of the baron d'Holbach.

It was there I first knew Diderot, Helvétius, Grimm, and J. J. Rousseau, before he had become a savage. Grimm, then the secretary and intimate friend of the young count de Frise, the nephew of marshal Saxe, used to give us a dinner every week at his own house; and at this bachelor's dinner reigned a frank liberty; but that was a dish of which Rousseau tasted but very temperately. No one ever observed more strictly than he the melancholy maxim of living with his friends as if they were one day to be his enemies. When I first knew him, he had just borne the prize of eloquence at the academy of Dijon, with that fine sophism in which he has imputed to the arts and sciences the natural effects of the prosperity and wealth of nations. Yet he had not then declared himself as he has since done, nor did he announce any ambition to form a sect. Either his pride was unborn, or he concealed it under the show of a timid politeness, that was sometimes even obsequious, and bordered on humility. But in this timid reserve distrust was evidently visible; his eyes observed everything with a suspicious attention. He was very rarely affable, and never open-hearted. He was not the less amicably received; as we knew he indulged a restless self-love, tetchy, easily hurt, he was humoured, and treated with the same attention and delicacy that we should use toward a beautiful woman, very vain and very capricious, whose favours we wished to obtain. He was then composing the music for the 'Devin du Village,' and sung to us at the harpsichord the airs he had written. We were charmed with them; we were not less so with the firm, animated, and profound manner, in which his first essay on eloquence was written. Nothing could be more sincere, I ought to say it, than our benevolence for his person, nor than our esteem for his talents. It is the recollection of these days that made me indignant against him, when I saw him, for foolish trifles, or wrongs of his own creating, calumniate men who treated him so kindly, and would have been so happy to love him. I have lived with them all their lives; I shall have occasion to speak of their minds and hearts. I never perceived in them anything like the character that his evil genius attributed to them.

As for me, the little time that we were together in their society passed, between him and me, coldly, without affection and without aversion for each other; the way in which we treated each other admitted neither of complaint nor praise: and, in what I have said, and in what I may still say of him, I feel myself perfectly free from all personality.

But the fruit I gathered, from his society and example, was a return of reflection on the imprudence of my youth. There, said I, is a man who has given himself time to think before he wrote; and I, in the most difficult and most perilous of arts, have hastened to write almost before I had thought. Twenty years of study and meditation, in silence and retreat, have amassed, ripened, and fertilized his knowledge; and I scatter my ideas when they are scarcely blown, and before they have acquired their vigour and growth. Thus in his first productions there is an astonishing abundance, a perfect virility; and in mine all savours of the greenness and feebleness of a talent that study and reflection have not sufficiently nurtured. My only excuse was my poverty, and the necessity of labouring incessantly and hastily to procure my subsistence. I resolved to extricate myself from this sad situation, were I even obliged to renounce poetry.

I had some access to the court, and the removal of M. Orri had not taken from me all hope of fortune. The same woman, by whose influence he had been dismissed, was pleased with me for having more than once been the echo of the public voice, in verses where I celebrated what was worthy of praise in the reign of her lover. A little poem, that I had written on the establishment of the military school, a monument raised to the glory of the king by the bosom friends of madame de Pompadour; this little poem, I say, had interested her, and installed me in her favour. The abbé de Berni and Duclos went together to see her every Sunday, and, as they had both some friendship for me, I used to go with them as a third. This woman, to whom the first nobility of the kingdom, and the princes of the blood themselves paid their court, at her toilet, though simple by birth, she who had the weakness to be ambitious of pleasing the king, and the misfortune to succeed, became, in her elevation, the best woman in the world. She received us all three familiarly, although with evident shades of distinction. To one she said, speaking short and with a light air, "How do you do, Duclos?" to another, in an air and tone more friendly, "How do you do, abbé?" giving him occasionally a little pat on the cheek; and to me more seriously, and in a lower voice, "How do you do, Marmontel?" The ambition of Duclos was to render himself important in his province of Britanny; that of the abbé de Bernis was to have a little lodging at the top of the Tuileries, and a pension of fifty pounds on the privy purse; mine was to be usefully occupied for myself and for the public, without depending on their caprice. The employment I solicited was assiduous and tranquil. "I feel that I have but an indifferent talent for poetry," said I to madame de Pompadour; "but I think I have sense and intelligence enough to fill an employment in the public offices; and, whatever application it may require, of that I am capable. Persuade them to make trial of me, madame; I dare assure you that they will be satisfied with me." She answered, I was born to be a man of letters; that my disgust for poetry was want of courage; that, instead of quitting the game, I should have taken my revenge, as Voltaire had more than once done, and like him rise from my fall by a successful effort.

I consented, from complaisance to her, to exert myself on a new subject. But I chose one that was too simple, and too much above my powers. The subjects afforded by history seemed to me exhausted: I found all the grand interests of the human heart, all the violent passions, all the tragic situations, in a word, all the great springs of terror and compassion employed before me by the masters of the art. I racked my brains to invent an action that should be new, and out of the common route. I thought I had found it in a subject purely of imagination, with which I was at first infatuated. It offered an exhibition of awful majesty *(les Funerailles de Sésostris;)* it gave me great characters to paint in favourable contrast, and an intrigue so nicely veiled that it was impossible to foresee its solution. This it was that blinded me on the difficulties of an action without love, wholly composed of politics and morality, and which, to be sustained with warmth during five acts, required all the resources of poetic eloquence. I did all I could; and, whether it were illusion or excess of indulgence, I was persuaded by my friends that I had succeeded. Madame de Pompadour often asked me how I went on with my new piece; when it was finished, she desired to read it; she made, in detail, some criticisms that were very just; but on the whole it pleased her.

I here recollect an incident that may enliven for a moment the recital of my misfortunes. While the manuscript of my tragedy was still in the hands of madame de Pompadour, I presented myself one morning at her toilet when the room was crowded by a conflux of courtiers who had just been at the king's levee. She was surrounded by them, and, whether she were displeased with some one near her, or wished to divert the weariness that this circle occasioned her, as soon as she saw me, "I want to speak to you," said she; and, quitting her toilet, went into her cabinet, whither I followed her. It was simply to return me my manuscript, on which she had pencilled her notes. She was five or six minutes showing me the passages she had marked, and explaining to me her criticisms. Yet the whole circle of courtiers were standing round her toilet, waiting for her. She reappeared, and I, concealing my manuscript, went modestly to resume my place. I suspected the effect that this singular incident would produce; but the impression it made on the whole company far exceeded my expectation. All eyes were fixed on me; on every side I was addressed by little imperceptible salutations, and gentle smiles of friendship; and before I left the room, was invited to dinner at least for the whole week. Shall I say it? a titled man, a man with a ribbon at his breast, with whom I had sometimes dined at M. de la Poplinière's, le M.D.S., standing by my side, took me by the hand and whispered to me: "What! you won't know your old friends?" I bowed, confused at his meanness, and said to myself, "Ah! what then is favour, if its shadow only gives me such singular importance?"

The players, as well as madame de Pompadour, were seduced at the reading of my piece by the beautiful morality with which I had decorated the last acts. But on the stage their feebleness was manifest, and it was the more sensibly felt because I had written the first with more vehemence and warmth. My combat of generosity and virtue had nothing tragic. The public were weary at not being moved, and my piece fell. For this time, I was convinced the public were right.

I returned home, determined to write no more for the stage; and I wrote instantly by an express to madame de Pompadour, who was at Bellevue, to inform her of my misfortune, and very urgently to renew the prayer I had made her to obtain for me some employment in which I might be more useful than in an art for which I was not born.

She was at table with the king when she received my letter, and the king having permitted her to read it, "The new piece is fallen," said she; "and do you know, sire, who it is that tells me so? The author himself. Unhappy young man! I would willingly have at this moment some place to offer him that might give him consolation." Her brother, the marquis de Marigny, who was at this supper, said to her, that he had a place of 'secretaire des bâtimens,' which he would give me, if she chose. "Ah!" said she; "write to him then tomorrow, I entreat you;" and the king appeared satisfied that they should afford me this consolation.

The letter in which M. de Marigny offered me, in the most engaging and obliging manner, a place of little value, as he said, but tranquil, and which would leave me leisure for my devotion to the muses, caused me an emotion of joy and gratitude, which I warmly expressed in my reply. I thought myself safe in port, after having been cast away, and blessed the hospitable earth that insured me gentle repose.

M. de la Poplinière did not learn without sorrow that I was about to leave him. In his complaints, he repeated what he had so often said to me, that I ought not to have been uneasy about the future, and that it had been his intention to provide for it. I answered that, in renouncing the profession of a man of letters, my intention had not been to live as an idle and useless man; but that I was not the less grateful for his kindness. Indeed, I should be most ungrateful, if, after recording the part he involuntarily had in the wrong I did myself, I did not add, that in many other respects the time I passed with him ought to be dear to my memory, as well from the sentiments of esteem and confidence which he personally showed me, as from the kindness with which he inspired all those who heard him speak of my good disposition; for this, above all, was what he praised in me.

At his house, as in a moving picture, there was a succession and a variety of persons, different in manners, mind, and character. I frequently saw there the ambassadors of the different courts of Europe, and from them gained instruction. It was there that I became acquainted with the count de Kaunitz, then ambassador from the court of Vienna, and since the most celebrated statesman in Europe.

He had admitted me to his friendship; I used often to go and dine at his house, the palais Bourbon; and he talked to me of Paris and Versailles like a man who had observed them. Yet I ought to confess that what struck me most in him was, the delicacy and vanity that usually accompany effeminate minds. I supposed him more occupied by the care of his health, his face, and particularly of his head-dress and complexion, than by the interests of his court. I surprised him one day, on his return from hunting, plastering his face with the yolk of an egg, to take off the tan; and I learnt a long time afterwards from the count de Par, his cousin, an ingenuous simple man, that, during the long and glorious ministry in which he was the soul of the cabinet of Vienna, he had preserved, in his luxury, in his effeminacy, in all the minute cares of his dress and his person, the same character which I had remarked. Of all the men I have seen, he it is in whom I have been the most grossly deceived. Yet I remember some of his observations, that might have taught me the temper of his mind and soul.

"What do they say of me in the society you frequent?" said he to me one day.—"They say that your excellency does not sustain the idea of magnificence that they had conceived of you on your arrival at Paris. The first ambassador in Europe, a great fortune, a palace for your residence, the ostentatious pomp you had displayed on entering it, announced more splendour and luxury in your house and in your manner of living. A sumptuous table, feasts, and assemblies, balls in particular, balls in your superb drawing rooms, these were what they expected, and they see nothing of all these. You frequent the society of financiers' wives, like a private man, and neglect the nobility of the court and city."—" My dear Marmontel," said he, " I am here only for two objects; for the affairs of my sovereign, which I transact properly, and my pleasures; and, on this last article, I have only to consult myself. Parade would weary me, and be a burden; it is for this reason that I avoid it. Of all the intriguing women at Versailles, there is not one worth the trouble of gaining. What should I do with those women? Sit down at their 'tri,' or their dull 'cavagnole?' I have two persons to court, the king and his mistress: I am well with them both." These were not the remarks of a frivolous and foolish man.

His little dinners were very good: Merci, Stahremberg, Seckendorf, his then secretaries of legation, or rather his pupils, treated me with kindness; we talked gaily together, and a flask of Tokay animated the close of the repast.

A man very different from the count de Kaunitz, more friendly and more engaging, was lord Albemarle, the English ambassador, who died at Paris, as much regretted among us as in his own country He was, in the highest sense of the phrase, an honest man; noble, feeling, generous, full of loyalty, frankness, politeness, and kindness; and in his person were united those qualities which the two characters of French and English contain of most estimable. He had an accomplished girl for his mistress, to whom envy never imputed any other fault than that of having yielded to him. I made a friend of her; it was a sure way of making a friend of lord Albemarle. The name of this charming girl was Gaucher; in her childhood she had been called Lolote, and this was still her name of endearment. It was to her that her lover one day said, as she was looking stedfastly at a star, "Don't look at it so, my love, for I cannot give it you." Never was love more delicately expressed. That of lord Albemarle honoured its object by the highest esteem, and the tenderest respect; and he was not the only one who had these sentiments for her. As prudent as beautiful, one man alone had ever succeeded in winning her love; and the most excusable of the errors into which extreme youth leads innocence, had assumed in her a character of nobleness and modesty that vice never had: Fidelity, decency, disinterestedness, nothing was wanting to her love to be virtuous but legal form: These two lovers would have been the most perfect models of wife and husband.

The character of mademoiselle Gaucher was ingenuously expressed in her whole person. She had, in her beauty, something so romantic and fabulous, that, till then, it had been seen only in idea. Her figure had the majesty of the cedar, yet the suppleness of the poplar; her gait was indolent; but in the negligence of her carriage there was a simplicity full of seemliness and grace. Her image was present to my fancy when I formerly painted the 'Shepherdess of the Alps,' which I thought tolerably imitated. A lively imagination and a cool judgment gave to her mind very much the air of that of Montaigne. His were her favourite works, and her habitual reading; her language was imbued with them; it had their simplicity, their colouring, their flow, very often their energetic turn and happiness of expression.

As much as it is possible to be charmed with a woman without being in love, so much was I charmed with her. After the conversation of Voltaire, the most enchanting to me was hers. We became intimate friends from the moment we knew each other.

Lord Albemarle died: he had secured to her, I believe, two hundred and fifty pounds a year: that was all her fortune. The grief she felt at his death was deep, but courageous; and, while I suffered with her, I aided her to bear her misfortune with becoming firmness. All the friends of lord Albemarle were hers; they all remained faithful to her. The duke de Biron, the marquis de Castries, and some others of the same class composed her society. Happy, had she not been thrown, by a kind of fatality, out of this calm state, with which she was content, into a situation not suitable to her.

Her health had become feeble; her friends were uneasy at it, and she was advised to go to Barège. In going and returning by Montauban, she was treated with particular attention by the commandant, the count de Héronville; and on arriving at Paris, she received from him a letter written nearly in these words: "I am poisoned: my servants are all poisoned too. Come, mademoiselle, hasten to my aid, and bring with you a physician. I have no confidence but in you." She set off in a post-chaise with an eminent physician, and M. de Héronville was saved. He had already felt that enthusiasm for her which in lively old men very much resembles love. The service she had rendered him did but increase it. He had seen her at the head of his house, re-establishing in it order and tranquillity, restoring hope to his domestics, who were tortured by the action of the verdigrise, encouraging himself, and, in concert with Dr Malouet, doing the office of a moral physician. So much zeal, and so much courage, had filled him with admiration; and, as soon as he was out of danger, he knew not how to express his gratitude better than by saying to her, like Medoro to Angelica:

"To serve you I only desire,
That hope I delight to renew,
To you I'm indebted for life,
I cherish it only for you."

She was prudent enough at first to resist his entreaties; but she at last had the weakness to yield, on condition that their marriage should be kept secret: it was so for some time, but she became a mother, and it was necessary to make it public.

The only prudent conduct for both of them to observe (and this was the advice I gave my friend) would then have been to confine themselves to a society of men, chosen as their mutual inclination guided, to render this society agreeable, and if possible attracting to women, or to be contented without them, and not to pretend to think of them. Madame d'Héronville felt perfectly that this conduct was the only one that suited her. But her husband, impatient to introduce her into society, would persist in doing violence to public opinion. Unhappy imprudence! he ought to have known that this opinion was interwoven with the dearest interests of women; and that, already too indignant that mistresses should steal their husbands and lovers, they were fully determined never to suffer them to come and usurp their condition, and enjoy it publicly. He flattered himself that, in favour of his wife, so charming a character, such rare merit, so many estimable qualities, and such modesty and prudence, in her, frailty itself would be forgotten. He was cruelly undeceived in his mad mistake. She endured humiliations, and died of grief.

It was likewise at the house of M. de la Poplinière that I became acquainted with the family of Chalut, in whose praise I shall often have occasion to speak in these memoirs, and which family I myself, alas, have seen extinct.

Finally, I owed to the vicinity of the country house in which I was to that of madame de Tencin, at Passy, the advantage of seeing that extraordinary woman tête-à-tête. I had refused the honour of being admitted to the dinners she gave to men of letters; but when she came to repose in her retreat, I used to go and pass with her the moments she was alone; and I cannot express to what degree I was deceived by her air of carelessness and indolence. Madame de Tencin, who, to obtain favour from the state, could put more springs in action both in town and at court than any other person in the kingdom, was to me only a lazy old woman. "You are not fond of these parties of men of wit," said she; "their presence intimidates you. Well! come and talk with me in my solitude, you will be there more at your ease; and the simplicity of your disposition will accommodate itself better to my dull good sense." She made me tell her the history of my life from my in-infancy, entered into all my interests, was touched at all my sorrows, reasoned with me on my views and hopes, and appeared to think only of what created my solicitude. Ah! how much acuteness of intellect, what suppleness and activity, were concealed under this appearance of calm and leisure! I still smile at my own want of penetration when I used to exclaim, on quitting her, What a good simple creature! The fruit I gathered from her conversations, without perceiving it, was a more perfect and deep knowledge of the world. For instance, I remember, two pieces of advice she gave me; one was to secure myself a livelihood independent of literary successes, and to put into this lottery only the overplus of my time. "Woe to him," said she, "who depends wholly on his pen; nothing is more casual. The man who makes shoes is sure of his wages; the man who writes a book or a tragedy is never sure of anything." Her other counsel was to seek friends among women rather than men. "For by means of women," said she, "you may do what you please with men; and then these are either too dissipated, or too much occupied with their own personal interests, to attend to yours; whereas women think of your interest, be it only out of indolence. Mention this evening to a woman, who is your friend, an affair that intimately concerns you; tomorrow, at her spinning-wheel, at her embroidery, you will find her thinking of and torturing her fancy to invent some means of serving you. But be careful to be nothing more than the friend of her whom you think may be useful to you; for, between lovers, where once there happens any cloud, dispute, or rupture, all is lost. Be then assiduous to her, complaisant, gallant even if you will, but nothing more; you understand me." Thus in all our conversations, the plainness of her language imposed on me so well, that I never took her subtle intellect for any other than good sense.

An acquaintance of another kind took place at the same time, between me and *les intendans des Menus Plaisirs*. It cost me dear, as will be seen in the sequel. For the present, I will only mention how it arose. Quinault was one of my favourite poets. Alive to the harmony of his beautiful verses, and charmed with the elegant facility of his style, I never read the beautiful scenes of 'Proserpine,' of 'Thésée,' and of 'Armide,' without feeling a strong desire to write an opera, nor without some hope of writing like him. Vain presumption of youth! but which spoke the praises of the poet that inspired me: for one of the characters of the truly beautiful, as Horace says, is to be in appearance easy to imitate, but, in fact, inimitable:

"―――― Ut sibi quivis
Speret idem, sudet multum, frustraque laboret
Ausus idem."

Besides, I was passing my life with Rameau; I saw him writing music to wretched poetry, and should have been happy to have given him better.

Such was the disposition of my mind, when, at the birth of the duke of Burgundy, the provost of merchants, Bernage, came to propose to me, at Passy, to write an opera jointly with Rameau, on this happy event, which should be susceptible of show and splendour. It was necessary that the words and music should be composed hastily, and within a given time.

You may suppose that we both laboured to sketch an opera. However, as 'Acanthe and Céphise' was an imposing exhibition, the varied motion on the stage, the beauty of the decorations, some great effects of harmony, and perhaps some interest in the piece itself, sustained it. It was played, I think, fourteen times, and that was much for a bespoken work.

I wrote somewhat better two detached acts that Rameau had again the kindness to set to music, 'La Guirlande' and 'Les Sybarites.' They both of them succeeded. But at our concerts, I heard pieces of melody after which French music appeared to me heavy and monotonous. Those airs, those duets, that measured recitative, all of which the Italians mingle in the lyric scene, charmed my ear and ravished my soul. I studied their forms, attempted to bend and accommodate our language to them, and wanted to persuade Rameau to undertake, with me, to enrich our stage with all their wealth and beauties. But Rameau, already an old man, was not disposed to change his manner; and, determined to see nothing but vice and abuse in that of the Italians, he feigned to despise it. The most beautiful airs of Leo, of Vinci, of Pergolese, or of Jomelli, made him tremble with impatience: it was not till long afterwards that I found composers who would understand and second me. However, from that time, I was known at the opera among the amateurs, at the head of whom, for singing, dancing, or voluptuousness, *les intendans des Menus Plaisirs* were distinguished in the green-room. I engaged in their society by that gentle inclination that naturally leads us to enjoy life; and their company had the more charm for me, because it offered, in the bosom of joy, traits of character and striking originality, with sallies of the most tasteful and delicate gaiety. Cury, the chief of the joyous band, was a man of talent, a merry companion, acute in his satire, with ironical gravity, and rather facetious than malicious. The epicurean Tribou, a disciple of father Porée and one of his favourite pupils, afterwards engaged at the opera, and then having resigned the scene to Géliote, living independent and content with little, he charmed us in his old age by an Anacreontic humour that never forsook him. He is the only man I have seen take leave gaily of the pleasures of youth and manhood, suffering himself to glide gently down the current of life, and preserving in his decline that philosophy, green, gay, and open-hearted, that Montaigne himself attributed only to youth. A character of another stamp, and as engaging in its way, was that of Géliote: gentle, good-humoured, *amistous*, to use one of his provincial words that paints him in his native colour, he bore in his front the serenity of happiness, and while breathing it himself, inspired it Indeed, were I asked who was the most completely happy man I have seen in my life, I should answer—Géliote. Born in obscurity, in his youth a singing boy in a church at Toulouse, he sprang at a bound to try his talents at the opera, and met with the most brilliant success: from that moment, he had been, and still was, the idol of the public. They leapt for joy when he appeared on the stage; they listened to him with the intoxication of pleasure; and applause always marked his pauses. His voice was the rarest that had been heard, for its volume and fulness as well as for its piercing brilliancy. He was neither handsome nor well made; but, in order to become both, he had only to sing; you would have said that the eyes as well as the ears were charmed. Young women were mad after him: you might see them leaning half out of their boxes, exposing to public view the excess of their emotion; and more than one, and of the most lovely, were pleased to express it to him. A good musician, his talent occasioned him no toil, and his profession had for him none of its vexations.

Beloved, esteemed by his comrades, with whom he was on the tone of amicable politeness without familiarity, he lived like a man of the world, received and welcomed everywhere. First it was his singing that all were desirous of hearing, and to afford that pleasure he had a complaisance that charmed as much as his voice. He had made it his study to choose and to learn the most beautiful of our songs; and he sang them to his guitar with delicious taste. But, in him, the singer was soon forgotton, in order to enjoy the engaging qualities of the man; and his wit and character gained him as many friends as he had admirers. These friends were of every class, from the citizen to the first nobility; he was everywhere simple, gentle, and modest, and everywhere at home. He had acquired by his talent, and by the favours it had procured him, a comfortable little fortune, and the first use he made of it was to extend his comforts to his family. In the offices and cabinets of the ministers, he enjoyed very considerable credit, for it was the credit that pleasure gives, and he employed it to render essential services to the province in which he was born. He was therefore adored in it. Every year he was permitted in summer to take a journey there, and from Paris to Pau his route was known; the time of his passing was marked from town to town; fêtes everywhere awaited him; and at this point I ought to mention what I knew of him at Toulouse, before my departure. He had two friends in that city, to whom no one was ever preferred: one was the tailor, at whose house he had lodged; and the other his music master while he was a singing-boy. The nobility and parliament disputed with each other the second supper that Géliote should partake of at Toulouse; but, for the first, they knew it was invariably reserved for his two friends. A man of intrigue, as much so and more than he could have wished, he was renowned for his discretion: and of his numerous conquests none have been known, but those who chose to proclaim themselves. Finally, amid so much prosperity, he never excited envy, and I never heard it said that Géliote had an enemy.

The rest of the society of the *Menus Plaisirs* were simply men of pleasure; and among these I may say that I occupied my corner with some distinction.

Imagine me now, after just partaking of a jovial dinner with these gentlemen, passing into the school of philosophers; and gliding, at the opera buffa newly arrived from Italy, into the queen's famous corner among the Diderots, the d'Alemberts, the Buffons, the Turgots, the d'Holbaches, the Helvétiuses, the Rousseaus, all burning with zeal for Italian music, and full of ardour for raising that immense edifice, the Encyclopédie, whose foundations they were laying, and you may say of me, in miniature, what Horace said of Aristippus:—

"Omnis Aristippum decuit color, et status, et res."

Yes, I confess, all was welcome to me; pleasure, study, the table, philosophy; I had a taste for wisdom with the wise, but I abandoned myself willingly to folly with the foolish. My character was still floating, variable, and discordant. I adored virtue; I yielded to the example and charm of vice. I was pleased and happy, when, in the little chamber of d'Alembert, at his good old glazier's, making a frugal dinner tête-à-tête with him, I heard him, after having been puzzled all the morning at his mathematics, talk to me like a man of letters, full of taste, intelligence, and science: or when, on moral subjects, displaying the wisdom of a ripe intellect, and the gaiety of a free and youthful soul, he surveyed the world with the eye of Democritus, and made me laugh at the expense of folly and pride. I was happy, too, but in a lighter and more fugitive way, when, surrounded by a covey of games and pleasures, just escaped from behind the scenes, at the supper of our amateurs, among the nymphs and graces, sometimes too of the bacchantes, I heard only the praises of love and wine. I quitted all this for Versailles. But, before I left the chiefs of the enterprise of the Encyclopédie, I engaged to contribute to it in the belles-lettres; and, encouraged by the praises they bestowed on my labours, I did more than either they or I expected.

Voltaire was then absent from Paris; he was in Prussia. The thread of my narrative has appeared to separate me from my connection with him; but till his departure it had remained the same, and the vexations he experienced seemed to have tightened the bond of our friendship. Of these vexations, the most severe for the moment was that of the death of the marchioness du Châtelet. But, to be sincere, I recognised on this occasion, as I often had done, the mobility of his soul. When I went to express to him the part I took in his affliction: "Come," said he on seeing me; "come and share my sorrow. I have lost my illustrious friend: I am in despair, I am inconsolable." I, to whom he had often said that she was like a fury that haunted his steps, and who knew that in their disputes they had more than once been at daggers-drawn, let him weep, and seemed to sympathize with him. Solely to make him perceive some motive of consolation in the very cause of her death, I asked him what she died of. "Of what! don't you know? Ah! my dear friend! the brute has killed her. He got her with child." It was Saint Lambert, his rival, of whom he spoke: and thus he continued to exhaust language in praise of that incomparable woman, redoubling his tears and sobs. At this moment arrives the intendant Chauvelin, who tells him some ridiculous story, and, at once, Voltaire is bursting with laughter. I laughed too, as I went away, to see in this great man the facility of a child, in passing from one extreme to another in the passions that agitated him. One only was fixed in him, and, as it were, inherent in his soul; it was an ardent love of fame, and, of all that flatters and feeds this passion, nothing to him was indifferent.

It was not enough for him to be the most illustrious of men of letters, he wanted to be a courtier. From his earliest youth, he had assumed the seductive habit of living with the great. First, marshal Villars, the grand prior de Vendôme, and afterwards the duke de Richelieu, the duke de la Vallière, the Boufflers, the Montmorency, had been in his society. He supped with them habitually, and you know with what respectful familiarity he had the art of writing and speaking to them. Verses lightly and delicately flattering, a conversation not less seducing than his poetry, made him beloved and welcomed among the nobility. Now, these noblemen were admitted to the royal suppers; and why was he not one of them? This he earnestly desired. He recollected the reception that Louis the Great had given to Boileau and Racine; he said that Horace and Virgil had the honour of approaching Augustus; that the Æneid had been read in the cabinet of Livia. Were Addison and Prior more worthy than he? And had they not both been honourably employed in their country, one in the ministry, and the other as ambassador? The place of historiographer was already a mark of confidence in him, and who before him had filled it with so much glory? He had bought a place of gentleman in ordinary of the king's chamber: this place, commonly very inactive, gave, however, the right of being sent to foreign courts on light commissions, and he had flattered himself that for a man like him these commissions would not be limited to bare compliments of felicitation and condolence. He wanted, as we say, to make his way at court; and, when he had a project in his head, he persisted in it obstinately: one of his maxims was these words of the Evangelist: " Regnum cœlorum vim patitur et violenti rapiunt illud :" he employed then all the means he could devise to approach the king.

When madame d'Etioles, afterward marchioness de Pompadour, was announced as the king's mistress, and even before she was declared so, he was eager in paying his court to her. He easily succeeded in pleasing her; and, while he celebrated the victories of the king, he flattered his mistress by writing pretty verses to her. He was persuaded that, through her, he should obtain the favour of being admitted to the little cabinet suppers, and I am persuaded this was her wish.

Transplanted to the court, and ignorant enough of the character and tastes of the king, she had at first hoped to amuse him by her talents. On a private theatre she used to play before him little acts of operas, some of which were written for her, and in which her acting, voice, and singing were justly applauded. Voltaire, in favour with her, took the fancy to wish to direct these performances. The alarm spread to the camp of gentlemen of the bedchamber and *les intendants des Menus Plaisirs*. It was trespassing on their rights, and a league was instantly formed among them to remove from the court a man that would have governed them all, if he had pleased the king as well as his mistress. But they knew the king did not like him, and that by his eagerness to increase his importance he only increased the prejudice against him. But the king, little touched with the praises he had lavished on him in his panegyric, only saw in him an impious philosopher, and an ambitious flatterer. He had at last consented, with great difficulty, that he should be received at the Academy. Without reckoning the friends of religion, who were not the friends of Voltaire, there were many about the king who were envious of the favour they saw him courting, and careful to censure what he did to please.

In their mind, the poem of Fontenoy was only a cold gazette; the panegyric on the king was inanimate, defective in colouring, and without eloquence. The verses to madame de Pompadour were taxed with impropriety and indiscretion; and in this verse in particular:—

"Be both without a foe,
Your conquests both retain,"

they persuaded the king that it was indecorous to put him on an equality with his mistress.

At the marriage of the dauphin with the infanta of Spain, it was easy to animadvert on the absurdity and folly of having given, as a play to the infanta, that 'Princesse de Navarre,' which really was not calculated to succeed. I do not say the same of the opera of 'Le Temple de la Gloire;' the idea of it was grand, the subject well conceived, and nobly executed. The third act, of which Trajan was the hero, presented an allusion flattering to the king; it was a hero, just, humane, generous, pacific, and worthy the love of the world, to whom the temple of glory was open. Voltaire doubted not but that the king would recognise his eulogy. After the play he met him in his way out, and seeing that the king passed without saying anything to him, he took the liberty of asking him, "Is Trajan satisfied?" Trajan, surprised and displeased that he should have dared to interrogate him, answered by a cold silence; and the whole court thought Voltaire very wrong, for having dared to question the king.

To remove him, it was only necessary to detach him from the mistress, and the way they took to do this was to place Crébillon in opposition to him.

Crébillon, old and poor, was living obscurely in the vilest part of the Marais, labouring by starts at that 'Catalina' which he had announced for ten years, and of which he read here and there some bits of scenes that were thought admirable. His age, his former success, his manners somewhat rough, his soldier-like character, his truly tragical face, the air, the imposing though simple tone in which he recited his harsh and inharmonious verses, the vigour, the energy he gave to his expression, all concurred to strike the mind with a sort of enthusiasm. I have heard applauded with transport, by men who were not fools, these verses, which he had put into the mouth of Cicero:—

"I think you are not guilty, Catiline;
But, if you be, how odious are you then!
In you I see the talents and renown
Of the first of men, or the first of villains."

The name of Crébillon was the rallying word for the enemies of Voltaire. 'Elèctre' and 'Radamiste,' which were sometimes still played, drew but thin houses; all the rest of Crébillon's tragedies were forgotten, while those of Voltaire, 'Œdipe,' 'Alzire,' 'Mahomet,' 'Zaire,' and 'Merope,' were often performed in all the splendour of full success. The partisans of old Crébillon were few, but noisy; and they did not cease to call him the Sophocles of our age; and even among men of letters, Marivaux used to say, that all the fine wit of Voltaire must bow before the genius of Crébillon.

It was mentioned before madame de Pompadour, that this great neglected man was suffered to grow old without support, because he was without art and intrigue. This was touching her in a tender part. "What say you?" cried she; "Crébillon poor and forsaken!" She instantly obtained for him from the king a pension of one hundred pounds from the privy purse.

Crébillon was eager to go and thank his benefactress. A slight indisposition kept her in bed, when he was announced: she desired he might come in. The sight of this fine old man touched her; she received him with an affecting grace. He was moved by it; and, as he leaned over her bed to kiss her hand, the king appeared. "Ah! madam," cried Crébillon, "the king has surprised us; I am ruined." This sally in an old man of eighty pleased the king. The fortune of Crébillon was decided. All the 'Menus Plaisirs' launched into praises of his genius and manners. "He had dignity," said they, "but no pride, and still less vain glory. His poverty was the proof of his disinterestedness. He was a venerable character, and truly the man whose genius honoured the reign of the king." 'Catiline' was mentioned as the wonder of the age. Madame de Pompadour wished to hear it. A day was fixed for the reading; the king, present but invisible, heard it also. It had complete success; and, on its first performance, madame de Pompadour, accompanied by a crowd of courtiers, attended with the most lively interest. A little time afterwards, Crébillon obtained the favour of an edition of his works at the press of the Louvre, the expense defrayed by the royal treasury. From that time, Voltaire was coldly received, and he left off going to court. You know the connection he had formed with the prince royal of Prussia. This prince expressed to him the same kindness when he was become king; and the infinitely flattering manner in which Voltaire answered it might well have contributed secretly to alienate from him the mind of Louis XV. The king of Prussia, then in correspondence with Voltaire, had not ceased, since his accession to the crown, to invite him to come and see him; and the favour which Crébillon enjoyed at court having cut him to the quick, had decided his journey. But before he set off, he had wished to revenge himself for this vexation, and he had undertaken it like a great man; he had attacked his adversary, hand to hand, to try his force with him on the subjects he had treated, abstaining only from 'Radamiste,' 'Atrie,' and

s

'Pyrrhus;' from one, doubtless from respect; from the other, out of horror; and from the third, out of disdain for so ungrateful and fantastic a subject.

He began by 'Semiramis;' and the grand and tragic manner in which the action of it, the sombre, stormy, and terrible colouring he spread over it, the magic style he employed, the religious and fearful majesty with which he filled it, the afflicting scenes and situations he drew from it,—in fine, the art with which he contrived to prepare, establish, and sustain the marvellous,—were well calculated to annihilate the cold and feeble 'Semiramis' of Crébillon. But the theatre was then not susceptible of an action of this kind. The stage was confined by a crowd of spectators, some placed on seats raised one above another, others standing at the bottom of the stage, and along the side scenes; so that the affrighted Semiramis, and the shade of Ninus coming from his tomb, were obliged to penetrate through a thick line of petits-maîtres. This impropriety threw ridicule on the gravity of the theatrical action. Without illusion there is no interest, and without probability there is no illusion: thus this piece, the masterpiece of Voltaire as a work of genius, had in its novelty so little success, that it might be said to fall. Voltaire shook with grief, but he was not disheartened. He wrote 'Oreste,' after Sophocles; and he rose above Sophocles himself in the part of Electra, and in the art of saving the indecorum and severity of the character of Clytemnestra. But in the fifth act, at the moment of the catastrophe, he had not sufficiently enfeebled the horror of parricide; and Crébillon's party being there everything but benevolent, whatever could give a hold to criticism was caught at with murmurs, and turned into derision. The performance was interrupted at every instant; and this piece, which has since been justly applauded, was hooted. I was in the amphitheatre, more dead than alive. Voltaire came in there; and at the moment when the pit were turning a pathetic line into ridicule, he rose and cried out, "Ah, barbarians, that's a line of Sophocles!"

Lastly, he gave 'Rome sauvée;' and in the characters of Cicero, Cæsar and Cato, he revenged the dignity of the Roman senate, which Crébillon had degraded, by making all these great characters subordinate to that of Catiline. I remember when he had just written the beautiful scenes of Cicero and Cæsar with Catiline, he read them to me with a perfection to which no actor ever approached; simply, nobly, without any affectation, better than I had ever heard him read. "Ah!" said I, "your conscience is quiet on these verses; and therefore you do not flourish them, and you are right; you never made any more beautiful." This piece, in the opinion of well-informed men, had the full success of merit; but it was not calculated to move the multitude; and that eloquence of style, that talent of having so learnedly observed the manners, and painted the characters, were lost on the mass of the public. Thus, with prodigious advantages over his rival, Voltaire had the pain of seeing the triumph disputed with him, and even refused.

These disappointments determined his journey into Prussia. One difficulty only still retarded it; and the way in which that was removed is curious enough to amuse you for a moment.

This difficulty consisted in the expenses of the journey, about which Frederic suffered himself to be a little baited. He was willing to defray Voltaire, and for that purpose he consented to give him a thousand pounds. But madame Denis wanted to accompany her uncle, and for this additional expense Voltaire asked for another thousand pounds. This was what the king of Prussia would not listen to. "I shall be very happy," said he in his answer, "that madame Denis accompanies you; but I do not ask it."—"Look," said Voltaire to me, "at this meanness in a king! He has barrels of gold, and he won't give a thousand poor pounds for the pleasure of seeing madame Denis at Berlin! He shall give them, or I myself will not go." A comical incident happened, which ended this dispute. One morning, as I was going to see him, I found his friend Thiriot in the garden of the Palais Royal; and, as I was always on the watch for literary news, I asked him if he had heard any. "Yes," said he, "some that is very curious: you are going to M. de Voltaire's, and there you shall hear it; for I shall come there as soon as I have taken my coffee."

Voltaire was writing in his bed when I went in: in his turn he asked me, "What's the news?"— "I know none," said I; "but Thiriot, whom I have met in the Palais Royal, says he has something very interesting to tell you. He is coming."

"Well, Thiriot," said he, "you have some curious news?"—"Oh! very curious, and that will please you in particular," answered Thiriot, with his sardonic laugh, and the nasal twang of a capuchin.— "Let's hear; what have you to tell!"—"I have to tell you that Arnaud-Baculard is arrived at Potsdam, and that the king of Prussia has received him with open arms."—"With open arms!"—"That Arnaud has presented him an epistle."—"Very bombastical and very insipid?"—"Not at all; very fine, so fine that the king has answered it by another epistle."— "The king of Prussia, an epistle to Arnaud! No, no, Thiriot; they have been making a jest of you." "I don't know what you call a joke, but I have the two epistles in my pocket."—"Let's see; quick; let me read these masterpieces of poetry. What insipidity! what meanness! how egregiously stupid!" said he, in reading the epistle of Arnaud: then, passing to that of the king, he read a moment in silence and with an air of pity. But when he came to these verses:

"Voltaire's a setting sun;
But you are in your dawn;"

he started up, and jumped from his bed, bounding with rage: "Voltaire a setting sun, and Baculard in his dawn! And it is a king who writes this enormous folly! Let him think only of reigning!"

It was with difficulty that Thiriot and I could prevent ourselves from bursting into laughter to see Voltaire in his shirt, dancing with passion, and addressing himself to the king of Prussia. "I'll go," said he; "yes, I'll go and teach him to distinguish between men:" and from that moment the journey was decided. I have suspected that the king of Prussia intentionally gave him this spur; and without that I doubt whether he would have gone, so angry was he at the refusal of the thousand pounds, not at all out of avarice, but out of indignation at not having obtained what he asked.

Obstinate to excess, by character and by system, he had even in little things an incredible repugnance to yield, and to renounce what he had resolved on. I again saw a singular instance of it just before his departure. He had taken a fancy to carry a cutlass with him on his journey; and, one morning, when I was at his house, a bundle of them was brought, that he might choose. But the cutler wanted twenty shillings for the one that pleased him; and Voltaire took it into his head that he would give but fifteen. He then begins to calculate in detail what it may be worth; he adds, that the cutler bears in his face the character of an honest man, and that, with such good faith written on his forehead, he cannot but confess that the instrument will be well paid at fifteen shillings. The cutler accepts the eulogy on his face, but answers that, as an honest man, he has but one word; that he asks no more than the thing is worth; and that, were he to sell it at a lower price, he should wrong his children. " What, you have children, have you?" asked Voltaire.—" Yes, sir, I have five; three boys and two girls, the youngest of whom is just twelve."—" Well! we'll think about placing your boys and marrying your girls: I have friends in the treasury, I have some credit in the public offices. But let's finish this little affair: here are your fifteen shillings; say no more about it." The good cutler was confused in thanking Voltaire for the protection with which he was pleased to honour him; but he still kept to his first word about the price of the cutlass, and did not abate one farthing. I abridge this scene, which lasted a quarter of an hour with the turns of eloquence and seduction that Voltaire employed in vain—not to save five shillings that he would have given to a beggar, but to prevail by the power of persuasion. He was obliged to yield, and with a troubled, indignant, confused air, threw the crown upon the table, which he relinquished so unwillingly. The cutler, when he had got his money, returned him thanks for his favours, and went away. " I am very glad," said I, in a low voice, as I saw him go out.—" Of what ?" said Voltaire, angrily. " What are you glad of?"— " That this honest man's family is no longer to be pitied. His sons will soon be placed; his daughters married; he, in the meantime, has sold his cutlass for what he wanted; and you have paid it in spite of all your eloquence."—" And this is what you are glad of, you obstinate Limosin !"—" Oh! yes, I am quite pleased; if he had yielded to you, I believe I should have beaten him."—" Do you know," said he laughing in his sleeve, after a moment's silence, " that if Molière had been witness to such a scene, he would have turned it to some profit?"—" Indeed," said I, " it would have been the counterpart to that of M. Dimanche." It was thus that with me his anger, or rather his petulance, always terminated in gentleness and friendship.

As I was in his secret with respect to the king of Prussia, and as I imagined I well understood that king, and the little sincerity there was in his caresses, I had some presentiment of the dissatisfaction they would both have on seeing each other near. A soul so imperious, and a mind so ardent, could scarcely be compatible; and I hoped to see Voltaire soon return, more discontented with Germany than he was with his own country. But the new vexation he experienced, on going to take leave of the king, and the anger he expressed at it, no longer left me that consoling hope. As gentleman in ordinary of the king's chamber, he thought he might venture to ask his orders for the king of Prussia; but the king, instead of answering, abruptly turned his back on him; and he in indignation, as soon as he was out of the kingdom, sent him back his warrant of historiographer of France, and accepted, without his consent, the cross of the order of merit, which the king of Prussia bestowed, though to despoil him of it a short time afterwards.

The example of so many crosses and vexations in the life of this great man, did but exhibit a more fearful picture of the life of a man of letters, and reconciled me to the mild though obscure repose I was going to enjoy at Versailles.

Here, thank heaven! finish the errors of my youth; here I begin a course of life, less dissipated, less irregular, more prudent, and, above all, less exposed to the tempest of the passions; here, in short, my character, too long mobile and unsteady, takes a little consistency, and my reason, on a solid base, becomes able to exert itself and regulate my morals.

BOOK V.

AFTER having seen M. de Marigny, my first care, on arriving at Versailles, was to go and thank madame de Pompadour. She was pleased to say that she was happy to see me tranquil, and added, with an air of kindness, "Men of letters have an imaginary system of equality, that often makes them forget decorum; I hope, Marmontel, that with respect to my brother you will always be aware of this." I assured her that my feelings accorded with my duties.

I already knew M. de Marigny. I had met him in the society of *les Intendants des Menus Plaisirs*, and from them I had learned the character of the man to whom his sister had recommended me, so far as to induce me never to be wanting in respect. Of my intention I was sure; gratitude alone would have inspired me with all the deference that my position and his place required. But to intention it was necessary to add the most scrupulous care, to humour in him a captious self-love; he being jealous, and susceptible to excess of suspicion. The weakness of fearing lest any one should not esteem him enough, or should maliciously and enviously say all that might be said of his birth and fortune, were inquietudes so excessive that, if a few words were but whispered in his presence, he was alarmed. Attentive to watch the opinion that was entertained of him, it often happened that he spoke of himself with a feigned humility, to see whether his auditors would be pleased to hear him undervalue himself; and then, if the least smile, the least equivocal word escaped, their wound was deep and without remedy. With all the essential qualities of an honest man, and even with some that were engaging; with talents, some cultivation, an enlightened taste in the arts, which he had made his study (for that had been the object of his journey into Italy) with frankness, rectitude, and rare probity of morals, he might have been as amiable as he was deserving; but his temper spoiled all, and sometimes betrayed him into rude and abrupt manners.

You may conceive, my dear children, what care was requisite to be always in favour with a man of this character. But I knew him, and this knowledge was the rule of my conduct. Besides, whether it were purposely or not, he indicated by his example the manner in which he wished me to behave. Were we alone, his air was friendly, free, and gay; in short, that of the society in which we had lived. Were we before witnesses, and, above all, were these witnesses artists, he spoke to me with esteem, with an air of affability; but in his politeness the consequence of the placeman and the superior was sensibly felt. This dictated the part I had to perform. I distinguished in myself *le secretaire des bâtimens* from the man of letters and the man of the world; and in public I gave to the two academies, of which he was the chief, and to all the artists employed under his orders, an example of the respect we all owed to his place. At his audiences, no one was more becomingly reserved in behaviour and language than I: tête-à-tête with him, or in the society of our common friends, I resumed the simple air that was natural to me; but neither my air nor my tone were ever familiar. As playfulness could never be equal between us, that I tacitly declined. He had a certain turn of pleasantry, that was not always sufficiently delicate and tasteful, which he loved to indulge; but this was a game at which he was not fitted to play. No joker ever took a joke so ill. No touch of raillery, however gentle, could strike without a wound. I perceived, that I must never exceed a moderate gaiety, and beyond it I never went. On his part, perceiving some delicacy in my reserve, he was always pleased to conform his language to mine.

Yet, he sometimes appeared desirous of learning my feeling and opinion on things that touched him nearly. For instance, when he obtained the order of the Holy Ghost, and I called to congratulate him on this subject: " M. Marmontel," said he, " the king has ennobled me." I answered, as I really thought, " that his nobility was in his soul, which was fully equivalent to that of blood." Another time, returning from the play, he told me that he had there passed a most painful moment; that, as he was sitting in the balcony at the theatre, thinking only of being entertained by the little piece they were performing, he had suddenly heard one of the characters, a drunken soldier, exclaim : ' What! I've a pretty sister, and shall I get nothing by her, when so many others make their fortunes by their great-grand cousins!' " Figure to yourself," added he, "my embarrassment and confusion ! Fortunately the pit took no notice of me."—" Sir," answered I, " you had nothing to fear; you justify so well what has been done for you, that no one thinks of taking offence." And indeed I saw him fill his place so worthily, that, with respect to him, favour appeared to me to be but simple equity.

In this manner I was five years under his orders, without the smallest dissatisfaction either on his part or mine; and, when I quitted the place he had granted me, I still remained his friend. I had even the happiness of serving him more than once with his sister, who reproached him with being harsh in the negative answers he returned to certain petitions. I replied, " It is I, madame, who drew up those answers;" which I showed to her. " But to these people," I added, " refusal seems bitter, however delicately it be seasoned."—" And why so many refusals ?" said she—" Have I not enemies enough already ? Why make me more ?"—" Madame," I answered ; " it is the misfortune of his place, but it is his duty : there is no medium; he must either dishonour himself, by betraying the interests of the king to please the people of the court, or he must refuse to incur the foolish expenses that are solicited from him on all sides."—"How did others do?" insisted this weak woman. "They did wrong, if they did otherwise; but observe, madame, that less was required of them; for abuses increase as they go, and perhaps they expect from him a more timid compliance. But I, who know his principles, dare assure you that he would quit his place rather than swerve from his duty."—"You are an honest man," said she; "and I am grateful to you for having so well defended him."

I have scarcely known a happier part of my life than the five years I passed at Versailles. Versailles was to me divided into two regions. One was that of intrigue, of ambition, of envy, and of all the passions that servile interest and necessitous luxury engender: I scarcely ever went there. The other was the abode of labour, of silence, of repose, and, after labour, of joy in the bosom of that repose; and there it was I passed my life. Free from inquietude, almost wholly to myself, having little more than two days in the week to give to the light employment of my place, I had created an occupation for myself that was no less pleasing than interesting: it was a course of study, in which methodically, with my pen in my hand, I surveyed the principal branches of ancient and modern literature, comparing them with each other, without partiality, without respect to persons, like an independent man, who should be of no country and of no age. It was in this spirit that, reading and collecting the traits that struck me, and the reflections that examples suggested to me, I formed that mass of materials which I first employed in my labours for the 'Encyclopedia,' from which I afterward drew my 'Art of French Poetry,' and which I have since amalgamated with my 'Elements of Literature.' In this employment, there was no restraint;

no anxiety about the opinion and judgment of the vulgar. I studied for myself: I noted down my thoughts and sentiments like a man under no shackles; and this course of reading and meditation had the more charm for me, because I thought I discovered, between the objects of the art and its means, between its march and that of nature, relations that might serve to fix the rules of taste. I had few books of my own, but I was abundantly furnished from the royal library. I used to make a good provision of them for the journies of the court; for in these journies I went in the suite of M. de Marigny: and the woods of Marly, with the forests of Campiègne and Fontainbleau, formed the secret shades in which I studied. I had not the same comfort at Versailles, and the only inconvenience I felt there was the want of walks. Who would believe it? Those magnificent gardens were impracticable in the summer season; particularly in the hottest weather, those pieces of water, that beautiful canal those marble basins, surrounded by statues where the bronze seemed to breathe, exhaled at a distance pestilential vapours; and the waters of Marly were conducted at an immense expense to stand in that valley, only to poison the air we breathed. I was obliged to seek a purer and more healthful air in the woods of Verières or of Sataury.

Yet these excursions of the court were to me sufficiently varied; at Marly, at Compiègne, I was solitary and temperate. I once indulged the whim of living for six weeks on milk at Compiègne when in full health. Never was my mind more calm, more peaceful, than during this regimen. My days flowed along in study with an unalterable equality; my nights were but one gentle sleep; and, after waking in the morning to drink an ample bowl of milk from my black cow, I again closed my eyes to slumber another hour. Discord might have overturned the world—it would not have shaken me. At Marly, I had but one single amusement: it was to be a bystander at the royal card table in the drawing room. There I used to look round the lansquenet table, and observe the torment of the passions restrained by respect; the greedy thirst of gold, hope, fear, the pain of losing, the ardour of winning, the joy that followed a good hand, and the despair that accompanied baffled expectation, rapidly succeeding each other in the souls of the players, under the stern mask of cold tranquillity.

My life was solitary and less prudent at Fontainbleau. The suppers of *les Menus Plaisirs*, the king's hunt, and the theatre, were frequent sources of dissipation, which I confess I had not the courage to avoid.

At Versailles too I had my amusements, but they were so regulated by my plan of study and employment as never to be more than recreations. My daily society was that of the first clerks in the public offices, most of them men of engaging manners, and emulous of giving excellent dinners. After their labours, they indulged in the pleasures of the table; they were epicures nearly for the same reason as priests. The abbé Delaville for instance was the most careful man in the world to insure to himself good wine. His house-steward used to go every year to collect the unpressed wine of the best cellars in Burgundy, and on his return he always kept within sight of the casks. At these dinners I was generally a guest, and played my part tolerably well.

Dubois, the head clerk in the war-office, was he whose friendship for me was the most frank; we were so familiar that 'thee' and 'thou' were our common terms. Being in place, there was no service he would not have rendered me, had I afforded him an opportunity. But for myself, personally, I only thought of amusement, and if I derived any advantage from the society of the head clerks, it

T

proceeded from their own free will, unsolicited by me. Of this I will give you an example.

Among these laborious sybarites, the most animated, the most seducing, and the most voluptuous, with the frailest health, was that Cromot who afterwards became so famous under successive ministers. The facility, the clearness, the celerity, with which he transacted the business of his office, and above all, his dexterity, captivated them in spite of themselves.

When I first knew him, he was the intimate and favourite secretary of M. de Machault. It was an acquaintance that many people might envy, but its chief value to me was the pleasure it gave. About the same time, fortune, who was watching over me without my knowledge, introduced me at Versailles to the tender favourite of Bouret, the farmer-general, who was charged with the distribution of places; an acquaintance not less useful. This woman, who soon became my friend, and who continued so till her last sigh, was the witty, the engaging madame Filleul. She was detained at Versailles, and I was invited to sup with her; but I excused myself, alleging that I was obliged to go to Paris. She immediately offered to take me there, and I accepted a place in her carriage. From this our acquaintance began; she spoke of me to her friend Bouret, and probably inspired him with some desire of knowing me. Thus circumstances concurred that favoured the object nearest my heart.

My eldest sister was of a marriageable age, and, though I had but little portion to give her, several suitable offers had been made her in my native town. I preferred him who in morals and talents I knew to be the best; and my choice happened to be the same my sister would have made, had she simply followed her own inclination. Odde, my old schoolfellow, ever since he left school, had been remarkable for piety, prudence, and application. His character was gentle, gay, and candid, with a perfect equality of temper: his manners were incorruptible, and his conduct uniform. He is still living, about my age, and I believe there is not a purer soul on earth. To him, the change and passage of life has only been from the age of innocence to the age of virtue. His father, when he died, left him but little property, but he inherited a rare and precious friend. This friend, in whose praise M. Turgot has often spoken to me, was one M. de Malesaigue, a true philosopher; who, in our isolated town, almost solitary, passed his life in reading Tacitus, Plutarch, Montaigne, and in taking care of his domains, and cultivating his gardens. "Who would believe," said M. Turgot to me, "that such a man should be concealed in a small town in Limosin? In matters of government, I have never seen any one wiser or better informed." The worthy friend of M. Odde, was he who in his name solicited the hand of my sister. It gave me pleasure, but I thought I could perceive from his letter that Odde indulged the hope of obtaining some place through my interest. I answered I would do all that I possibly could, but that as my credit was not what it was supposed to be in the country, I was sure of nothing myself, and could make no promise. M. de Malesaigue replied, that my good faith was better than light promises, and the marriage was concluded.

A month afterwards, Bouret, being come to consult with the minister of finance about filling the vacant places, I dined with him at his friend Cromot's. It would have been difficult to have brought together men of more lively native wit, more ready, and more fertile in ingenious traits, than these two. In Cromot, there was the superior ease of habitual grace and facility: in Bouret, more ardour in the desire of pleasing, and more happiness in the pertinence of wit. This dinner was animated by the gaiety of both, and I insensibly assumed the tone that they inspired. But, as we rose from table, Bouret displayed a long list of candidates for the vacant offices, and of solicitors for them all. These solicitors were all people of rank. It was this duke, that marquis, the princes of the blood, the royal family, in short, the town and the court. "How mad then have I been," exclaimed I, "who, on marrying my sister to a young man, well informed, versed in business, replete with talents and good sense, and, what's more, an honest man, to have given him, as her dowry, the hope of obtaining a place by my feeble interest! I'll write to him instantly, and tell him to flatter himself no longer."—"Why so?" replied Bouret. "Why do your sister so ill a turn as to afflict her husband? Love, when sad, is very cold; leave them hope, 'tis a happiness, till they can get something better."

They left me to transact business with the minister, and, after I was gone home, a boy from the office came to me on their part to inquire the name of my brother-in-law. He had a place given him the same evening. I need not tell you what was the transport of my joy and my gratitude on the following day. It was the epoch of a long friendship between Bouret and myself. I shall speak of it more at leisure.

The place, that was granted to M. Odde, appeared to me too indolent and too obscure for a man of his talents. I changed it for one more difficult and of less value, in order that, by making himself known, he might contribute to his own advancement. The place of his destination was Saumur; on their way thither, he and his wife came to see me at Paris; and I cannot express the joy with which my sister was penetrated when we met. They staid with me some days. I sensibly felt the reception my friends so kindly gave them. At the dinners to which they invited us, it was affecting to behold the eyes of my sister continually fixed on me, unable to satiate themselves with the pleasure of looking. It was not fraternal, it was filial love.

She was scarcely arrived at Saumur when she formed a tender friendship with a person related to madame de Pompadour; whose husband had, in that town, a place of two hundred and fifty pounds a year. It was an employment in the salt office. This young man, whose name was de Blois, was attacked by the disorder of which my father, mother, and brother, had died. We too well knew that it was incurable, and madame de Blois did not conceal from my sister that her husband had but a short time to live. "It would at least be some consolation to me, my dear friend," said she, "if M. Odde could succeed him in the place he holds. It will be disposed of by madame de Pompadour; persuade your brother to ask it for your husband." My sister gave me this intimation, by which I profited and had a promise of the place: but, at the death of M. de Blois, madame de Pompadour's steward informed me that she had just granted this same place, as a dowry, to a young lady, whom she protected. Thunderstruck at this intelligence, I went to her house; and as she passed to go to mass I asked her with a respectful assurance for the place she had promised me for my sister's husband. "I have forgotten you," said she, as she ran along, "and have given it to another; but I'll make you amends." I waited her return, and begged a moment's audience. She permitted me to follow her.

"Madame," said I, "it is neither place nor money that I now ask of you; it is my honour which I conjure you to save, for, by depriving me of that, you would give me a death blow." This preface astonished her, and I continued. "As sure of the place you had promised me as if I had obtained it, I have announced it to my brother-in-law. He has said publicly at Saumur that I had your word for it;

he has written to his family and to mine; two provinces are informed of it; I myself, in speaking of your beneficence, have boasted of it at Versailles and at Paris. No one, madame, will be persuaded that you would have granted to another the place you had formally promised to me. All the world knows that you have a thousand ways of benefiting whom you please. It is I, then, whom they will accuse of vain boasting, of violated faith, and of falsehood; and thus you will see me dishonoured. Madame, I have conquered adversity, I have lived in indigence, but I cannot live in the shame and contempt of men. You are pleased to express your desire of indemnifying my brother-in-law; but I shall first have passed for an impudent liar: will you, madame, restore to me the reputation of an honest man, the thing of which I am most desirous? Can your beneficence efface the spot my fame will have received? Indemnify, madame, the other persons you patronize, for the place you promised them in a moment of forgetfulness. It will be very easy for you to procure them one more advantageous. Do not do me an irreparable injury, that would reduce me to the deepest despair." She wanted to persuade me to wait, telling me that my sister should suffer no loss; but I persisted in replying " that it was the place at Saumur that I had boasted of having, and that I would accept no other, were it ten times its value." At these words I withdrew, and the place was granted me.

I had, as you perceive, and as you will soon perceive yet more clearly, facilities for making my own fortune, that might well have excited my ambition; but, having provided for the well-being of my family, I was so contented, so tranquil, that I desired nothing more.

My most intimate and most habitual society at Versailles was that of madame de Chalut; an excellent woman, of no brilliant understanding, but of great good sense, and of a gentleness, an equality, a truth of character that were inestimable. After having been the favourite femme-de-chambre of the first dauphiness, she had passed to the second, and she was still more beloved by her. That princess had no friend more faithful, more tender, more sincere, or, rather, she was the only true friend the dauphiness had in France. Of this the latter was sensible; and her heart was always open to her, even to the most secret of her thoughts; and in the most delicate and most difficult circumstances, she had only her for counsel, consolation and support. These sentiments of esteem, of confidence, and of friendship, were communicated by sympathy from the dauphiness to the dauphin. That they might marry mademoiselle Varanchan (that was her maiden name) and give her a rich dowry, they were both determined to have sold their most precious jewels, had not the comptroller-general prevented them, by obtaining from the king the post of farmer-general for the man she should marry. This sufficiently proves how great her credit was with the princess, and I may add, that there was nothing she would not have done for me; I have been her friend twenty years, and I have made no request. I had formed to myself so noble, so pure an idea of friendship, and it was to me a sentiment so generous, that I should have thought it profaned had I mixed with it any view of ambition; and the more prodigal madame de Chalut would have been to me of her good offices, the more I thought it became me to be discreet and disinterested.

I seized every occasion of paying my court to those who patronized her, but solely out of complaisance to her; and, if I sometimes wrote verses for them, it was never but when she inspired them. This brings to my memory a scene that was somewhat curious.

Madame de Chalut, after the marriage of the

dauphiness, still continued in her service. She was even more assiduous in her attention to her. The princess was so fond of her that she was afflicted when she was absent. Madame Chalut, therefore, constantly kept a house at Versailles, and whenever I went thither, previously to my residence there, her house was mine. The recovery of the dauphin from the small-pox was there celebrated by a fête, to which I was invited. I found madame de Chalut full of joy, and delighted by the conduct of her mistress, who, day and night, by the pillow of her husband, had watched him with the tenderest care during his malady. I was affected by the animated recital she made, and wrote some verses on this subject. The interest of the picture insured the success of the painter; and these verses gained, at court at least, the applause of the moment, and had the merit of being opportune. On reading them, the prince and princess were moved even to tears. Madame de Chalut was commissioned to tell me how great an effect this reading had produced, and to inform me they should be very happy to tell me so in person. "Be in their dining-room tomorrow at dinner time," said she; "you will be satisfied with the reception they intend to give you." I did not fail. There was very little company. I was placed opposite to them, at two paces from the table, quite isolated and full in view. On seeing me, they whispered each other; then cast their eyes on me, and whispered again. I perceived they were speaking of me, but they both seemed alternately to let what they wished to say expire on their lips. Thus passed their dinner, till the moment when I was obliged to retire with the rest of the company. Madame de Chalut had waited on them at table, and you may judge what impatience this long mute scene caused her. I was to dine with her, and we were to rejoice together at the reception they had given me. I went and waited for her, and when she arrived,

"Well! madame," said I, "ought I not to be extremely flattered by all the obliging things that were said to me?"—"Do you know," answered she, "how their dinner passed? In trying to engage each other to speak to you, but they had neither of them the courage!"—"I did not think myself so imposing a personage," said I; "and certainly I ought to be proud of the respect with which I inspire the prince and the princess." This contrast of ideas appeared to us so comical, that we laughed at it heartily; and I took for granted, all that they had the courteous intention to say.

The kind of benevolent feeling with which I was regarded in this court, was of service to me in one particular instance; I was listened to and believed in an affair that interested me. The register in which the baptism of Aurore, the daughter of mademoiselle Verrière, was recorded, attested that she was the daughter of marshal Saxe; and, after the death of her father, it was the intention of the dauphiness to provide for her education; which the mother greatly desired. But the dauphin took the whim to affirm that she was my daughter, and this made its impression. Madame de Chalut told me of it laughing; but this pleasantry of the prince made me very serious. I accused him of levity; and offered to prove I had only known mademoiselle Verrière during the marshal's journey into Prussia, and about a year after the birth of this child. I alleged it would be inhumanly depriving her of her real father, were she made to pass for my daughter. Madame de Chalut undertook to plead this cause to the dauphiness; and the dauphin yielded. Thus Aurore was educated at their expense in a convent of nuns at Saint Cloud; and madame de Chalut, who had a country-house at that village, had the kindness, for love of me and at my request, to take charge of the details of her education.

I have two other acquaintances to mention whom

I had at Versailles: the one, of simple convenience, with Quesnai, madame de Pompadour's physician; the other with madame de Marchais, and her intimate friend the count d'Angiviller, a young man of a noble character. The latter soon became a union of sentiment; and, during the forty years it has lasted, I may cite it as an example of friendship that neither years nor events have changed or diminished. Let us begin by Quesnai, for it is the less interesting. Quesnai lodged very incommodiously in madame de Pompadour's *entresol*, and was occupied the whole day with little but political and rural economy. He thought he had reduced his system to calculations and axioms, the evidence of which was irresistible; and, as he was forming a school, he was pleased to give himself the pains of explaining his new doctrine to me, that I might be his disciple and proselyte. I, who wished to make him my mediator with madame de Pompadour, applied the whole power of my mind to understand the truths which he thought so evident, but in which I could only discover vagueness and obscurity. To pretend to comprehend what I really did not, was beyond me, but I listened with patient docility, and left him the hope of finally enlightening me, and of instilling his doctrine. This would have been enough to gain me his good will. I did more, I used to applaud a labour that I really found estimable; for it tended to give vogue to agriculture in a country where it was too much disdained, and to turn a variety of valuable minds to this study. He afforded me an opportunity of flattering him on his weak side.

An Irishman, whose name was Patulo, had written a book, in which he developed the advantages of English over French agriculture; and, through Quesnai, he had obtained the permission of dedicating it to madame de Pompadour; but he had written the dedication ill. Madame de Pompadour, after having read it, told him to apply to me, and to beg me, on her part, to retouch it with care I found it easier to write him another; and, in speaking of husbandmen, I showed their condition to be so truly interesting, that madame de Pompadour had tears in her eyes, as she read this dedication. Quesnai perceived it, and I cannot tell you how delighted he was with me. His way of serving me with the marchioness, was to drop here and there a word that seemed to escape him, but which left its impression. With respect to his character, I will mention but one trait by which it will be sufficiently marked. He had been placed in his situation by the old duke de Villeroy, and the countess d'Estrade, the friend and devoted companion of madame d'Estioles, who not suspecting she was warming a serpent in her bosom, had extricated her from poverty and brought her to court. Quesnai was then attached to madame d'Estrade by gratitude, when this intriguing woman forsook her benefactress to abandon herself to the count d'Argenson, and to conspire with him against her benefactress.

It is difficult to conceive how so frightful a woman, in every sense, could, in despite of the deformity of mind and features, seduce a man of the character, the talents, and the age of M. d'Argenson. But in his eyes she had the merit of sacrificing the friend to whom she owed everything, and of being, for love of him, the most ungrateful of human beings.

At the same time Quesnai, without being agitated by these hostile passions, was, on one side, the incorruptible servant of madame de Pompadour, and, on the other, faithful by gratitude to madame d'Estrade, who answered for him to M. d'Argenson; and, though he used to go and see them sometimes openly, it did not make madame de Pompadour uneasy. On their part, they had as much confidence in him as if he had been held by no tie to madame de Pompadour.

The following was told me, after the exile of M.

d'Argenson, by Dubois, who had been his secretary. It is he himself who is about to speak; I well remember his recital, and you may think you hear him.

To supplant madame de Pompadour, M. d'Argenson and madame d'Estrade had contrived to inspire the king with a desire of obtaining the favours of the young and beautiful madame de Choiseul, the wife of Menin. The intrigue had made a rapid progress: it was near its dénouement. The rendezvous was given; the lady in all her youth and beauty was gone to it; she was there at the very moment that M. d'Argenson, madame d'Estrade, Quesnai, and I were together in the minister's closet. We two were mute witnesses; but M. d'Argenson and madame d'Estrade were exceedingly busied and anxious about what might have passed. After some considerable time of eager expectation, madame de Choiseul arrives, dishevelled and in the disorder which marked her triumph. Madame d'Estrade runs to meet her with open arms, and enquires, if her victory be complete. 'Oh! yes,' answered she, 'entirely; I am loved; he is happy: she's to be discharged; for this he has given me his word.' At these words, there was a great burst of joy in the closet. Quesnai alone sat unmoved. 'Doctor,' said M. d'Argenson to him, 'there will be no change for you, and we sincerely hope that you will remain with us.'—'I count!' answered Quesnai as he rose. 'I have been attached to madame de Pompadour in her prosperity, and I shall be so still under misfortune;' and he instantly went away. We remained petrified; but no one conceived any mistrust. 'I know him,' said madame d'Estrade; he is not a man that will betray us.' And indeed it was not through him that the secret was discovered, and that the marchioness de Pompadour was delivered of her rival. This was the story of Dubois.

While storms were formed and dissipated beneath Quesnai's *entresol*, he was sketching his axioms and calculations on rustic economy, as tranquilly, and as indifferent to these passions of the court, as if he had been a hundred leagues distant. While below they were deliberating on peace and war, the choice of generals, and the removal of ministers, we, in his little apartment, were reasoning on agriculture, calculating the neat produce, or perhaps dining gaily with Diderot, d'Alembert, Duclos, Helvétius, Turgot, or Buffon; and madame de Pompadour, who could not induce this troop of philosophers to descend into her saloon, would come herself to see and converse with them at table.

The other connection I mentioned was infinitely dearer to me. Madame de Marchais was not only, in my opinion, the most witty and the most engaging of women, but the best and most essential of friends; the most active, the most constant, the most ardently occupied with all that interested me. Imagine to yourselves all the charms of character, of wit, of eloquence, united in their highest degree, and even those of the person, though she was not beautiful; above all, in her manners, a most attractive grace: such was this young fairy. Her mind, active beyond all expression, gave to the traits of her countenance a dazzling and enchanting mobility. Not one of her features was that which the pencil would have chosen, but altogether they had a charm that the pencil could not have expressed. Her short and slender form was inimitably turned, and her carriage communicated to her whole person a character of imposing dignity. Add to this a mind exquisitely cultivated; varied and copious, from the light and brilliant part of literature to the highest conceptions of genius; a clearness in her ideas, an acuteness, an accuracy, a rapidity that astonished; a facility, a choice of language that was always happy, flowing from an abundant source, and as quick of thought. She had besides an excellent heart, inexhaustible in kindness, an ardent and invariable desire to oblige.

an exertion that never wearied, and that had so unaffected, seducing, flattering an air, that one would have been tempted to suspect it of artifice, if art could ever have given itself that continued unalterable equality, which was always the distinctive mark of nature, and the only one of its characters that art could never imitate.

Her society was composed of the most engaging people of the court, and of those men of letters who were most estimable for their morals, or most distinguished for their talents. With courtiers, she was a model of the most noble and most delicate politeness; the young women came to her house to study her air and manner. With men of letters, she was on a par with the most witty, and with the best informed. No one conversed with more ease, more precision, or more method. Her silence was animated by the fire of an acute attentive look; she divined the idea, and her replies were darts that never missed their aim. But the wonder of her conversation was its variety, the feeling of propriety, pertinence, measure; the word best suited to the thing, the moment, and the person; the difference of things, the finest shades of expression, and what could best be said to all and to each in particular: such was the manner in which this incomparable woman knew how to animate, to embellish, and, as it were, to enchant her society.

Well skilled in music, with a taste for singing and a sweet voice, she had adorned the little private theatre of madame de Pompadour; and, when that amusement ceased, she remained as her friend: she was more careful than myself to cultivate her kindness for me, and never missed an opportunity of engaging her to serve me.

Her young friend, M. d'Angiviller, was the more interesting because, with all that can render man amiable, with all that can render man happy, a fine form, a cultivated understanding, a taste for letters and the arts, a noble mind, a pure heart, the king's esteem, the confidence and intimate favour of the dauphin, and with a fame and consideration at court rarely acquired at his age, he never ceased to be, or at least to appear, unhappy at heart. Inseparable from madame de Marchais, but sad, speechless in her presence, the more serious the more she was gay, timid and trembling at her voice; he, whose character had such boldness, such power, and such energy, was troubled when she spoke to him, looked at her with an air of suffering, and answered her in a feeble, hesitating, and half-extinguished voice. In her absence, on the contrary, he displayed his fine physiognomy, conversed well and with animation, and abandoned himself, with all the liberality of heart and soul, to the gay enjoyment of society. Nothing then resembled the lover treated with rigour, and imperiously governed. Yet they passed their lives in the most intimate union; and he was, very evidently, the man to whom no other was preferred. If this character of the unhappy lover had lasted but a little while, we should have thought it acted; but it was the same for fifteen successive years, and continued after the death of M. de Marchais, the same as while he was living, and till the moment that M. d'Angiviller made her his wife. The scene was then completely changed; the whole authority was transferred to the husband; and the wife became all deference and complaisance, with the submissive air of respect. I have never in my life seen anything so singular in moral conduct, as this voluntary and sudden mutation that has since been an equally happy destiny for both.

Their sentiments towards me were always in perfect harmony, and are still the same. Those I feel for them will never change.

Among my recreations, I have reckoned the theatre; though I had always every facility of enjoying it, I went rarely, and only mention it here to mark the epoch of an interesting revolution in the art of declamation.

I had long been in the habit of disputing with mademoiselle Clairon, on the manner of declaiming tragic verse. I found in her playing, too much violence and impetuosity, with not enough of variety and discrimination, and above all, a loud continued exertion, which was more akin to rant than feeling. This I modestly endeavoured to make her understand. "You have," I used to say, "every means of excelling in your art; and great as you are, it would be easy for you still to rise above yourself, by managing more carefully the powers of which you are so prodigal. You tell me of your brilliant successes, and of how much I have profited by them; you oppose me by the opinion of the town and the suffrages of your friends, nay by the authority of M. de Voltaire, who himself recites his verses with emphasis, and who pretends that tragic verses require, in declamation, the same pomp as in the style; and I can only answer, I have an irresistible feeling, which tells me that declamation, like style, may be noble, majestic, and tragic, with simplicity; that expression, to be lively and profoundly penetrating, requires gradations and shades, with unforeseen and sudden traits, which it cannot have when it is stretched and forced." She used to answer sometimes impatiently, that I should never let her rest, till she had assumed a familiar and comic tone in tragedy. "No, mademoiselle," said I, "that you will never have; nature has forbidden it; you even have it not, while you are speaking to me; the sound of your voice, the expression of your countenance, your pronunciation, your gestures, your attitudes, are naturally noble. Dare only to confide in this charming native talent, and I dare warrant you will be the more tragic."

Other counsels than mine prevailed, and, tired of being importunate without utility, I had given up the point, when I saw the actress suddenly and voluntarily come over to my opinion. She came to play Roxana at the little theatre at Versailles. I went to see her at her toilet, and, for the first time, I found her dressed in the habit of a sultana, without hoop, her arms half-naked, and in the truth of oriental costume: I congratulated her. "You will presently be delighted with me," said she. "I have just been on a journey to Bourdeaux; I found there but a very small theatre; to which I was obliged to accommodate myself. The thought struck me of suiting my action to its size, and of making trial of that simple declamation you have so often required of me. It had there the greatest success: I am going to try it again here, on this little theatre. Go and hear me. If it succeed as well, farewell to my old manner."

The event surpassed her expectation and mine. It was no longer the actress, it was Roxana herself, whom the audience thought they saw and heard. The astonishment, the illusion, the enchantment, were extreme. All inquired, where are we? They had heard nothing like it. I saw her after the play, and was about to congratulate her on her success. "Ah!" said she, "don't you see that it ruins me? In all my characters, the costume must now be observed; the truth of declamation requires that of dress; all my rich stage-wardrobe is from this moment rejected; I lose twelve hundred guineas' worth of dresses; but the sacrifice is made. You shall see me here within a week playing Electra after nature, as I have just played Roxana."

It was the Electra of Crébillon. Instead of the ridiculous hoop, and the ample mourning robe, in which we had been accustomed to see her in this character, she appeared in the simple habit of a slave, dishevelled, and her arms loaded with long chains. She was admirable; and, some time afterwards, she was still more sublime in the Electra of Voltaire.

This part, which Voltaire had made her declaim with a continued and monotonous lamentation, acquired, when spoken naturally, a beauty unknown to himself; for on seeing her play it on his theatre at Ferney, where she went to visit him, he exclaimed, bathed in tears and transported with admiration, "It is not I who formed this being, 'tis she: she has created her part!" And, indeed, by the infinite shades she introduced, and by the expression she gave to the passions with which this character abounds, it was perhaps that of all others in which she was most astonishing.

Paris, as well as Versailles, recognised in these changes the true tragic accent, and the new degree of probability that the strict observance of costume gave to theatrical action. Thus, from that time, all the actors were obliged to abandon their fringed gloves, their voluminous wigs, their feathered hats, and all the fantastic paraphernalia that had so long shocked the sight of all men of taste. Lekain himself followed the example of mademoiselle Clairon; and from that moment their talents, thus perfected, excited mutual emulation, and were worthy rivals of each other.

It may easily be conceived that a mixture of peaceful occupations and varied amusements would have more than indemnified me for the pleasures of Paris. But, to crown the advantages I enjoyed, I had still the liberty of going there when I pleased, to pass the time that was unoccupied by the duties of my place. M. de Marigny himself, at the solicitation of my old acquaintances, engaged me to go and see them.

I did not cease to remark in his conduct, with respect to me, a particularity to which perhaps another's pride would not have accommodated itself; but a little philosophy made me feel the reason of it. When from home, he, of all men, delighted to be in my society. At dinner, at supper, at the houses of our common friends, he enjoyed, more than I did myself, the esteem and friendship that were shown me: he was flattered by, and grateful for them. It was he who introduced me to madame Geoffrin; and, from respect to him, I was admitted to the dinners she gave to artists, as well as to those she gave to men of letters: in short, from the moment I ceased to be his secretary, as will be seen in the sequel, no one expressed more eager desire to have me for his companion and friend. Yet, as long as I held the place of secretary under him, he never once permitted himself to invite me to dinner. The ministers never dined with their clerks; he had assumed their etiquette, and, had he made an exception in my favour, all the persons employed in his offices would have been jealous and dissatisfied. He never explained himself to me on this subject, but you have just seen that he had the kindness to make it perfectly intelligible to me.

The years I passed at Versailles, were those in which the spirit of philosophy was in its greatest activity. D'Alembert and Diderot had hoisted its standard in the immense laboratory of the Encyclopedia, and all who were most distinguished among men of letters were there rallied round them. Voltaire, on his return from Berlin, from which place he had chaced the unhappy Arnaud, and where he himself could not remain, had retired to Geneva; and from thence he blew that spirit of liberty, innovation, and independence, that has since made such progress. In his spite against the king, he had been guilty of imprudences; but they were guilty of much greater, who obliged him to remain in a land of liberty, when he would fain have returned to his country. The king's answer, " let him remain where he is," was not sufficiently deliberate. His attacks were not such as could there be prevented. Versailles, where he would have been less bold than in Switzerland or Geneva, was the place of exile they should have given him. The priests should have opened to him that magnificent prison : it was thus that cardinal de Richelieu acted towards the first nobility.

When Voltaire reclaimed his title of gentleman in ordinary of his majesty's chamber, he himself held out to them the end of the chain with which they might have attached him if they would. It becomes me to testify of madame de Pompadour, that he was exiled against her will. She interested herself for him ; she sometimes enquired after him of me, and, when I answered that it depended only on her to make her enquiries unnecessary, " Ah! no, it does not depend on me," said she, with a sigh.

Thus, it was from Geneva that Voltaire animated the co-operators of the Encyclopedia. I was of the number ; and my greatest pleasure every time I went to Paris, was to find myself in their society. D'Alembert and Diderot were satisfied with what I wrote, and our relations strengthened more and more the bonds of that friendship, which ended but with life : they were more intimately, more tenderly, more assiduously cultivated by d'Alembert; but not less sincere, not less unalterable with the good Diderot, whom I was always so delighted to see, and charmed to hear.

I felt at last, I confess, that the distance, from Paris to Versailles, occasioned unpleasant intervals, which too long and too often delayed the happiness I tasted in the society of men of letters. Those among them whom I loved and honoured most had the kindness to say we were formed for mutual friendship; and they represented the French academy as a prospect that ought to attract and fix my attention. Thus, from time to time, I felt the desire of engaging again in the career of literature revive. But I first wanted to insure myself an independent and certain existence; and madame de Pompadour and her brother would have been happy to procure it me, of which the following is a sensible proof.

In 1757, after the outrage committed on the person of the king, and the remarkable change in the ministry, when M. d'Argenson and M. de Machault were removed on the same day, M. Rouillé was appointed postmaster-general, the secretariship of which was a sinecure worth two hundred and fifty pounds a-year, and was held by old Moncrif. It came into my head to ask for the reversion of it, persuaded that M. Rouillé, being newly appointed, would not refuse madame de Pompadour the first thing she should ask. I therefore employed doctor Quesnai to request her to grant me an audience. I was put off till the evening of the following day; and all night long was dreaming of what I should say to her. My brain took fire, and losing sight of my object, I became wholly occupied with the misfortunes of the state, and resolved to profit by this audience to tell some useful truths. The greater part of my night was employed in meditating my speech, and my morning in writing it, in order that it might be fully present to my mind. In the evening I went to Quesnai's at the appointed hour, and sent up word that I was there. Quesnai, busy in tracing the zigzag of the neat produce, did not even ask me what I was going to do at madame de Pompadour's. She sends for me; I descend, and am introduced into her closet: "Madame," said I, "M. Rouillé is appointed postmaster-general; the secretariship depends on him: Moncrif, who holds it, is very old. Would it be abusing your kindness, were I to entreat you to obtain the reversion of it for me? Nothing can suit me better than this place, and to this I entirely limit my ambition." She answered that she had promised it to Darboulin (one of her familiars), but that she would make him renounce it, if she could get it for me.

After having returned my thanks, "Madame,"

said I, "I am going to astonish you; the favour that I ask of you is not what occupies and interests me most in the present moment: it is the situation of the kingdom, it is the trouble into which it is plunged, by this never-ending dispute between the parliaments and the clergy; in which I see the royal authority like a vessel beaten by the storm between two rocks, and not a man in the council capable of governing it." I expatiated on this picture; and also drew that of the war, which called forth all the land and maritime forces of the state, and rendered peace and concord, the union of minds and the concurrence of wills, so necessary at home. After which, I added, "As long as M. d'Argenson and M. de Machault were in place, to their divisions and misunderstanding might be attributed the intestine dissensions with which the kingdom has been torn, and all those acts of rigour, which, instead of calming, have but exasperated them. But, now that these ministers are removed, and that the men who replace them have neither ascendency nor influence, recollect, madame, it is on you that all eyes are turned: it is henceforth to you that all will address their reproaches, and their complaints, if the evil continue, or their public benedictions, if you apply its remedy, and make it cease. In the name of your glory and repose, madame, hasten to produce this happy change. Do not wait till necessity command it, or till some other than you effect it; you will lose the merit of it, and they will accuse you alone of the ill you will not have done. All those who are attached to you have the same fears, and form the same vows with me."

She answered, she had courage sufficient, and that she wished her friends to have no fears, but to act like her; and added, that she was pleased with the zeal I expressed; but that I might be very tranquil, as the government was then labouring to pacify all. She promised she would speak to M. Rouillé on that very day, and bade me call again on the following morning.

"I have no good news for you," said she, on seeing me again; "the survivorship of Moncrif's place is disposed of. It was the first thing that the new postmaster-general asked of the new king, and he has obtained it in favour of Gaudin, his former secretary. See if there be anything else that I can do for you."

It was not easy for me to find a place that suited me so exactly as this. Yet, a little time after, I thought myself sure of obtaining one that I liked better, because I should create it, and should leave honourable traces of my labours. This obliges me to introduce a personage that has shone like a meteor, and whose lustre, though very much enfeebled, is not yet extinguished. If I spoke only of myself, all would soon be said; but, as the history of my life is a walk that I am taking with my children, I must shew them the passengers with whom I have had some relations in society.

The abbé de Bernis, just escaped from the seminary of Saint-Sulpice, where he had succeeded ill, was a gallant chubby-cheeked poet; fresh coloured, much of a beau, and with the agreeable Bernard, made pretty verses for the jovial suppers of Paris. Voltaire used to call him the flower-girl of Parnassus, and in society he was more familiarly called 'Babet,' from the name of a pretty flower-girl of that time. From this point he started, and became a cardinal and an ambassador from France to the court of Rome. He had in vain solicited from the old bishop of Mirepoix (Boyer) a pension on some abbey. This bishop, who set but little value on gallant poetry, and who knew the life that this abbé led, had harshly declared to him, that so long as he (Boyer) should continue in place, he had nothing to hope for; to which the abbé had answered, "My lord, I shall wait;" a reply that became current in society, and was considered as peculiarly happy. His fortune then consisted of a prebendary at Brioude, which was worth nothing to him on account of his absence, and a little sinecure at Boulogne-sur-mer, that he had got I know not how.

This was his situation, when he learnt, that, at the hunting parties in the forest of Senart, the beautiful madame d'Estioles had been the object of the king's attention. The abbé immediately solicits the permission to go and pay his court to this engaging young woman, and the countess d'Estrade, to whom he was known, obtained for him this favour. He arrives at Estioles by the public barge, his little packet under his arm. They engage him to recite some of his verses; he amuses, and exerts every effort to make himself agreeable; and, with that superficies of wit, and varnish of poetry, which was his sole talent, he succeeded so well, that, in the absence of the king, he was admitted into the secret of the letters that passed between the two lovers. Nothing could better suit the turn of his mind and character, than this species of ministry. And thus, as soon as the new mistress was installed at court, one of the first effects of her favour was to obtain for him a pension of one hundred pounds on the privy-purse, and apartments at the Tuilleries, which she furnished at her own expense. I saw him lodged under the roof of the palace, the happiest of men, with his pension and 'brocatelle' furniture. As his birth was noble, his protectress advised him to pass from the chapter of Brioude to that of Lyons; and for the latter she obtained, in favour of the new canon, a new decoration. At the same time, he was the favoured and declared lover of the beautiful princess de Rohan; which, in the great world, put him on the footing of a man of quality, and he was suddenly named ambassador to Venice. There he received with distinction the nephews of the pope

Ganganelli, and by that means procured himself the favour of the court of Rome. Recalled from Venice to assist in the councils of the king, he concluded the treaty of Versailles with count Stahremberg: as a reward, he was appointed minister for foreign affairs, on the resignation of M. Rouillé; and, a short time afterwards he obtained a cardinal's hat, at the nomination of the court of Vienna.

On his return from his embassy, I saw him, and he treated me as he had done before his prosperity, yet with a tint of dignity that arose from a feeling of excellence; and nothing was more natural. After he had signed the treaty of Versailles, I congratulated him on it; and he told me that I should oblige him by celebrating, in an epistle addressed to the king, the advantages of that great and happy alliance. I answered that it would be more easy, and more graceful to me, to address it to himself. He did not dissemble that he should be flattered by it. I wrote my epistle; he was pleased with it, and his friend madame de Pompadour was enchanted with it; she insisted on its being printed, and presented to the king: which did not at all displease the diplomatic abbé. (I pass over in silence the embassies of Spain and Vienna, to which he was named, but where he did not go, because he had something better to do at Versailles.) He soon afterwards, on an urgent occasion, wanted a man, sure, discreet, and diligent, who wrote a good style, and he did me the honour to have recourse to me. The circumstances were these: the king of Prussia, on entering Saxony with an army of sixty thousand men, had published a manifesto, to which the court of Vienna had answered. This answer, translated into a kind of Teutonic French, had been sent to Fontainbleau, where the court then was. It was to be presented to the king on the following Sunday, and the count de Stahremberg had five hundred copies of it to distribute on that day. It was on the Wednesday evening that the abbé de Bernis sent to beg me to call on him. He was closeted with the count de Stahremberg. They both expressed how much they were afflicted at having to publish a manifesto written in such bad French; and they told me that I should do something very agreeable to the two courts of Versailles and Vienna, if I would correct and get it printed with all possible speed, to be presented and published in four days. We read it together, and independently of the Germanisms with which it was filled, I took the liberty of observing to them a number of reasons badly deduced or obscurely presented. They gave me a carte-blanche for all these corrections, and, after having fixed a rendezvous for the next day at the same hour, I went and set myself to work. At the same time, the abbé de Bernis wrote to M. de Marigny, to request him to resign me to him for the rest of the week, as he wanted me for an urgent work that I had kindly undertaken.

I employed almost the whole night and the following day in retouching and getting transcribed this ample manifesto; and, at the hour of rendezvous, I carried it to them, if not elegantly, at least more decently written. They praised to excess my performance and my diligence. "But this is not all," said the abbé; "this memoir, printed, must be here in our hands on Sunday morning at the hour of the king's levee, and it is by effecting this, my dear Marmontel, that you must crown your work."—"Count," said I; "in half an hour I will be ready to go off. Order that a post-chaise may come and take me, and write with your own hand two words to the minister of police, in order that the censor may not retard the impression. I promise you to be here on Sunday as soon as you are up." I kept my word with him; but I arrived worn out with fatigue and watching. A few days afterwards, he asked me for the note of the expenses of my journey, and of those of the printing. I gave it him very exactly, article by article, and he as exactly paid me the amount. It was never mentioned afterwards.

However, he did not cease to repeat on his part, that one of the advantages of the favour he enjoyed would be the power of being useful to me. For this reason, when he became secretary of state for foreign affairs, I thought that if in his department there were any means of employing me usefully to the public, to himself, and to me, I should find him well disposed. It was on these three bases that I established my project and my hope.

I knew that at that time the office for foreign affairs presented a chaos, in which the oldest clerks could with great difficulty find their intricate way. Thus to a new minister, whoever he might be, his place was a long school. In speaking of Bernis himself, I heard Bussy, one of these oldest clerks, say, "This is the eleventh scholar that the abbé de la Ville and I have had given us." And this scholar was the master the dauphin had taken to teach him politics: a very strange choice for a prince who appeared desirous of being solidly instructed!

I should therefore have served the minister, the dauphin, the king, and the state itself, could I have established order and thrown light into this chaos of the past. It was this that I proposed in a precise and clear memorial which I presented to the abbé de Bernis.

My project consisted first of all, in regulating and arranging the objects of the negociations according to their different relations. By their dates, with respect to time, and by their order, with respect to place. Then, from time to time, commencing from an epoch more or less remote, I undertook to extract from all those portfolios of dispatches and memorials whatever was interesting; to form successively an historical table of them, sufficiently developed to pursue by it the course of negociations; and to observe the spirit of the different courts, the system of their cabinets, the policy of their councils, the character of their ministers, with that of their kings, and of their reigns; in a word, the springs that, at such and such periods, had put the great powers of Europe in motion. Three volumes of this course of diplomacy would have been deposited every year in the hands of the minister; and perhaps, written with care, they might have formed a satisfactory reading to the dauphin himself. Finally, to render the objects yet more visible, a book of tables would have presented at one view all the respective negociations under their mutual relations, and their simultaneous effects on the courts and cabinets of Europe. For this immense work, I required only two secretaries, a lodging in the office itself, and enough to live frugally at home. The abbé de Bernis appeared charmed with my project. "Give me this memorial," said he, after he had heard it read; "I feel its utility and excellence more than yourself. I wish to present it to the king." I did not doubt of its success, and waited the answer, but waited in vain; and, when impatient to know the decision of the king, I inquired how it had been received; "Ah!" said he, with a careless air, as he stepped into his chair to go to the council, "it depends on a general arrangement, on which nothing is yet determined." This arrangement has since taken place; the king has built two hotels, one for the war-office, and the other for foreign affairs. My project has been executed, at least in part, and another has reaped the fruit of it. *Sic vos non vobis.* After this answer of the abbé de Bernis, I saw him once again it was on the day, when, in the habit of a cardinal, in a cap, red stockings, and with a rochet trimmed with the richest point lace, he was going to present himself to the king. I traversed his antichambers between two long rows of servants in new scarlet dresses laced with gold. On entering his closet, I found him vainglorious as a peacock, more chubby-cheeked than ever, admiring himself in his glory, and, above all, unable to weary himself with looking at his rochet and scarlet stockings. "Don't you think me well dressed?" said he.—"Exceedingly well," I answered; "your new dignity sits admirably on you, and I come, my lord, to congratulate you."—"And what do you think of my livery servants?"—"I took them," answered I, "for the tinsel troop, who were come to compliment you." These are the last words that passed between us.

I easily consoled myself for not owing anything to him, not only besause I saw in him nothing but a coxcomb invested with the purple, but because I soon beheld him rude and ungrateful to her who had created him; for nothing weighs so heavily as gratitude, when we owe it to the ungrateful.

More happy than he, I found, in study and application, consolation for the little frowns I endured from fortune. But, as my character was never that of a stoic, I every year less patiently paid the tribute of pain which nature imposed. Though I had habitually good and full health, I was subject to a head-ache of a very singular species. This disorder is called the *clavus*: its seat is under the eyebrow. It is the beating of an artery, each of whose pulsations is a dart that seems to pierce to the very soul. I cannot express the pain it gives; and, acute and severe as it is, one single point only is affected by it. This point is above the eye, the place to which the pulsation of an interior artery corresponds. I explain all this, the better to make you understand an interesting phenomenon.

For seven years, this head-ache returned to me at least once a year, and lasted twelve or fifteen days; not continually, but by fits, like a fever, and every day at the same hour with little variation: it continued about six hours, announcing itself by a tension in the neighbouring veins and fibres and by pulsations, not quicker but stronger, in the artery where the pain was seated. At its commencement, this pain was almost insensible; and it gradually increased, and diminished in the same way before it eft me: but during four hours at least, it was in all its force. What appeared astonishing was, that the fit once finished, no trace of pain was left in the part; and that neither the rest of the day, nor the following night, till the next day at the usual hour, were the least remains of it felt. The physicians whom I consulted had in vain attempted to cure me. Bark, bleeding at the foot, emollient liquors, fumigations, sneezing powders, were all tried without success. Some of these medicines, the bark for instance, only served to irritate my complaint.

One of the queen's physicians, whose name was Malouin, a very skilful man, but a greater Purgon than Purgon himself, conceived the idea of prescribing for me injections made of the infusions of herbs. These did me no good; but at the end of its accustomed period the disease had ceased: and there was Malouin proud of so fine a cure. I did not disturb his triumph; but he took this opportunity to give me a gentle reprimand. "Well! my good friend," said he, "will you in future have faith in medicine and in the knowledge of physicians?" I assured him that my faith was very strong. "No," replied he; "you sometimes suffer yourself to speak of it rather lightly. This does you harm in the world. Among men of letters and science, the most illustrious have always respected our art." To prove this, he cited some great names. "Voltaire himself," added he; "one who censures so many things, has always spoken with respect of medicine and of physicians."—"Yes, doctor," answered I; "but there was one Molière!"—"Aye," said he, looking at me with a fixed eye, and pressing my hand; "and how did he die?"

At last, for the seventh year, my complaint again

attacked me, when one day, whilst the fit was on me, I saw Genson, the farrier of the dauphin's stables, enter my room. Genson gave some distinguished articles to the 'Encyclopedia' on the objects relative to his art. He had made a particular study of the comparative anatomy between the man and the horse. Not only of the diseases, but also the food and treatment of horses, no one was better informed than he; but he was little practised in the art of writing, and he had recourse to me to retouch his style. He came with his papers at the moment when, for three hours, I had been suffering torture. "M. Genson," said I, "it is impossible for me to peruse your labours with you to-day: I suffer too cruelly." He saw my right eye inflamed, and all the fibres of the temple and the eyelid palpitating and spasmodic. He asked me the cause of my complaint; I told him what I knew of it; and after some account of my constitution, my manner of living, and my habitual health, "Is it possible," said he, "that the physicians can have suffered you to linger so long under a disease of which it was so easy to cure you?"—"What!" answered I with astonishment, "do you know its remedy?"— "Yes: nothing is more simple. In three days you shall be cured, and even tomorrow you shall be relieved."—"How?" asked I with a feeble and still timid hope. "When your ink is too thick and does not run," said he, "what do you do?"—"I put water to it."—"Well then, put water to your lymph: it will flow, and will no longer choke the glands of the pituitary membrane, which at present confines the artery, the pulsations of which bruise the neighbouring nerves, and cause you so much pain."— "Is that indeed," asked I, "the cause of my disease?"—"Certainly," said he. "You have there in the bone a small cavity, called the *sinus frontal*. It is lined with a membrane which is a tissue of little glands. This membrane, in its natural state, is so thin as a leaf. It is now thick and choked; it wants to be disengaged; and the means are easy and sure. Dine temperately today,—no ragôuts, no pure wine, nor coffee, nor liqueurs; and, instead of supper this evening, drink as much clear and fresh water as your stomach can properly bear: tomorrow morning drink the same; observe this regimen for a few days, and I predict that tomorrow the pain will decrease, that the day after tomorrow it will be almost insensible, and that the next day it will be gone."— "Ah! M. Genson, you will be my guardian angel," said I, "if your prediction be realised." It indeed was realised. Genson called on me again, and, as I embraced him and announced my recovery, "It is not enough to have cured you," said he; "you must be preserved from a future attack. This part will still be feeble for some years; and, till the membrane shall have resumed its spring and elasticity, it will be there that the thickened lymph will again lodge. This must be prevented. You have told me that the first symptom of your complaint is a tension in the veins and fibres of the temple and the eyelid. From the moment you feel this inconvenience, drink water, and resume your regimen as least for a few days. The remedy of your disorder will be its preventive. Besides, this precaution will only be necessary for a few years. The organ once re-established, I ask nothing more of you." His prescription was exactly observed, and I obtained from it the full success that he had predicted.

This year, in which by the virtue of a few glasses of water I had relieved myself from so great an evil, was otherwise magical; inasmuch as, with a few accidental words, I conferred a great benefit on an honest man, with whom I had no acquaintance.

The court was at Fontainbleau, and there I used often to go and pass an hour in the evening with Quesnai. One evening when I was with him, madame de Pompadour sent for me, and said, "Do you know that La Bruyére is dead? He died at Rome. It was he who held the patent of the 'Mercure:' this patent was worth a thousand a year to him; there is enough to make more than one happy man; and we intend to add to the new patent of the 'Mercure' a few pensions for men of letters. You who know them, name to me those who would want such pensions, and would be well calculated to receive them." I named Crébillon, d'Alembert, Boissy, and some others. As for Crébillon, I knew it was unnecessary to recommend him; as for d'Alembert, perceiving she made a little sign of disapprobation, "He is," said I, "madame, a geometrician of the first order, a most distinguished writer, and a perfectly honest man."—"Yes," replied she, "but a little hot-headed." I answered, very mildly, that without some warmth in the head, there was no great talent. "He indulges a passion," said she, "for Italian music, and has put himself at the head of a party of the Buffons."—"It is not the less true," answered I, modestly, "that he has written the preface of the Encyclopedia." She said no more; but he had no pension. I believe that a graver subject of exclusion was his zeal for the king of Prussia, of whom he was the declared partisan, and whom madame de Pompadour personally hated. When we came to Boissy, she asked me, "Is not Boissy rich? I thought him at least in easy circumstances: I have seen him at the theatre, and always quite well dressed!"—"No, madame, he is poor; but he conceals his poverty."—"He has written so many theatrical pieces," insisted she. "Yes, but all these pieces had not the same success; and he had himself to maintain. In short, madame—shall I say it?—Boissy is so far from rich that, had not a friend discovered his situation, he would last winter have perished for want. Without bread, and too proud to ask it of any one, he had shut himself up with his wife and son, resolved to die together; and they were going to kill themselves in each other's arms, when this helping friend forced the door and saved them."—" Ah, God!" cried madame de Pompadour, " you make me shudder. I'll go, and recommend him to the king."

The next morning I saw Boissy enter my room, pale, wild, disordered, with an emotion that resembled joy upon the face of grief. His first impulse was to fall at my feet. I, who thought he fainted, hastened eagerly to aid him, and raising him up, asked him what could put him in such a state. "Ah! sir," said he, " don't you know? You, my generous benefactor, you who have saved my life, you who, from an abyss of misery, have raised me to a situation of comfort and unexpected fortune! I came to solicit a moderate pension on the ' Mercure;' and M. de Saint Florentin announced to me that it is the privilege, the patent itself, of the ' Mercure' which the king has just granted me. He informs me that I owe it to madame de Pompadour; I go to return her my thanks; and then M. Quesnai tells me that it is you who, as you spoke of me, so touched madame de Pompadour that she had tears in her eyes."

I endeavoured to interrupt him by embracing him; but he continued: " What then have I done, sir, to merit from you so tender an interest? I have scarcely seen you; you hardly know me; and in speaking of me you have the eloquence of sentiment, the ardour of friendship!" At these words he would have kissed my hand. " This is too much," said I; " it becomes me, sir, to moderate this excess of gratitude; and when your heart shall be more at ease, I will explain myself in turn. I certainly wished to serve you; but in that I have been but just; and without it I should have abused the confidence with which madame de Pampadour honoured me by consulting me. Her sensibility and goodness have done the rest. Suffer me to rejoice with you at the smiles of fortune; and let us both return thanks to her to whom you are indebted."

As soon as Boissy had taken leave of me, I went to the minister's; and perceiving that he received me as if he had nothing to say to me, I first asked if I had not something to thank him for? He answered no. If the pensions on the 'Mercure' were disposed of? Yes, they were. If madame de Pompadour had not mentioned me? He assured me she had not said a word about me, and that, if she had named me, he would willingly have put me on the list which he had presented to the king. I was confounded, I confess; for though I had not named myself when she consulted me, I thought myself very sure of being of the number of the persons she meant to propose. I went to her house; and very fortunately I found in her drawing-room madame de Marchais, to whom I related circumstantially my mischance. "And this really astonishes you?" said she: "for my part I am not at all surprised; it is her very self. She has forgotten you." At the same instant she runs to the dressing-room, where madame de Pompadour was; and immediately after I hear bursts of laughter. I thought this a happy presage; and indeed madame de Pompadour, in her way to mass, could not look on me without laughing again at her palpable forgetfulness. "I divined it exactly," said madame de Marchais, on seeing me again; "but it shall all be repaired." I had but a pension of fifty pounds on the 'Mercure,' and I was happy.

M. de Boissy, as editor of the work, did not sufficiently exert himself. It soon became necessary to give him support; and for this purpose he had neither the connections, the resources, nor the activity, of the abbé Raynal, who, in the absence of La Bruyére, conducted it, and conducted it well.

Destitute of assistance, finding nothing passable.

in the papers that were left him, Boissy wrote me a letter, which was a true picture of distress. "You will in vain have given me the Mercure," said he; "this favour will be lost on me, if you do not add that of coming to my aid. Prose or verse, whatever you please, all will be good from your hand. But hasten to extricate me from the difficulty in which I now am; I conjure you in the the name of that friendship which I have vowed to you for the rest of my life."

This letter roused me from my lethargy; I beheld this unhappy editor a prey to ridicule, and the 'Mercure' decried in his hands, should he let his penury be seen. It put me in a fever for the whole night; and it was in this state of crisis and agitation that I first conceived the idea of writing a tale. After having passed the night without closing my eyes, rolling in my fancy the subject of that I have entitled 'Alcibiade,' I got up, wrote it at a breath, without laying down my pen, and sent it off. This tale had an unexpected success. I had required that the name of its author should be kept secret. No one knew to whom to attribute it; and at the dinner of Helvétius, where the best connoisseurs were assembled, they did me the honour of ascribing it to Voltaire, or to Montesquieu.

Boissy, overjoyed at the increase which this novelty had given to the sale of the 'Mercure,' redoubled his prayers to obtain some more pieces of the same kind. I wrote the tale of 'Soliman II' for him, then that of 'Le Scrupule,' and some others. Such was the origin of those moral tales which have since obtained so much repute in Europe. In this instance Boissy did me more benefit than I did him. But he did not long enjoy his good fortune: and at his death, when it became necessary to appoint his successor, "Sire," said madame de Pompadour to the king, "will you not give the 'Mercure' to him who has supported it?" The patent was granted me. I was then obliged to resolve to quit Versailles. At the same time an employment was offered me, which at the moment appeared better and more solid. I know not what instinct, an instinct that has always conducted me tolerably well, prevented me from preferring it.

Marshal Belleisle was minister of war; his only son, the count de Gisors, the best educated and most accomplished young man of the age, had just obtained the lieutenancy and command of the carabineers, of which the count de Provence was colonel. The regiment of carabineers had a secretary attached to the person of the commander, with a salary of five hundred a year; and this place was vacant. A young man of Versailles, whose name was Dorlif, proposed himself, and said that he was known to me. ".Well!" replied the count de Gisors; "engage M. Marmontel to come and see me; I shall be very happy to speak with him." Dorlif wrote little verses, and used to come sometimes to shew them to me: this was all our acquaintance. As for the rest, I believe him an honest, good man; and that was the testimony I gave him. "I am going," said the count de Gisors, whom I saw for the first time; "to speak to you with confidence. This young man would not suit the place: I want a man who from this instant should be my friend, and on whom I can depend as on another self. The duke de Nivernois, my father-in-law, has proposed me one; but I am a little distrustful of the indulgence of the great in their recommendations; and if you can indicate a man, sure, and such as I ask,—not daring," added he, "to pretend to have you yourself—I will take him on your word."

"A month ago, count," answered I, "it would have been for myself that I should have solicited the honour of being attached to you. The patent of the 'Mercure de France,' which the king has just granted me, is an engagement that, without levity, I cannot so soon break; and I'll go and see if among my acquaintance I can find the man who will suit you."

Among my young friends, there was one at Paris, whose name was Suard, of an active mind, penetrating, accurate, and prudent of an amiable character, a gentle and engaging companion, tolerably well imbued with classical learning, eloquent, writing a pure, easy, natural, and elegant style; above all, discreet and reserved, with exemplary morals. I fixed my eyes on him. I begged him to call on me at Paris, whither I went in order to save him the journey. On one side, this place appeared to him very advantageous; on the other, he thought it slavish and painful. France was at war; it would be requisite to follow the count de Gisors in his campaigns; and Suard, naturally indolent, was desirous enough of fortune, but not at the expense of his liberty and repose. He asked for twenty-four hours to reflect on it. The next morning he came to tell me that it was impossible for him to accept of the place; that M. Delaire, his friend, solicited it; and that he was recommended by the duke de Nevernois. I knew Delaire to be a man of understanding, very honest, of a sure and solid character, and great severity of morals. "Bring your friend to me," said I to Suard; "I will propose him, and he will certainly have the place." We agreed with Delaire to say simply, that my choice happened to coincide with that of the duke de Nivernois. M. de Gisors was charmed at this coincidence, and Delaire was accepted. "I must go to him," said the brave youth; "a battle may soon take place, and I am desirous of being present. You will come and join me as soon as possible." Indeed, a few days after his arrival, the battle of Crevelt was fought, in which, at the head of the carabineers, he was mortally wounded. Delaire arrived but to bury him.

I asked M. de Marigny if he thought my place of

secretary compatible with the patent and management of the 'Mercure.' He answered, that he thought it impossible to attend to both. "Then give me my discharge," said I; "for I have not the courage to discharge myself." He gave it me; and madame Geoffrin offered me a lodging in her house. I accepted it with gratitude, but praying her to have the kindness to permit me to pay rent; a condition to which I brought her to consent.

Behold me once again pushed back into that Paris from which I had been so delighted to remove! Behold me more dependent than ever on that public, from whom I thought myself disengaged for life! What then were become of my resolutions? Two sisters in a convent, of an age to be married; the excessive indulgence of an old aunt in giving credit to all comers, and ruining the trade by contracting debts that I was every year obliged to pay; my future comfort, to which I was obliged to look forward, having as yet only reserved four hundred guineas, which I had employed in giving security for M. Odde; the French Academy, at which I could only arrive by the career of letters; lastly, the charm of that literary and philosophic society which recalled me to its bosom,—were the cause, and must be the excuse of that inconstancy that induced me to renounce repose, so gentle and delicious, in order to go and be the editor of a journal at Paris; that is, to condemn myself to the labour of Sisyphus, or to that of the Danaïdes.

BOOK VI.

If the 'Mercure' had been only a simple literary journal, I should have had, in composing it, but one endeavour to fulfil, and but one route to pursue. But formed of different elements, and calculated to embrace a vast variety of objects, it was necessary that in all its relations it should fulfil its functions; that, according to the various tastes of the subscribers, it should supply the place of newspapers to the lovers of news; that it should render an account of the theatres to those who took pleasure in the drama; that it should give a just idea of literary productions, to those who, select in their reading, wished to be instructed or amused; that to the sane and prudent part of the public, who delight in the progress and discoveries of the useful and salutary arts, it should communicate their attempts at improvement, and the happy inventions of the time; that to the lovers of the fine arts, it should announce new productions, and sometimes the writings of authors. The popular parts of science, which might present objects of curiosity to the public, were also a part of its domain. But, above all, it was requisite that it should have a local and social interest for the provincial subscribers, and that the poetic talent of this or that city of the kingdom should there find inserted, from time to time, its enigma, its madrigal, or its epistle:—this part of the 'Mercure,' in appearance the most frivolous, was the most lucrative.

It would have been difficult to imagine a periodical work more diversified, more attractive, and more abundant in resources. Such was the idea I gave of it in the preface to my first volume, in the month of August 1758. "Its form," said I, "renders it susceptible of all that is useful and agreeable; and genius has neither flowers nor fruits with which the 'Mercure' does not adorn itself. Literary, civil, and political, it extracts, it collects, it announces, it embraces all the productions of talent and of taste; it is, as it were, the rendezvous of the arts and sciences, and the channel of their commerce. . . . It is a field that may become more and more fertile, both by the cares employed in its cultivation and by the riches that may be spread over the soil. . . . It may be considered as an extract, or as a collection: as an extract, it is I whom it concerns; as a collection, its success depends on the aid I shall receive. In the critical part, the worthy man whom I succeed, without daring to pretend to replace him, leaves me an example of precision and prudence, of candour and honesty, which to me shall be law. . . . . To men of letters I propose to speak the language of truth, decorum, and esteem; and my attention to notice the beauties of their works, will justify the freedom with which I shall observe their defects. I do not blush to avow, that no one knows better than I how much a young author is to be pitied, who, when abandoned to insult, has modesty enough to forbid himself personal defence. Such an author, whoever he may be, will find in me, not a passionate avenger, but, according to my abilities, an equitable judge. An irony, a parody, a raillery, prove nothing, and enlighten no one; they are traits that sometimes amuse: they are even more interesting to vulgar readers than an honest and sensible criticism; the moderate tone of reason has nothing consoling for envy, nothing flattering for malignity; but my design is not to prostitute my pen to the envious and malicious. . . . . With respect to the collective part of the work, although I purpose to contribute to it as much as I am able, if it be but to supply what may be deficient, I do not depend on my own exertions; all my hope is in the benevolence and the aid of men of letters; and I dare trust that hope is well founded. If some of the most estimable have not disdained to confide to the 'Mercure' the amusements of their leisure, often even the fruits of serious study, at a time when the success of this journal was advantageous to one man only,—what assistance ought I not to expect from the concourse of talents interested to give it support? The 'Mercure' is no longer a private fund; it is a public domain, of which I am but the farmer and steward."

Thus was my work announced: and it was well seconded. The moment was favourable A flight of young poets began to try their wings. I encouraged their first efforts, by publishing the brilliant essays of Malfilatre; and thus raised hopes which he would not have deceived, if a premature death had not torn him from us. The just praises that I gave to the poem entitled 'Jumonville,' revived in the feeling and virtuous Thomas that great talent which inhuman critics had frozen. I presented to the public the first offerings of the Translation of Virgil's Georgics; and I venture to predict, that if this divine poem could be translated into elegant and harmonious French verse, it would be done by the abbé Delille. By inserting in the 'Mercure' a *héroïde* of Colardeau, I made the public feel how nearly the style of this young poet approached, by its melody, its purity, its grace, and its dignity, to the perfection of the models of the art. I spoke advantageously of the *héroïdes* of la Harpe. Finally, when the 'Hypermnestre' of Lemierre was performed with success, "Behold at present," said I, "three new tragic poets, who create the fairest hopes: the author of 'Iphigénie en Tauride,' by his sage and simple manner of gradually increasing the interest of the action, and by bursts of poetic fire worthy of the greatest masters; the author of 'Astarbé,' by animated poetry, by a full and harmonious versification, and by the dignity and boldness of a character which wanted nothing to put it in action, but worthy contrasts; and the author of 'Hypermnestre,' by pictures of the greatest force. It should be the public care," added I, "to protect, to encourage, to console them for the lunacy of envy. The arts want the torch of criticism, and the spur of glory. It is not to the 'Cid' persecuted, it is to the 'Cid' triumphant after persecution, that

'Cinna' owed its birth. Encouragement inspires neglect and presumption only in little minds; to elevated souls, to lively imaginations, in a word, to great talents, the intoxication of success becomes the intoxication of genius. For them, there is but one poison to fear; it is that which cools them."

While I pleaded the cause of men of letters, I did not fail to mix with temperate praises a tolerably severe but innocent criticism and in the same tone that a friend would have assumed with his friend. By conciliating the favour of young men of letters in this spirit of benevolence and equity, I had them almost all for co-operators.

The tribute of the provinces was yet more abundant. It was not all precious; but if, in the pieces of verse or prose that were sent me, there were only some marks of negligence, some incorrectness, some faults in detail, I was careful to retouch them. Sometimes, even if a few good verses or interesting lines occurred to me, I slipped them in without saying a word; and never did the authors complain to me of these little infidelities.

In the arts and sciences I had likewise a variety of resources. In medicine, at that time, the problem of inoculation was agitated. The comet predicted by Hally, and announced by Clairault, fixed the eyes of astronomers; natural philosophy afforded me curious observations to publish: for instance, I gave considerable satisfaction by making public the means of cooling liquors in summer. Chemistry communicated a new remedy for the bite of vipers, and the invaluable secret of restoring the drowned to life. Surgery imparted her bold experiments, and her astonishing success. Natural history, under the pencil of Buffon, afforded me a multitude of pictures, of which I had the choice. Vaucanson gave me his ingenious machines to describe and present to the public: the architect Leroi, and the engraver Cochin, after having travelled, to observe with the eyes of artists, one the ruins of Greece, and the other the wonders of Italy, came emulous with each other to enrich me with brilliant descriptions or learned remarks; and my extracts from their travels formed an amusing journey for my readers. Cochin, a man of understanding, and whose pen was scarcely less pure and correct than his graver, wrote me some excellent disquisitions on the arts that were the objects of his studies. I recollect two of them that painters and sculptors have surely not forgotten; one 'On reflected light;' the other 'On the difficulties of painting and sculpture, compared with each other.' It was he who dictated the account I gave to the public of the exhibition of pictures in 1759; one of the most beautiful that had ever entered, or that had since been seen, in the hall of the arts. This account was a model of sound and benevolent criticism; it justly indicated the defects, and extolled the beauties. The public were not deceived, and the artists were satisfied.

At this time, a new career was opened for eloquence. The French Academy invited all young orators to celebrate the praises of great men; and what was my joy in having to announce that in these lists the first who had just borne the prize, by a worthy eulogy on Maurice de Saxe, was the interesting youth whose courage I had so often animated, the author of the poem of 'Jumonville,' who was not less pleased with the sincerity of my counsels than with the equity of my praise, and who, in the secrecy of most intimate friendship, had made me the confidant of his thoughts, and the censor of his writings!

I had formed a correspondence with all the academies of the kingdom, as well for the arts as for letters; and, without reckoning their productions which they were pleased to send me, the bare subjects for their prizes were interesting to read, on account of the sagacious and profound views announced by the questions they proposed for solution, whether in morality, in political economy, or in the useful, domestic, and salutary arts. I myself was sometimes astonished at the luminous extent of these questions, that were sent us from every side and from the remotest corners of the provinces. Nothing, in my opinion, better marked the direction, the tendency, and the progress, of the public mind.

Thus, without ceasing to be amusing and frivolous in its light part, the 'Mercure' did not fail by its utility to acquire consistence and weight. On my part, contributing all in my power to render it at once agreeable and useful, I often added to it one of those tales, in which I always endeavoured to mix some portion of interesting morality. The apology for the theatre, which I wrote in answer to Rousseau's letter to d'Alembert on the stage, had all the success that truth could have when it was engaged with sophistry, and reason when, hand to hand and in close contest, it combats eloquence.

But as we should never be either so proud or forgetful as to be guilty of ingratitude, I will honestly tell you what was occasionally one of my resources. At Paris the republic of letters was divided into several classes, that had little or no communication with each other. I neglected none of them; and the little verses that were made in inferior societies, all that had grace or nature, were dear to me. At a jeweller's in the place Dauphine I had often dined with two poets of the old Opera Comique, whose genius was gaiety, and whose poetic fire never was so vivid as under the vine-arbour of a tavern. To them the happiest of all states was intoxication; but, before they were too far gone, they used to have moments of inspiration that seemed to confirm what Horace has said of wine. One of them, whose name was Galet, passed for an idle rake. I never saw him but when at table, and I mention him only as the friend of Panard, who was a good man, and whom I loved.

This idle rake, however, was an original whose singularity may occupy a moment. He was a grocer in Lombard street, who, more attentive to the theatre of 'La Foir' than to his shop, had ruined himself before I knew him. He was in a dropsy, and did not drink the less, nor was he the less jovial: he was equally indifferent about death or life; and in penury, in captivity, on the bed of sickness, and almost in the agonies of death, his gaiety did not forsake him; to him these things were sport.

After his bankruptcy, he fled to the Temple, then the asylum for insolvent debtors: and as he every day received bills from his creditors, "Here I am," said he, "lodged in the Temple, where bills are booked." When his dropsy was on the point of suffocating him, the vicar of the Temple came to administer the extreme unction: "Ah! Mr abbé," said he, "what! you come to clean my boots? You need not have troubled yourself, for I am going by water." The same day he wrote to his friend Collé; and wishing him a happy new year in some couplets to the air of *Accompagné de plusieurs autres*, he thus terminated his merry career:

> "Receive, dearest Collé, my farewell in rhyme,
>   I'm just setting off to go home;
> It should be much longer, if I had more time,
>   But the grave-digger waits till I come."

The good Panard, as heedless as his friend, as forgetful of the past, and as negligent of the future, had, in his misfortunes, rather the tranquillity of a child, than the indifference of a philosopher. The care of feeding, lodging, and clothing himself, did not give him any concern. They were the business of his friends: and he had some so kind as to merit this confidence. In his manners, as in his mind, he had a great deal of the simple and unaffected nature of La Fontaine. No exterior ever announced less delicacy; yet it was inherent in his fancy and in his language. More than once at table, when rosy with the vapours of wine, I have heard issue from that heavy mass, and that thick covering, impromptu couplets full of ease, grace, and delicacy. For this reason, when, compiling the 'Mercure' of the month, I wanted some pretty verses, I used to go and see my friend Panard. "Rummage the litter in my wig-box," he used to say. This box was indeed a true litter, in which the verses of this amiable poet, scrawled on dirty strips of paper, lay heaped in confusion. Seeing almost all his manuscripts spotted with wine, I reproached him with it. "Oh! take those, take those," cried he; "they have the seal of genius." He had so tender an affection for wine, that he always spoke of it as of the friend of his heart; and with the glass in his hand, looking at the object of his worship and delight, he would suffer himself to be so moved by it, that the tears would start into his eyes. I have seen him shed them for a very singular reason. And do not take for a tale the following trait, which will give you the finished portrait of a drunkard.

After the death of his friend Galet, meeting him in my walks, I wished to express the part I took in his affliction. "Ah! sir," said he, "it is very lively and very profound. A friend of thirty years, with whom I passed my life! In my walks, at the theatre, at the wine shop, always together! I have lost him. I shall sing no more, I shall drink no more with him. He is dead. I am alone in the world. I don't know what to do with myself." As he complained thus, the good man melted into tears: and so far, nothing could be more natural. But observe what he added: "You know that he died at the Temple? I went there to weep and lament over his tomb. But what a tomb! Ah! sir, they have laid him under a water-spout: he who never since he understood reason, tasted water!"

You are now going to behold me living at Paris with people of very different characters; and I should have a beautiful gallery of portraits to paint, if I had colours lively enough for that purpose. But I will at least attempt to sketch their features.

I have said that so long as madame de Tencin lived, madame Geoffrin was in the habit of going to see her; and the cunning old woman penetrated so well the motive of her visits, that she used to say to her guests, "Do you know why la Geoffrin comes here? It is to see what she shall be able to collect from my inventory." And indeed, at her death, a part of her company, and the best part of what remained (for Fontenelle and Montesquieu were no longer living) had passed into the new society; which was not limited to that little colony. Rich enough to make her house the rendezvous of letters and of the arts, and perceiving that it would be the means of affording to her old age an amusing society and an honourable existence, madame Geoffrin had two weekly dinners at her own house; one on Mondays, for artists; the other on Wednesdays, for men of letters; and it is a remarkable thing, that without any tincture either of letters or the arts, this woman, who in her life had never studied anything but very superficially, did not appear ignorant in either of these societies: she was even at her ease; but she had the good sense never to speak but of what she well knew, and to listen, on all other subjects, to the better informed; always politely attentive, without even appearing wearied at what she did not understand; but still more adroit in presiding, in watching over, and in holding under her command, these two societies, naturally inclined to a freedom that borders on licence. She knew the art of setting bounds to this freedom, and by a word, or a gesture, as by an invisible thread, of restoring order and decorum. " Come, that's well," was commonly the signal of prudence that she gave to her guests; and whatever might be the vivacity of a conversation that passed the limit, at her house you might say what Virgil has said of bees:

" Hi motus animorum, atque hæc certamina tanta
Pulveris exigui jactu compressa quiescent."

Her's was a singular character, and difficult to comprehend and paint, because it was all in demi-tints and shades; and, though very decided, it had not one of those distinguishing traits by which disposition is usually marked and defined. She had kindness, but very little sensibility; she was beneficent, but without one of the charms of benevolence; eager to aid the unfortunate, but without seeing them, for fear of being moved by them; a sure, faithful, even an officious friend, but timid, disturbed, while in the very act of serving her friends, with the fear of compromising either her credit or her repose. She was simple in her taste, dress, and furniture, but nice in her simplicity; having the delicacies of luxury in all their refinement, but nothing of their brilliancy or their vanity; modest in her air, carriage, and manners, but with a fund of pride, and even a little vainglory. Nothing flattered her more than her commerce with the great. At their houses she saw them but rarely; there she was not at her ease; but she had the secret of attracting them to her's by a coquetry imperceptibly flattering; and in the easy, natural, half-respectful and half-familiar air with which she received them, I thought I saw an extreme address. Always free, and on the verge of propriety, yet it was never overstepped. To be in favour with heaven, without being out of favour with her society, she used to indulge in a kind of clandestine devotion: she went to mass as privately as others go to an intrigue; she had an apartment in a convent of nuns, and a tribune, or pew, in the church of the Capuchins, with as much mystery as the gallant women of that day had their private houses for their amours. All kind of state disgusted her. Her greatest care was to make no noise. She was ardently desirous of celebrity, and of acquiring a great consideration in the world; but she would have it tranquil. A little like the lunatic who fancied himself made of glass, she avoided, as so many rocks, all that could expose her to the shock of human passions: and thence her indolent timidity, whenever a good office required courage. The man for whom, with a full heart, she would have freely opened her purse, was not equally sure of the support of her tongue; and on this point she consoled herself by ingenious excuses. For example, it was her maxim that, when we hear our friends abused in company, we should never undertake warmly their defence, nor contend with the defamer; for that was the sure way to irritate the viper and refine its venom. She used to say that a man should praise his friends but very temperately, and for their qualities, not for their actions; for on hearing it is said of some one that he is sincere and beneficent, each can say to himself, I too am beneficent and sincere. "But," said she, "if you cite of him a laudable act, an act of virtue, since each cannot say that he has done as much, he takes this praise for a reproach, and seeks to depress it." What she most esteemed in a friend, was an attentive prudence, so that she might never be compromised; and as an example she used to cite Bernard, the man of all others most coldly precise in his actions and words. "With him," she used to say, "one may be at ease; no one complains of him; it is never necessary to defend him." This was a hint for heads a little too hot, like mine, of whom there were more than one in her society; and if any one of those she loved happened to be in danger, or in trouble, whatever might be the cause, and whether he were right or wrong, her first impulse was to accuse him herself: on which point, perhaps too warmly, I one day took the liberty of telling her, that her friends ought to be all infallible and always fortunate.

One of her foibles was the desire of intermeddling in the affairs of her friends, of being their confidant, their counsel, and their guide. By initiating her in your secrets, and suffering yourself to be guided and sometimes scolded by her, you were sure of touching her in the most sensible part. But indocility, however respectful, cooled her instantly; and by a little dry anger, she showed how much she was offended. It is true that, to conduct yourself according to the rules of prudence, you could not do better than consult her. The knowledge of life was her supreme science; her notions on all other subjects were trivial and common; but, in the study of manners and customs, in the knowledge of men, and above all of women, she was profound, and capable of giving good and useful instruction. If then a little self-love were mixed with this desire of counselling and guiding, it was likewise accompanied by kindness, by a wish to be useful, and by sincere friendship.

With regard to her mind, although cultivated solely by her commerce with the world, it was delicate, accurate, and penetrating. A natural taste, a right understanding, gave her, when she spoke, the appropriate word and turn of expression. She wrote purely, simply, and in a concise and clear style; but like a woman who had been badly educated, and who liked to show it. In a charming eulogy that your uncle has written of her, you will read that an Italian abbé being come to offer to her the dedication of an Italian and French grammar: " To me, sir," said she, " the dedication of a grammar! to me who do not even know how to spell!" It was the simple truth. Her peculiar talent was that of telling a story well; in this she excelled, and willingly exerted herself to enliven the table, but without affectation, without art, without pretension, solely to set the example; for she neglected none of the means she possessed to render her society agreeable.

Of this society, the gayest man, the most animated, and the most amusing in his gaiety, was d'Alembert. After having passed his morning in algebraic calculations, and in solving the problems of mechanics or astronomy, he came from his study like a boy just loose from school, seeking only to enjoy himself; and by the lively and pleasant turn that his mind, luminous, solid, and profound as it was, then assumed, he soon made us forget the philosopher and the man of science, to admire in him every quality that can delight and engage. The source of this natural gaiety was a pure mind, free from passion, contented with itself, and in the daily enjoyment of some new truth that recompensed and crowned his labours; a privilege which the mathematics exclusively possess, and which no other kind of study can completely obtain.

The serenity of Mairan, and his gentle and cheerful temper, had the same causes and the same principle. Age had done for him what nature had done for d'Alembert. He was temperate in all the emotions of his soul; and what warmth he had left was in the vivacity of Gascon wit, but steady, sage, and correct, of an original turn, and of sweet and delicate flavour. It is true, that the philosopher of Béziers was sometimes disturbed about what was passing in China; but, when any letters from his friend father Parennin arrived, and calmed his inquietude, his eyes sparkled with joy.

Oh! my children! what souls are those that are agitated only about the motion of the ecliptic, or the manners and arts of the Chinese! No vice degrades them, no regret decays them, no passion saddens and torments them; they are free, with that freedom which is the companion of joy, and without which there never was any pure and lasting gaiety.

Marivaux would have been very glad to have had this jovial humour too; but he had a business in his head that incessantly pre-occupied him, and gave him a sullen air. As he had acquired by his works the reputation of a subtle and refined wit, he thought himself obliged to give perpetual proofs of this wit, and he was continually on the watch for ideas susceptible of opposition or analysis, in order to turn or wind them as his fancy dictated. He would agree that such a thing was true, as far as a certain point, or in a certain view; but there was always some restriction, some distinction to make, which no one perceived but himself. This exertion of the attention was laborious to him, and often painful to others; but it sometimes gave birth to happy perceptions, and brilliant flashes of genius. Yet it was easy to discover by the inquietude of his looks, that he was in pain about the success he already had, or about that he was about to obtain. There never was, I believe, self-love more delicate, more wayward, or more fearful; but as he carefully humoured that of others, we respected his; and we only pitied him that he could not resolve to be simple and natural.

Chastellux, whose mind never was sufficiently clear, but who had a vast deal of understanding, and in whom very lively glimmerings would pierce from time to time the light vapour that enveloped his ideas, brought into our society the most engaging character, and the most lovely candour. Whether he were mistrustful of the accuracy of his opinions, and sought to assure himself of it, or whether he wished to refine them by discussion, he was fond of debate, and willingly engaged in it, but with grace and good faith; and as soon as his eye caught a glimpse of truth, whether it came from you or from himself, he was happy. No man ever employed his understanding better in enjoying that of others. A witticism, an ingenious story opportunely told, charmed him; you might see him leap for joy at them; and in proportion as conversation became more brilliant, the eyes and countenance of Chastellux became animated: all success flattered him as if it had been his own.

The abbé Morellet, with more order and clearness in a very rich magazine of every kind of knowledge, possessed in conversation a source of sound, pure, profound ideas, that, without ever being exhausted, never overflowed. He showed himself at our dinners with an openness of soul, a just and firm mind, and with as much rectitude in his heart as in his understanding. One of his talents, and the most distinguishing, was a turn of pleasantry delicately ironical, of which Swift alone had found the secret. With this facility of being severe, if he had been inclined, no man was ever less so; and, if he ever permitted himself to indulge in personal raillery, it was but a rod in his hand to chastise insolence or punish malignity.

Saint Lambert, with a delicate politeness, though a little cold, had in conversation the same elegant turn, the same acuteness of mind, that you remark in his writings. Without being naturally gay, he became animated by the gaiety of others; and, on philosophical or literary subjects, no one conversed with sounder reason or a more exquisite taste. This taste was that of the little court of Luneville, where he had lived, and the tone of which he had preserved.

Helvétius, preoccupied by his ambition of literary celebrity, came to us, his head heated with his morning's work. To write a book that should be distinguished in his age, his first care had been to seek for some undiscovered truth to publish, or some bold and novel idea to broach and support. But, as new truths have been infinitely rare for the last two thousand years, he had taken for his thesis the paradox which he had developed in his work 'De l' Esprit.' Whether it were that by force of contention he had persuaded himself of what he wished to persuade others, or whether he were still struggling against his own doubts, and sought to conquer them, we were amused at seeing him bring successively on the carpet the questions that occupied or the difficulties that embarrassed him; and, after having afforded him for some time the pleasure of hearing them discussed, he suffered himself to be carried along with the current of our conversation. He then gave himself wholly to it with infinite warmth; as simple, as natural, as ingenuously sincere in his familiar converse, as you see him systematic and sophistical in his writings. Nothing less resembles the simplicity of his character, and of his habitual life, than the premeditated and factitious singularity of his works; and this want of harmony will always be found between the manners and opinions of those who fatigue themselves by imagining strange things. Helvétius had in his soul the complete contrary of what he had said. There never was a better man: liberal, generous without ostentation, and beneficent because he was good, he conceived the idea of calumniating all honest men and himself, by giving to moral actions no motive but self-love. Abstracted from his writings, we loved him such as he really was, and you will soon see what an asylum his house was for men of letters.

A man still more ambitious of glory than he, was Thomas; but, more in tune with himself, he expected success only from the rare talent he possessed of expressing his sentiments and thoughts; being sure of giving to common subjects the originality of lofty eloquence, and to known truths new development, new extension, and new lustre. It is true, that, absorbed in meditation, and incessantly pre-occupied by that which might acquire him ample fame, he neglected the little attentions and the trifling merit of being engaging in society. The gravity of his character was gentle, but reserved; silent, smiling but seldom at the gaiety of conversation to which he never contributed. He even scarcely ever spoke freely on subjects that were familiar to him, unless it were in an intimate and confined circle: it was there only that he shone by the splendour of intellect, and astonished by grandeur of capacity. At our dinners he was of our number, and it was only by reflection on his literary merit, and on his moral qualities, that he there enjoyed consideration. Thomas always sacrificed to virtue, truth, glory, but never to the graces; and he lived in an age when, without their influence and favour, a brilliant reputation in literature was scarcely attainable.

I cannot mention the graces without speaking of one who had all their gifts, both in mind and language, and who was the only woman that madame Geoffrin had admitted to her dinners of men of letters; it was the friend of d'Alembert, mademoiselle Lespinasse: a wonderful composition of correctness, reason, prudence, with the liveliest fancy, the most ardent soul, the most inflammable imagination that has existed since the days of Sappho. That fire, that circulated in her veins, and which gave to her mind such activity, brilliancy, and so many charms, has prematurely consumed her. I will tell you hereafter what regret her loss occasioned. Here I only mark the place she occupied at our dinners, where her presence excited inexpressible interest. The continued object of attention, whether she listened or whether she spoke (and no one spoke better) without coquetry, she inspired us with the innocent desire of pleasing her; without prudery, she made freedom feel how far it might venture, without disturbing modesty or wounding decorum.

It is not my intention to describe the whole circle of our convivial friends. There were some idle ones, who scarcely did anything but enjoy: men well informed however, but covetous of their riches, and who, without giving themselves the trouble of sowing, came but to reap. The abbé Raynal was most certainly not of this number, and in the use he made of the vast fund of knowledge he possessed, if he sometimes indulged in excess, it was not an excess of economy. The robust vigour of his philosophy had not then shown itself; the great mass of his information was not completely formed; sagacity, accuracy, precision, were then the most distinguishing qualities of his mind, and he added to them a goodness of heart and an amenity of manners that made him dear to us all. It was observed, at the same time, that the facility of his elocution, and the stores of his memory, were not sufficiently tempered. His brilliant flow of expression was rarely susceptible of the dialogue; it has been only in his old age, that, less vivid and less abundant, he has understood the pleasures of conversation.

Whether it had entered into the plan of madame Geoffrin to attract to her house the most distinguished foreigners who came to Paris, and by that means to render it celebrated throughout Europe, or whether it were the consequence and natural effect of the charm and lustre this house received from the society of men of letters, there arrived neither prince, nor minister, nor men nor women of distinction, who, on going to see madame Geoffrin, were not ambitious of being invited to our dinners, and who did not feel great pleasure at seeing us there assembled. It was particularly in those days that madame Geoffrin displayed all the charms of her understanding, and used to say to us, "Let us be agreeable." And it was rare indeed that these dinners failed to be animated by excellent conversation.

Among those foreigners who came to make Paris their residence, or to reside there some time, she selected the most learned, and the most engaging, and they were admitted as being of the number of her convivial friends. I shall distinguish three of them, who, for the charm of wit and abundance of information, were not surpassed by the most cultivated of the French: they were the abbé Galiani, the marquis of Caraccioli, since ambassador from Naples, and the count de Creutz, the Swedish minister.

The abbé Galiani was in his person the prettiest little harlequin that Italy ever produced; but on the shoulders of this harlequin was the head of Machiavel. An epicurian in his philosophy, and with a melancholy soul, having looked at everything on the side of ridicule, there was nothing either in politics or in morality on which he had not some good story to tell; and these stories had always the merit of pertinence, and the wit of an unforeseen and ingenious allusion. Figure to yourself too the prettiest little natural graces in his manner of relating the gesticulation, and you may conceive what pleasure we derive from the contrast between the profound sense of the story and the bantering air of him who told it. I do not at all exaggerate, when I say that we forgot everything in order to hear him, even for whole hours. But when his part was played, he was like a cypher in the company; and, sad and mute in a corner, he had the air of impatiently waiting the watchword to re-enter on the stage. It was with his arguments as with his stories; he would be listened to. If he were sometimes interrupted, he would say, "But let me finish; you shall soon have full leisure to answer me." And when, after having described an ample circle of inductions (for that was his way) he at last concluded, if any one showed an inclination to reply, you might see him slide in among the crowd, and quickly escape.

Caraccioli, at first sight, had in his physiognomy the thick and massive air with which you would paint stupidity. To animate his eyes and disengage his features, it was necessary that he should speak.

But then, and in proportion as that lively, piercing, and luminous intelligence with which he was gifted awoke, it sent forth beams of light; and acuteness, gaiety, originality of thought, simplicity of expression, the grace of an animated smile, and a look of sensibility, all united to give an engaging, intelligent, and interesting character to ugliness. He spoke our language ill, and painfully; but he was eloquent in his own; and when the French term did not occur to him, he used to borrow the word, the turn, the image, he wanted, from the Italian. Thus he every moment enriched his discourse with a thousand bold and picturesque expressions that excited our envy. He accompanied them too with those Neapolitan gestures that, in the abbé Galiani, so well animated expression; and it was said of both that they had wit even to their fingers' ends. Both too had excellent stories, and they had almost all a delicate, moral, and profound object. Caraccioli had studied men as a philosopher; but he had observed them more as a politician and a statesman, than as a satirical moralist. He had contemplated the manners, the customs, and the policy of nations on a large scale; and if he cited some particular features of them, it was only as examples, and in support of the inferences he drew. In knowledge, his riches were inexhaustible, and he distributed them with the most engaging simplicity; besides, he had in our eyes the merit of being an excellent man. Not one of us would have thought of making a friend of the abbé Galiani; each of us was ambitious of the friendship of Caraccioli; and I, who have long enjoyed it, cannot express how desirable it was.

But one of the men to whom I was most dear, and whom I most tenderly loved, was the count de Creutz. He too was of the literary society and dinners of madame Geoffrin: less eager to please, less occupied with the care of attracting attention, often pensive, still oftener absent, but the most charming of the convivial circle, when without distraction he gave himself freely to us. It was on him that nature had really bestowed sensibility, warmth, the delicacy of moral sentiment and of taste, the love of all that is beautiful, and the passion of genius as well as that of virtue: it was to him that she had granted the gift of expressing and painting in touches of fire, all that had struck his imagination or vividly seized on his soul: never was a man born a poet, if this man were not so. Still young, his mind ornamented with a prodigious variety of information, speaking French like ourselves, and almost all the languages of Europe like his own, without reckoning the learned languages; versed in all kinds of ancient and modern literature; talking of chemistry as a chemist, of natural history as a pupil of Linnæus, and of Sweden and Spain distinctly as a curious observer of the properties of climates and of their divers productions: he was to us a source of knowledge, embellished by the most brilliant elocution.

This may suffice to make you feel what interest, and what a charm this rendezvous of men of letters must have had. As to myself, I kept my corner there, neither too bold nor too timid; gay, simple, even somewhat free; well liked in the society, dear to those I most esteemed and most loved. With respect to madame Geoffrin, though I lived in her house, I was not one of the first in her favour; yet she was pleased with me, for animating in my turn, and tolerably often too, our dinners and conversations, either by little stories, or by traits of pleasantry that I accommodated to her taste; but, as to my personal conduct, I had not enough complaisance in consulting her, and in following the advice she gave me: and, on her part, she had so little confidence in my prudence, that she feared lest I should occasion her some of those vexations she sometimes suffered from the want of caution in her friends. With me, therefore, she was on a footing of timid and cautious kindness; and I, reserved towards her, endeavoured only to be agreeable: I would not suffer myself to be governed.

At the same time she saw me a favourite with her whole society: and at her Monday's dinner I was not less kindly welcomed than at her literary banquet. The artists liked me, because, at once curious and docile, I talked to them incessantly of what they knew better than I. I have forgotten to say that, under my lodgings at Versailles, was a large room filled with pictures that were taken successively to decorate the palace, and which were almost all from the pencil of the greatest masters. This room was my recreation, and my morning's walk; I used to pass hours together there with the good Portail, the worthy guardian of this treasure, in conversing with him on the genius and style of the different schools of Italy, and on the distinctive character of the great masters. In the gardens I had formed some comparative ideas of ancient and modern sculpture. These preliminary studies enabled me to reason with our artists; and by leaving them the advantage and the amusement of instructing me, I had in their eyes the merit of being delighted to listen to them, and to profit by their lessons. With them I took great care to display no other literary knowledge than that which interested the fine arts. I had no difficulty in perceiving that, with good natural understandings, they almost all wanted information and culture. The good Carle Vanloo possessed in a high degree all the talents that a painter could have without genius; but he had no inspiration; and to supply it, he had cultivated but few of those studies that elevate the soul, and fill the imagination with great objects and great ideas.

Vernet, admirable in the art of painting water, air, light, and the play of the elements, had all the models of his compositions very vividly present to his fancy; beyond that, although gay enough, he was but a common man. Soufflot was a man of sense, very circumspect in his conduct, a skilful and learned architect; but his ideas were all commensurate by the rule and compass. Boucher had some fire in his imagination, but little truth, and still less dignity; the graces he had seen were not of a good family; he painted Venus and the Virgin after the nymphs of the theatre; and his language, as well as his pictures, savoured of the manners and tone of his models. Lemoine, the sculptor, tenderly inclined our hearts to friendship by the modest simplicity that accompanied his genius; but even on his art, which he knew so well, he spoke little; and he scarcely made an answer to the praises that were given him: a touching timidity in a man whose look was all mind and soul. Latour had some enthusiasm, and he employed it in painting the philosophers of that time. But his brain was so disturbed about politics and morality, on which he reasoned most learnedly, that he fancied himself humbled if you talked to him of painting. You, my dear children, have a sketch of my portrait painted by him: it was in return for the complaisance with which I listened to him, regulating the destinies of Europe. With the other guests I instructed myself on what concerned their art; and hence these dinners of artists had for me the interest of pleasure and utility.

Among the amateurs who partook of these dinners, there were some well stored with profitable studies. With these I had no difficulty in varying the conversation, nor in reviving it when it languished; and they seemed to be well pleased with my manner of conversing. One only, showed me no kindness; and in his cold politeness I perceived aversion: it was the count de Caylus.

I cannot say which of the two had anticipated the other; but I had scarcely known his character when

I conceived as strong a dislike to him as he ever felt to me. I never gave myself the trouble of examining in what I could have displeased him. But I well knew what displeased me in him. It was the importance he gave himself for the most futile merit, and the most trivial of talents; it was the value he attached to his minute researches, and to his antique gewgaws; it was the kind of sovereignty he had usurped over the artists, and which he abused, by favouring ordinary talents that paid their court to him, and by depressing those who, more confident in themselves, did not stoop to solicit his support. It was, in short, a very adroit and refined vanity, and a most bitter and imperious pride, under the rough and simple forms in which he had the art of enveloping it. Supple and pliant with the placemen on whom the artists depended, he obtained a credit with the former, the influence of which was dreaded by the latter. He insinuated himself into the company of men of information, and persuaded them to write memorials on the toys he had bought at his brokers; he made a magnificent collection of this trumpery, which he called antique; he proposed prizes on Isis and Osiris, in order to have the air of being himself initiated in their mysteries; and with this charlatanism of erudition, he crept into the academies, without knowing either Greek or Latin. He had so often said, he had so often published, by those whom he paid to praise him, that in architecture he was the restorer " of the simple style, of simple beauty, of beautiful simplicity," that the ignorant believed it; and by his correspondence with the dilettanti, he made himself pass in Italy and all Europe for the inspirer of the fine arts. I therefore felt for him that species of natural antipathy which ingenuous and simple men always feel for impostors.

After having dined at madame Geoffrin's with men of letters or with the artists, I was again with her in the evening in a more intimate society; for she had also granted me the favour of admitting me to her little suppers. The feast was very moderate; it was commonly a chicken, some spinage, and omelet. The company were not numerous; they consisted at most of five or six of her particular friends, or of three or four men and women of the first fashion selected to their taste, and reciprocally happy to be together. But, whatever these convivial circles might be, Bernard and I were admitted to them. One of them only had excluded Bernard, but had approved of me. The group that composed it consisted of three ladies and but one gentleman. The three ladies, who might well be likened to the three goddesses of Mount Ida, were the beautiful countess de Brionne, the charming marchioness de Duras, and the fascinating countess d'Egmont. Their Paris was the prince Louis de Rohan. But I suspect that at that time he gave the apple to Minerva; for, to my mind, the Venus of the supper was the seducing and engaging d'Egmont. She was the daughter of marshal Richelieu, and had the vivacity, wit, and graces of her father: she had too, as was said, his volatile and voluptuous disposition; but this was what neither madame Geoffrin nor myself had any appearance of knowing. The young marchioness de Duras, with as much of modesty as madame d'Egmont had of charming grace, gave us the idea of Juno, by her noble severity, and by a character of beauty that had neither elegance nor delicacy. As for the countess de Brionne, if she were not Venus herself, it was not that in the perfect regularity of her form, and of all her features, she did not unite all that can be imagined to paint ideal beauty. Of all charms, she wanted but one, without which there is no Venus on earth, and which made the witchery of madame d'Egmont; it was the air of voluptuousness. As to the prince de Rohan, he was young, active, wild, with a good heart, lofty by starts when in concurrence with dignities that rivalled his own, but gaily familiar with men of letters who were free and simple like myself.

You may readily conceive, that at these little suppers, my self-love was in league with all the means I might have of being amusing and agreeable. The new tales that I was then writing, and of which these ladies had the first offerings, formed, before or after supper, entertaining readings. They met one another to hear them, and when the little supper was prevented by any accident, they assembled at dinner at madame de Brionne's. I confess, that no success ever flattered me so sensibly as that which these readings obtained in this little circle, where wit, taste, beauty, all the graces, were my judges, or rather my applauders. There was not a single trait, either in my colouring or my dialogue, however minutely delicate and subtle, that was not forcibly felt; and the pleasure I gave had the air of enchantment. What enraptured me was, to see in such perfection the most beautiful eyes in the world swimming in tears at the little touching scenes where I made love or nature weep. But, in spite of the indulgence of an excessive politeness, I well perceived too the cold and feeble passages which they passed over in silence, as well as those where I had mistaken the word, the tone of nature, or the just shade of truth; and these passages I noted, to correct them at my leisure.

From the idea I give you of madame Geoffrin's society, you will doubtless imagine that to me it might well have supplied the place of all other company. But I had some old and good friends at Paris, who were very happy to see me again, and with whom I was highly delighted to pass again some of my leisure hours. Madame Harenc, madame Desfourniels, mademoiselle Clairon, and particularly madame d'Heronville, had a right to partake of my dearest moments. I had made myself, too, some new friends, whose society was very charming.

Besides I had well observed, that to be estimated by madame Geoffrin at your real value, it was necessary to preserve with her a certain medium between negligence and assiduity; neither to let her complain of the one, nor weary herself with the other; and, in the attentions you shewed her, to neglect nothing, but to be prodigal of nothing. Eager attentions oppressed her: even of the most engaging society, she would only take just what suited her inclination, at her own hours and at her ease. I therefore imperceptibly sought occasion of having some sacrifice to make to her; and, in talking of the life I led in society, I made her understand, without affectation, that the time I passed at her house might have been very gratefully spent elsewhere. It is thus that, during the ten years I was her tenant, without inspiring in her any very tender friendship, I never lost either her esteem or her favour; and till her unfortunate paralytic affection, I never ceased to be of the number of those men of letters who were her convivial companions and friends.

Yet I should tell the whole truth: madame Geoffrin's society wanted one of the pleasures that I esteem most highly, the liberty of thought. With her mild " Come, that's well," she never ceased to keep our minds as it were in leading strings; and I partook of dinners elsewhere at which there was more freedom.

The freest, or rather most licentious of all, was that which was given every week by a farmer-general, whose name was Pelletier, to eight or ten bachelors, all jovial friends. At this dinner, the men of the wildest heads were Collé and young Crébillon. Between them it was a continual assault of excellent pleasantry, and he that pleased might enter the lists. They never indulged in personality;

the self-love of talent was alone attacked, but it was attacked without indulgence; and it was requisite to shake it off and sacrifice it to these combats. Collé was brilliant beyond all expression; and Crébillon, his adversary, had singularly the address of animating by exciting him. Wearied of being an idle spectator, I sometimes darted into the circle at my peril, and received lessons of modesty that were rather severe. Sometimes too, a certain Monticourt would engage in the dispute; he was adroit and delicate in his pleasantry, and what was then called a banterer of the first rate. But the literary vanity which he attacked with the arm of ridicule, afforded us no hold on him: in avowing himself destitute of talents, he rendered himself invulnerable to criticism. I used to compare him to a cat, that, lying on his back, with his paws in the air, presented only his claws. The rest of the company laughed at our attacks, and this pleasure was permitted them; but when gaiety, ceasing to indulge in raillery, quitted the arm of criticism, all were emulous of contributing to it. Bernard alone (for he too was of these dinners) kept himself always in reserve.

The contrast between the character of Bernard and his reputation is a very singular thing. The nature of his poetry might well have procured him in his youth the epithet of '*gentil*,' but he was anything rather than '*gentil*,' when I knew him. With women he had then only a worn out gallantry; and when he had told one that she was fresh as Hebe, or that she had the complexion of Flora; and to another that she had the smile of the Graces, or the figure of the Nymphs, he had said his all. I have seen him at Choisy, at the *fête des roses*, which he celebrated there every year in a kind of little temple which he decorated with opera scenes, and which on that day he ornamented with so many garlands of roses that the whole company complained of the head-ache. This *fête* was a supper, where the women fancied themselves all the divinities of spring. Bernard was the high-priest. Most certainly it was for him the moment of inspiration, had he been in the least susceptible of it: yet, even there, not a single sally, not one stroke of gaiety, nor a lively touch of gallantry, ever escaped him; he was there coldly polite. With men of letters, even in their most engaging mirth, he was still only polite; and in our serious and philosophical conversations, no one could be more sterile. In literature, he had but a light superficial knowledge; he knew only his Ovid. Thus reduced almost to silence on all that was not circumscribed within the sphere of his ideas, he never had an opinion, and on no question of importance could any one ever say what Bernard had thought. He lived, as we say, on the reputation of his gallant poetry, which he had the prudence not to publish. We had foreseen its fate, when it should be printed: we knew that it was cold; an unpardonable vice, most particularly in a poem on the art of love: but such was the benevolence which his reserve, his modesty, his politeness inspired in us, that not one of us, so long as Bernard was living, ever divulged this fatal secret. I return to the dinner, where Collé displayed a disposition so different from that of Bernard.

Never was the fire of gaiety of so regular and so fruitful a warmth. I cannot now tell you at what we laughed so much; but I well know that at every turn he made us all laugh till the tears started in our eyes. His fancy, when once exalted, made everything appear comic and ridiculous. It is true, he often sinned against decency; but at this dinner we were not excessively severe on that point.

A singular incident broke up this jovial society. Pelletier fell in love with a fair adventurer, who made him believe she was the daughter of Louis XV. She used to go every Sunday to Versailles, to see, as she said, her sisters the princesses; and she always returned with some little present; it was a ring, a case, a watch, or a box with the portrait of one of these ladies. Pelletier, who had some understanding, but a weak and light head, believed all this; and in great mystery he married this little gipsy. From that time, you may well suppose that his house no longer suited us; and he, soon afterwards, having discovered his mistake, and the shameful folly he had committed, became mad, and retired to die at Charenton.

A more decent and more engaging freedom, a gaiety less wild and yet very lively, reigned at the suppers of madame Filleul, where the young countess de Séran shone in all the lustre of her nascent beauty and mirthful simplicity. At these suppers, no one dreamt of displaying his wit; that was the least of the cares either of the hostess or her guests; and yet there was an infinity of it, and of the most natural and delicate kind. But, before I describe the pleasures of this society, there is another whose charm is soon to cost me so dear that it cannot escape my memory. Observe, my dear children, by what a chain of circumstances, fortuitously united, one of the most remarkable events of my life was introduced.

In the society of madame Filleul, I again saw Cury; he was in misfortune, and I loved him the more tenderly. I have already said, that in the time of his prosperity he had shown me much kindness. Very lately again, he had invited me to pass with him and his intimate friends, a few charming days at Chénevière, his country-house, near Andresis, where he had a liberty for sporting. It was there that, within sight of a picturesque cottage, I invented the tale of the 'Shepherdess of the Alps.' Happy moment of calm and serenity, that was soon to be followed by a violent storm! There all the party were sportsmen, except myself: but I followed the sport, and on an island of the Seine, where it passed, seated at the foot of a willow, my pencil in my hand, fancying myself on the Alps, I meditated on my tale, and took care of the dinner of our sportsmen. At their return, the keen and pure air of the river had served me for exercise, and gave me an appetite as voracious as theirs.

In the evening, a table covered with game they had killed, and crowned with bottles of excellent wine, offered a free field for mirth and licence. These, for Cury, were the last caresses and deceitful adieus of faithless prosperity:

> "Hinc apicem rapax
> Fortuna cum stridore acute
> Sustulit."

A little gaiety, in which he had permitted himself to indulge at the theatre at Fontainbleau in a prologue of his own, by turning into ridicule the gentlemen of the king's chamber, had alienated them from him; and after they had pretended to laugh at his pleasantry, they revenged themselves by compelling him to quit his place of intendant of the *Menus Plaisirs*. The most stupid of these gentlemen, the most vain and the most choleric, was the duke d'Aumont. He was obstinately bent on Cury's ruin; he was its principal cause, and he gloried in it. This alone made me conceive an aversion to this little duke. But I had personally some reason to be offended with him: the circumstances were these.

Madame de Pompadour having expressed a desire that the 'Venceslaus' of Rotrou should be purified of the coarseness of manners and of language which disfigured that tragedy; I had undertaken, out of complaisance to her, that ungrateful task; and, the players themselves having at the reading approved my corrections, the tragedy had been got up and rehearsed with these changes, in order to be played at Versailles. But le Kain, who detested me (I have told the reason elsewhere) having pretended to adopt the corrections of his part, had played me the perfidious trick of re-establishing, without my knowledge, the old part as it used to be, which had bewildered all the other actors, and destroyed at every instant the continuity of dialogue, and all the effects of the scene. I had loudly complained of it as a strange unheard-of insolence; and, finding myself compromised in the debates it excited among the performers, had resolved, through the channel of the 'Mercure,' to lay the conduct of le Kain before the public, and give the lie to the reports that were spread by his cabal, when the duke d'Aumont, who favoured him, imposed silence on me. I too then had some good reason for not liking him.

Cury, in his adversity, had preserved as his friends the other intendants of the *Menus Plaisirs*. One of them, with whom I was particularly intimate, Gagny, an amateur of painting and French music, and one of the most habitual frequenters of the opera-house, had taken a fair candidate of that theatre for his mistress; and he wanted to bring her out in the great parts of Lully, beginning with that of Oriane. He invited her, Cury, and myself, and some other amateurs, to go and pass the Christmas holidays at his country-house at Garges, to hear the new Oriane, and give her some instruction. You must take notice, that Laferté, intendant of the *Menus*, and the beautiful Rosetti, his mistress, were of this party of pleasure. The good cheer, the good wine, the good looks of our host, made us listen with admiration to the voice of mademoiselle Saint Hilaire. Gagny thought he heard le Maure, and when exhilirated by wine, we were all of his opinion.

All went on as well as possible, when one morning I learnt that Cury was attacked with a cruel fit of the gout. I instantly went down to him. I found him by his fire-side with both his legs wrapped up in flannels, but writing on his knee, and laughing with the air of a satyr, for he had all the features of one. I would have spoken to him about his fit of the gout, but he made me a sign not to interrupt him, and with a crooked hand he finished what he was writing. "You have suffered very much," said I, then; "but I see that the pain is abated."—"I suffer still," answered he; "but I do not laugh the less. You shall laugh too. You know with what fury the duke d'Aumont has pursued me? I think it not too much to revenge myself by a little malice; and here is what I have been ruminating on the whole night, in spite of the gout."

He had already written some thirty verses of the famous parody of 'Cinna;' he read them to me, and I confess that, having found them very comic, I engaged him to continue. "Then let me write," said he; "for I am in the humour for it." I left him; and when, on hearing the bell, I descended to dinner, I found him, who had himself hobbled down, muffled up in his fur, and who, before the company assembled, was reading to Laferté and Rosetti what he had read in the morning to me, and some more verses that he had added. At this second reading, I easily retained these mischievous verses from one end to the other, aided by the verses of Corneille, of which these were the parody, and which I knew by heart. The next day Cury went on with his work, and I was always his confidant; so that on my return to Paris I carried away about fifty of these lines that my memory retained.

I know that, in rolling, the snow-ball increases in size; but this is all that I believe came from the hand of Cury. I ought to add, that in his verses there was no abuse, and I have seen some of the grossest in the copies that were multiplied of them.

In these copies, the general idea of the parody was preserved, but its details were almost all changed and disfigured. There were even passages that, not being parodies of the verses of Corneille, had absolately escaped the copyists. For example, in imitating the manner of giving his opinion, which had procured d'Argental the name of *Gobe-Mouche*, they had indeed strung together words without sense; but, in these broken words, there was no ingenuity, and not a feature that resembled the passage of the parody where d'Argental opened thus:

"Why, yes, I should think . . . . . yet I will not dissemble,
One might find . . . . . . for indeed you should
. . . . . but I tremble.
For, 'tis not, after all, as you well may conceive,
That I care for indulgence; or wish to deceive;
My cold prudent zeal is not made for extremes;
But the poets themselves, and the players, it seems. .
I cannot determine, and yet I surmise
That the all safest course is the course of the wise.
It is for this reason alone that I doubt.
You well know, my lord, that my wit, when half out,
Debates and consults ere I dare to decide.
Le Kain, without doubt, would be your better guide:
Has aught e'er escap'd his acuteness? 'Tis he
That to you's so convincing, so striking to me.
I always maintain that in all our debates . . . .
We think we can see what the fancy creates.
This is the opinion, my lord, which I give.
'Tis your's to resolve."

This was the style and tone of Cury's pleasantry. All those who were acquainted with him knew it as well as myself. And, when the duke d'Aumont was made to say to his confidents:

"And by your counsels, sirs, I shall be, this year,
A great stage-manager, or simple duke and peer:"—

when he replied to d'Argental, in admiring his eloquence:

"You know not what to say! Ah, that's saying much.
You always say more than you think, great sir:"—

I cannot conceive how those who every day heard

Cury's pleasantry did not recognise his ironical and delicate humour. In his earliest youth, this turn of mind had signalized itself by a remarkable trait, which was known.

His mother was on terms of very particular friendship with M. Poultier, the intendant of Lyons. One day, when she was dining at his house in grand gala, and her son with her, he by the side of the intendant's wife, and his mother by the side of the intendant, M. Poultier having attracted the eyes of the company to a snuff-box they had never yet seen, said, that it came from a hand that was infinitely dear to him.

"Madame, is it your's or my mother's, he means?"

asked the young Cury, addressing himself to the intendant's wife. One of the party, wishing to give a proof of his erudition, observed, that this was a verse from 'Rodogune.' "No," replied M. Poultier, "it is l'Etourdi." This was checking impertinence with a deal of wit.

This trait and several others had rendered the talent of Cury celebrated for ingenious allusions. Fortunately it was forgotten. My head full of the parody that had just been confided to me, I arrived at Paris at madame Geoffrin's, and the next day I there heard this curious piece mentioned. The two first verses only were quoted:

"Let each then retire, and none enter: do you
Le Kain stay with me, and you d'Argental too."

But this was enough to persuade me that it was already current in society, and I happened to say smiling, "What! do you know no more than that?" They instantly pressed me to tell what I knew of it. There were none present, they said, but confidential friends; and madame Geoffrin herself answered for the discretion of her little circle. I yielded; I recited to them what I knew of the parody; and the next day I was denounced to the duke d'Aumont, and by him to the king, as the author of this satire.

I was listening tranquilly at the opera house to the rehearsal of 'Amadis,' in order to hear our Oriana, when some of my friends came to tell me that all Versailles was in arms against me; that I was accused of being the author of a satire against the duke d'Aumont; that the first nobility of the court cried aloud for vengeance; and that the duke de Choiseul was at the head of my enemies.

I instantly returned home, and wrote to the duke d'Aumont to assure him that the verses that were attributed to me were not mine; and that, never having written a satire against any one, I certainly should not have begun with him. I should have stopped there. But, in writing, I recollected that on the subject of 'Venceslaus,' and the falsehoods that were published against me, the duke d'Aumont had himself written to me to say that I ought to despise such trifles, and that they would die of themselves if they were not kept alive by controversy. I thought it natural and just to return him his maxim, in which I was very foolish; and thus my letter was taken for a fresh insult, and the duke d'Aumont produced it to the king, as a proof of the resentment that had dictated the satire. Did I not accuse myself, by ridiculing him while I disavowed it? My letter then did but inflame his anger and that of the whole court. I did not fail to go immediately to Versailles, and on arriving there I wrote to the duke de Choiseul.

"My lord duke,

"I am told that you lend your ear to the voice that accuses me, and that solicits my ruin. You are powerful, but you are just; I am unfortunate, but I am innocent. I intreat you to hear me and to judge. "I am, &c."

The duke de Choiseul wrote, for answer, at the bottom of my letter, "In half an hour," and sent it back to me. In half an hour I went to his hotel, and was introduced.

"You are desirous that I should hear you," said he; "I am willing to do so. What have you to say?"—"That I have done nothing to merit the severe reception I experience from your grace, who has a soul so noble and so generous, and who never took pleasure in humbling the unfortunate."—"But Marmontel, how do you expect I should receive you after the infamous satire that you have just written against the duke d'Aumont?"—"I never wrote that satire; I have told him so himself."—"Yes; and in your letter you have added a fresh insult, by offering him, in his own words, the counsel he had given you."—"As that counsel was wise, I thought I might be allowed to recal it to his memory; I intended by it no insult."—"Yet it is nevertheless an impertinence, permit me to tell you so."—"I felt it so too after my letter was gone."—"He is very much offended at it; and with reason."—"Yes, to this I plead guilty, and I reproach myself with it as a total neglect of decorum. But would this neglect be a crime in the eyes of your grace?"—"No; but the parody?"—"The parody is not mine; I declare it to you as an honest man."—"Is it not you who have recited it?"—"Yes, what I knew of it, in a society where each tells all he knows; but I would not permit my hearers to take a copy, although they were very desirous."—"Yet it is current."—"Then those who give it currency have it from some other person."—"And who gave you a copy?" I was silent. "You," added he, "are said to have been the first who recited it, and recited it in such a way as to discover you were its author."—"When I told what I knew of it," answered I, "it was really the subject of conversation, and the first verses were quoted. As to the manner in which I recited, it would prove just as well that I wrote the 'Misantrope,' the 'Tartuffe,' and 'Cinna' itself; for I boast, my lord, of reading each of those pieces as if I were its author."—" But, to be short, from whom did you hear this parody? This is what you should tell."—" Pardon me, my lord, that is exactly what I should not tell and what I shall not tell."—" I would wager it was from the author."—" Well, my lord, if it were from the author, ought I to name him?"—" And how, without that, will you persuade the world that it is not your's? You had been irritated against the duke d'Aumont; the cause of it is known; you have sought to revenge yourself. You have written this satire, and finding it comic, you have recited it: this is what the world says, this is what the world believes, and this is what the world has a right to believe. What do you answer to this?"—" I answer, that such conduct would be that of a madman, a fool, a wretched idiot, and that the author of the parody is far from either of these characters. What! my lord, would the man that wrote it have had the simplicity, the imprudence, the extravagance, of going to recite it himself, without mystery, in society? No; disguising his hand-writing, he would have made a dozen copies of it, which he would have addressed to the players, and to the other malcontents about the court. I know, as well as another, these means of concealment; and, had I been culpable, should have adopted them. Be pleased then to say to yourself; 'Marmontel, before six persons who were not his intimate friends, had recited what he knew of this parody: therefore he is not its author. His letter to the duke d'Aumont is the letter of a man who fears nothing : he therefore felt himself strong in his innocence, and had thought he had nothing to apprehend.' This reasoning, my lord, is the reverse of that which is opposed to me, but it is no less conclusive. I have committed two imprudent mistakes; one is, that of reciting verses that my memory had caught, and having given them publicity without the author's consent."—" Then you really had them from the author?"—" Yes, from the author himself; for I will not tell you a falsehood. It is to him then that I am culpable, and that is my first fault. The other is, that of having written to the duke d'Aumont in a tone that seemed like irony, and was not sufficiently respectful. These are my two faults; I confess them; but I have no others."—" I believe you," said he; "you speak like an honest man. Yet you are to be sent to the Bastile. Call on M. de St Florentin; he has received the order from the king."—" I will go to him," said I; "but may I flatter myself that you will no longer be among the number of my enemies?" He promised it me with a good grace, and I went to the office of the minister, who was to expedite my *lettre de cachet*.

He was well inclined to favour me. Without difficulty, he believed me innocent. " But what can I do," said he; "the duke d'Aumont accuses you, and insists on your being punished. It is a satisfaction he asks, as a recompense for his services and the services of his ancestors. The king has chosen to grant it him. Go to M. de Sartine's. I address the king's order to him. You will tell him that you come to receive it by my direction." I asked him if I might be allowed to dine first at Paris, and this he permitted.

I was invited to dine that day with my neighbour M. de Vaudesir, a man of talents and learning, who, under a forbidding exterior, concealed an exquisite fund of literature, with much politeness and amiability. Alas! his only son was that unfortunate St James, who after having madly dissipated the great fortune he had left him, had gone to die insolvent in that Bastile to which they were sending me.

After dinner, I confided my adventure to Vaudesir,

who tenderly bade me adieu. I then went to M. de Sartine's, whom I did not find at home: he had gone out to dinner and would not be back till six o'clock. It was then five; I employed the interval in going to tell my good friend madame Harenc of my misfortune, and to comfort her. At six, I returned to the minister of police. He knew nothing of my business, or he feigned to know nothing. I related it; he appeared concerned. "When we dined together," said he, "at baron Holbach's, who could have foreseen that the first time I should see you again would be to send you to the Bastile? But I have not received the order. Let us see if it has come to my office in my absence." He sent for his secretaries, and as they had heard nothing of it; "Go and sleep quietly at home," said he, "and return hither tomorrow at ten; that will serve just as well."

I wanted that evening to prepare the 'Mercure' of the month. I sent then to ask two of my friends to supper; and, waiting their arrival, I went to madame Geoffrin's to announce my calamity to her. She already knew something of it, for I found her cold and sorrowful. But, although my misfortune had taken its rise in her society, and that she herself had been the involuntary cause of it, I did not touch on that point, and by this conduct I believe she was pleased.

The two friends I expected were Suard and Coste; the latter a young Toulousian, and with whom I had been acquainted in his native city; the other, on whom I thoroughly depended, was the friend my heart had chosen. He loved to keep me in that gentle illusion, by spontaneously giving me opportunities of being useful to him He would have offended me if he had appeared to doubt the full right he had to command me. The desire of employing them usefully to themselves had induced me to undertake a collection of the most curious pieces in the old 'Mercures.' They selected them at their leisure; and the one hundred and twenty guineas, clear, that this part of my domain produced, was divided between them.

We passed a part of the night together in disposing everything for the printing of the next 'Mercure;' and, after having slept a few hours, I rose, packed up my necessaries, and went to M. de Sartine's, where I found the officer who was to accompany me. M. de Sartine wished that we should go to the Bastile in separate carriages. It was I who refused this obliging offer; and my conductor and I arrived at the Bastile in the same hackney-coach. I was received in the council chamber by the governor and his staff-officers; and there I began to perceive that I was well recommended. This governor, M. Abadie, after having read the letters which the officer had presented to him, asked me whether I wished to have my servant left, but on condition that we should be in the same chamber, and that he should only quit the prison with me. This servant was Bury. I consulted him about it; he answered that he would not leave me. My parcels and books were then lightly examined, and I was conducted into a large room, the furniture of which consisted of two beds, two tables, the bottom of a chest of drawers, and three straw chairs. It was cold; but a jailor made us a good fire, and brought me wood in abundance. At the same time they gave me pens, ink, and paper, on condition of giving an exact account of the employment and number of sheets with which they should furnish me.

Whilst I was preparing my table to set myself to write, the jailor came back to enquire whether I was satisfied with my bed. After having examined it, I answered that the mattresses were bad, and the blankets dirty. In a minute they were all changed; they sent to ask too at what hour I dined? I answered at their usual hour. The Bastile had a library; the governor sent me the catalogue, giving me the choice of the books that composed it. I thanked him for myself; my servant asked for the novels of Prévost, and they were brought him.

On my part, I had provision enough to save me from weariness. I had long been impatient at the contempt that men of letters expressed for the poem of 'Lucan,' which they had never read, and which they knew only by the barbarous and bombastic version of Brebœuf; and I had resolved to translate it more decently and more faithfully in prose; and this employment, that would occupy without fatiguing me, appeared well suited to the solitary leisure of my prison. I had therefore brought with me the 'Pharsalia;' and, to understand it better, I had taken care to add 'Cæsar's Commentaries.'

Here then I was by the side of a good fire, meditating on Cæsar's dispute with Pompey, and forgetting mine with the duke d'Aumont. There was Bury, on his part, as much a philosopher as I, amusing himself with making our beds, placed in the two opposite angles of my chamber, which was lighted at that moment by a clear winter's day, notwithstanding the bars of two strong iron grates that just left me a view of the Fauxbourg Saint-Antoine.

Two hours afterwards, the bolts of the two doors that inclosed me awoke me by their noise from my profound reverie; and two jailors, loaded with a dinner, which I supposed mine, came and served it in silence. One places before the fire three little dishes covered with plates of common earthenware; while the other lays a coarse but clean cloth on the table that was vacant. I saw him put on the table a clean pewter spoon and fork, some good household bread and a bottle of wine. Having done this the two jailors retire, and the two doors are again closed with the same sound of locks and bolts.

Bury then invites me to place myself at table, and he serves me up the soup. It was on a Friday;

this soup *en maigre* was a white bean soup, made with the freshest butter, and a dish of these same beans was the first that Bury put on my table. I found all this very good. The dish of cod-fish that he brought for my second course was still better. A little point of garlic seasoned it with a delicacy of flavour and smell, that would have flattered the palate of the most dainty Gascon. The wine was not excellent, but it was passable. No desert; it was requisite to be deprived of something. On the whole I found that one dined very well in prison.

As I rose from table, and as Bury was going to seat himself at it (for there was enough for his dinner in what remained) behold my two jailors, who re-enter with pyramids of new dishes in their hands. At the appearance of this service in fine linen, in beautiful porcelain, silver spoon and fork, we recognised our mistake; but we took no notice of it, and when our jailors had set all this down, and were retired; "Sir," said Bury to me, " you have just eaten my dinner; allow me in my turn to eat your's."—" That is but just," answered I; and the walls of my chamber were, I believe, quite astonished to re-echo a laugh.

This dinner was *gras;* it consisted of an excellent soup, a slice of juicy beef, the leg of a boiled capon swimming in its gravy, and melting in the mouth, a little dish of fried artichokes in marinade, one of spinage, a very fine Crésanne pear, some grapes, a bottle of old Burgundy, and some of the best Mocha coffee; this was Bury's dinner, with the exception of the coffee and the fruit, which he chose to reserve for me.

In the afternoon, the governor came to see me, and inquired if I were satisfied with my dinner, assuring me that it should be served from his table, that he would take care to carve for me himself, and that no other person should touch it. He proposed a chicken for my supper; I thanked him, and said that the fruit I left at my dinner would suffice for me. You see what was my ordinary fare at the Bastile, and you may conclude with what mildness, or rather with what repugnance, they consented to inflict on me the anger of the duke d'Aumont.

I had every day a visit from the governor. As he had some tincture of literature, and even of Latin, he took pleasure in observing the progress of my work; he was delighted with it. But soon stealing himself from these little recreations, "Adieu," said he; "I am going to console those who are far more unfortunate than you." The attentions he shewed to me might well be no proof of his humanity; but I had besides a very faithful testimony of it. One of the jailors had conceived a friendship for my servant, and he soon became familiar with me. One day, as I was speaking to him of the feeling and compassionate disposition of M. Abadie, "Ah!" said the jailor, "he is the best of men; he has accepted this painful office, only to soften the lot of the prisoners. He has succeeded a hard and avaricious man, who treated them very ill; so that, when he died, and M. Abadie took his place, the change was felt even to the dungeons; you would have said (a very strange expression in the mouth of a jailor) that a sun-beam had penetrated into these cells. People to whom we are forbidden to tell what passes without, asked us what then has happened? In short, sir, you see how your servant is fed; almost all our prisoners are as well fed as he; and the comforts it depends on him to give them, comfort himself; for he suffers when he sees them suffer."

I need not tell you that this jailor himself was a good man in his profession; and I took great care not to disgust him with that profession, in which, compassion is so precious and so rare an ingredient.

The manner in which I was treated, at the Bastile, made me well conceive that I should not be there long; and my translation, intermixed with interesting reading (for I had with me Montaigne, Horace, and la Bruyére) left me but few weary moments. There was one thing only that sometimes plunged me in malancholy; the walls of my chamber were covered with inscriptions that all bore the character of the sad and sombre reflections with which, before me, some unhappy sufferers had doubtless been oppressed in this prison. I used to think I still saw them wandering and lamenting, and their shades encompassing me.

But a circumstance that was personal to myself, occurred to torment my fancy more cruelly. In speaking of the society of madame Harenc, I have not mentioned an excellent man, whose name was Durant, who had some friendship for me, but who was otherwise remarkable only for a charming simplicity of manners.

One morning then, on the ninth day of my captivity, the major of the Bastile entered my chamber, and with a grave and cold air, without any preamble, asked me if a man of the name of Durant was known to me. I answered that I knew a man of that name. Then, seating himself to write, he continued his interrogatory. The age, the height, the features of this Durant, his profession, his abode, how long I had known him, in what house; nothing was forgotten, and at each of my answers the major wrote with a face of marble. At last, having read to me my interrogatory, he presented to me the pen in order to sign it; I signed it, and he withdrew.

He had scarcely left my room, when all the most sinister possibilities seized on my imagination. What then can this good Durant have done? He goes every morning to the coffee-house; he has there undertaken my defence; he has spoken with too much warmth against the duke d'Aumont; he has indulged in murmurs against a partial, unjust, oppressive authority, that crushes a feeble and innocent man to gratify the powerful. On the imprudence of these remarks, he has been arrested; and on my account, and for my sake, he will groan in a prison more rigorous than mine. Weak as he is, much older, and much more timid than I, melancholy will seize him, and he will sink under it; I shall be the cause of his death. And poor madame Harenc, and all our good friends, in what a situation must they be! Great God! what evils my imprudence will have created! It is thus that in the fancy of a captive, solitary man, in the bonds of absolute power, reflection gives every evil presage a gigantic form, and encircles his soul with dire presentiment. From that moment, I did not get one gentle sleep. All the dishes that the governor reserved for me, with so much care, were steeped in bitterness. All that was most vital in me felt wounded; and, if my detention at the Bastile had continued a week longer, it would have been my tomb.

In this situation, I received a letter that was forwarded to me by M. de Sartine. It was from mademoiselle S * *, a beautiful and interesting girl, with whom I was on the point of being united before my imprisonment. In this letter she expressed in the most touching manner, the sincere and tender part she took in my misfortune, assuring me that it had not alarmed her courage, and that, far from enfeebling her sentiments for me, it rendered them more lively and more constant.

I answered, first by expressing all my sensibility for so generous a friendship. But I added that the great lesson I received from adversity was, never to associate any one with the unforeseen dangers, and sudden revolutions, to which the perilous condition of a man of letters exposed me; and that if, in my situation, I felt some courage, I owed it to my isolated existence; that my senses would have been already lost, if I had left without my prison a wife and children in affliction; and that, at least on that side, which to me would be the most cruelly tender, I never would give adversity any hold on me.

Mademoiselle S * * was more stung than wounded at my answer; and a little while afterwards she consoled herself by marrying M. S * *.

At length, on the eleventh day of my detention, at the close of day, the governor came to announce that my liberty was restored; and the same officer who had conducted me, took me back to M. de Sartine's. This minister expressed some joy at seeing me again, but his joy was mixed with sadness. "Sir," said I, " in your kindness, for which I am very grateful, there is something that still afflicts me; while you congratulate me, you have the air of pitying me. Have you some new misfortune to announce to me?" (I thought of Durant.)— "Alas! yes," answered he; "and do you not suspect it? The king has taken the 'Mercure' from you." These words comforted me, and expressing my resignation, by gently inclining my head, "So much the worse for the Mercure," answered I.—"The evil," added he, "is perhaps not without remedy. M. de St Florentin is at Paris: he interests himself for you; go and call on him tomorrow morning."

On quitting M. de Sartine's, I ran to madame Harenc's, impatient to see Durant. I found him there, and, amid the joyous acclamations of the whole society, I saw only him. "Ah! there you are," said I, throwing myself into his arms; "then I am indeed comforted!" This transport, at the sight of a man for whom I had entertained no very passionate sentiment, astonished the whole company. They thought that the Bastile had disordered my brain. "Ah! my dear friend," said madame Harenc, embracing me; "what heart-felt joy it gives me to see you again at liberty! And the 'Mercure?'"—"The 'Mercure' is lost," said I. "But, madame, permit me to occupy myself a moment with this unfortunate man. What can he have done to cause me so much affliction?" I related the history of the major. The truth was, that Durant had gone to solicit from M. de Sartine the permission to see me, and he had said that he was my friend. M. de Sartine had sent to enquire of me who this Durant was; and of this very simple question the major had made a string of interrogatories. Enlightened and tranquil on that subject, I employed my courage in raising the hopes of my friends; and, after having received from them a thousand marks of the most tender interest, I went to see madame Geoffrin.

"Well, here you are again," said she; "heaven be praised! The king has taken the 'Mercure' from you! The duke d'Aumont is highly delighted, and this will teach you to write letters."—"And to recite verses," added I, smiling. She inquired if I were not going to commit some new folly. "No, madame, but I am going to try to remedy those I have already committed." As she was really afflicted at my adverse fortune, she was obliged to quarrel with me in order to comfort herself: "Why had I written these verses?"—"I never wrote them," said I.—"Why then did you repeat them?" "Because it was you who requested it,"—"But, did I know that they contained so severe a satire? Was it necessary for you, who knew it, to boast of that knowledge? What imprudence! And then your good friends, de Presle and Vaudesir, go publishing it everywhere that you are sent to the Bastile on your parole, with all kinds of attention and indulgence!"—"Ought it then, madame, to be believed, that I was dragged to prison like a criminal?"—"They should have been silent: people in power must not be braved. Marshal Richelieu has taken care to observe, that he has been twice led to the Bastile like a culprit, and that it was very singular that you should be treated better than he."

"Truly, madame, I am a most worthy object of envy for marshal Richelieu!"—"Ah! yes, sir, people are hurt at any indulgence shewn to him who offends them, and employ all their credit to be revenged on him; that is natural. Do you expect they will suffer themselves to be injured, without indulging resentment?"—"I pity them!" cried I, with an air of contempt. But soon perceiving that my replies irritated her, I thought proper to be silent. At last, when she had wholly unburdened her heart, I rose with a modest air, and wished her a good evening.

The next morning, I was scarcely awake, when Bury, entering my chamber, announced madame Geoffrin. "Well, my dear neighbour," said she, "and how did you sleep?"— "Exceedingly well, madame; neither the sound of the bolts, nor the cry of the centinels has interrupted my rest."—"And I," said she, "I have not closed my eyes."—"Why so, madame?"—"Why! don't you know the reason? I have been cruel and unjust. Yesterday evening I loaded you with reproaches. 'Tis thus we are: from the moment a man is unfortunate, we crush him, and turn all his conduct into crime" (and she began to weep).—"Good God! madame," said I, "do you still think of what passed yesterday? I myself had forgotten it. If it ever recur to me, it will be only as a mark of your kindness for me. Each has his way of loving: your's is to scold your friends for the misfortunes they bring on themselves, as a mother scolds her child when he falls." These words consoled her. She asked me what I was a going to do. "I am going," said I, "to follow the advice M. de Sartine has given me, and call on M. de St Florentin; from thence I shall go to Versailles, and see, if possible, madame de Pompadour and the duke de Choiseul. But I am perfectly cool, and am fully master of my feelings; I shall behave as I ought, never fear." Such was this conversation;

which, I think, does as much honour to the character of madame Geoffrin, as any one of the good actions of her life.

M. de St Florentin appeared concerned at my fate. He had done for me all that his weakness and timidity had permitted; but neither madame de Pompadour nor M. de Choiseul had seconded him. Without explaining himself; he approved my going to visit both of them, and I hastened to Versailles.

Madame de Pompadour, to whose house I first went, sent me word by Quesnai, that, under the present circumstances, she could not see me. I was not surprised at it; I had no right to expect that she should make herself powerful enemies for my sake.

The duke de Choiseul received me, but to load me with reproof. " It is truly with regret," said he, " that I again see you in misfortune; but you have done everything you could to deserve it; and your faults are so aggravated, by your imprudence, that those who were most inclined to favour you have been obliged to abandon you."—" What then have I done, my lord? What can I have done within the walls of my prison, to have added another fault to those of which I accused myself before you?"— " First," replied he, " on the day you should have gone to the Bastile, you went to the opera, to boast, with an insulting air, that you were sent to the Bastile only in derision, and out of vain complaisance for a duke and peer, against whom you had never ceased to declaim in the lobbies of the theatre, against whom you have written the most abusive letters to the army, and against whom you have made, not alone, but with others, the parody of Cinna, at a supper at mademoiselle Clairon's, with the count de Valbelle, the abbé Galiani, and other jovial companions: this is what you did not tell me, and what we are assured is true."

While he was speaking, I endeavoured to recollect

myself; and, when he had finished, addressed him thus: " My lord duke, your favour is dear to me; your esteem is still more precious than your favour, and I consent to lose both your favour and esteem if there be one word of truth in all these tales that have been told you."—" What!" cried he, proudly raising himself, " there is no truth in what I have just said to you?"—" Not one syllable; and I entreat you to permit me to sign, on your table, article by article, what I am going to answer to these charges.

" The day on which I should have gone to the Bastile, I certainly had no desire to go the opera." And after having given him an exact account of the employment of my time after I had left him;— " Send to know," added I, " of M. de Sartine and of madame Harenc, the time I passed with them: it was precisely the hours of the opera."

" As to the lobbies of the theatre, it happens by accident, that for six months I have never set foot in them. The last time that any one has seen me there (and the epoch is present to me) was at the *début* of Duranci, and, even before, I defy any man to cite one injurious expression of mine against the duke d'Aumont.

" By an accident no less fortunate, my lord, it happens, that since the campaign opened, I never have written to the army; and if any one can show me a letter, or a note, that he has received there from me, I consent to be dishonoured.

" With respect to the parody, it is a complete falsehood that it was written at the suppers, or in the company of mademoiselle Clairon. I even assert, that I never heard a single verse of this parody at her house; and, if it have been talked of there since it became known, as is very possible, it has not been before me.

" These four assertions, my lord, I will write and sign on your table, if you will allow me; and be assured that no man on earth can prove the contrary, nor will dare to maintain it to my face, and before you."

You will easily believe that, in listening to me, the vivacity of the duke de Choiseul was a little moderated. "Marmontel," said he, "I see that I have been imposed on. You speak to me in a tone that leaves me no doubt of your sincerity; truth only could hold that language. But you must put it in my power to affirm that the parody is not your's. Tell me its author, and the 'Mercure' is restored to you."—"The 'Mercure,' my lord, will never be restored to me at that price."—"Why so?"—"Because I prefer your esteem to six hundred a-year."— "By heaven," said he, "since the author has not the honesty to avow himself, I know not why you should be so tender of him."—"Why, my lord, because, after having imprudently abused his confidence, to betray it would be the height of injustice. I have been indiscreet, but I will not be perfidious. He did not confide to me these verses to publish. It is a larceny that my memory committed on him; and, if this larceny deserve punishment, it is I who should suffer: heaven forbid that he should declare himself, or that he should be known! I should then be indeed culpable! I should die with grief at his misfortune, for I should have caused it. But, at present, what is my crime? That of having done what each does in society without mystery. And you yourself, my lord, permit me to ask you whether in a convivial circle, you have never repeated the epigram, the comic verse, or the satirical couplet you had heard? Who, before me, was ever punished for that? 'Les Philippiques,' you well know, was an infernal work. The regent, the second person in the kingdom, was calumniated in it in an atrocious manner; and this infamous work was in every mouth; it was dictated and transcribed; there were a thousand copies of it; and yet who, besides the author has ever been punished for it? I happened to know some verses, I recited them; I suffered no one to copy them: and the whole crime of these verses, is to turn the vanity of the duke d'Aumont into ridicule. Such is the brief state of the case. If a plot of murder, or a crime of magnitude were in question, you would have a right to compel me to denounce its author. But for a joke, in truth, it is not worth the while to take upon myself the infamous part of an informer; and were not only my fortune, but my life at stake, I would say with Nicomède:

"The man by whom my youth was taught,
Ne'er taught me meanness."

I perceived that the duke de Choiseul thought there was something comic in my little pride; and, to make me feel it, he asked me, smiling, who had been my Hannibal? "My Hannibal, my lord," answered I, "is adversity, that has long tried and taught me to suffer."

"Come," said he, "this is what I call an honest man." Seeing then that he was shaken: "It is this honest man," answered I, "whom they oppress in order to gratify the duke d'Aumont, without any other motive than his complaint, without any other proof than his word. What dreadful tyranny!" Here the duke de Choiseul stopped me. "Marmontel," said he, "the patent of the 'Mercure' was a favour from the king; he withdraws it when he pleases; there is no tyranny in that."—"My lord," replied I, "from the king to me the patent of the 'Mercure' is a favour; but between the duke d'Aumont and me the 'Mercure' is my property, and he has no right to deprive me of it by a false accusation. . . . . . But no, it is not I whom he despoils, it is not I whom they immolate to his vengeance. To glut his appetite, they sacrifice more innocent victims Know, my lord, that at the age, of sixteen, having lost my father, and seeing myself surrounded with orphans like myself, and with a poor and numerous family, I promised to serve them all as a father. I called heaven and nature to witness my promise, and from that time to the present moment it has been faithfully fulfilled. I live on little; I can reduce my wants and expenses. But this crowd of unfortunate beings who subsist on the fruit of my labour, two sisters to whom I was about to give a little dowry to settle them in life, other women whose age needed a little repose; my mother's sister, a widow, poor and burdened with children, what will become of them? I had flattered them with the hope of comfort; they already felt the influence of my fortune; the favour to which I owed it was a spring that should never cease to flow for them; and they will now suddenly learn! . . . . Ah! 'tis there the duke d'Aumont should go to relish the fruits of his vengeance; 'tis there that he will hear doleful cries and see tears flow. Let him go thither and count his victims, and the wretches he has plundered; let him go and drink the tears of infancy and age, and insult the miserable beings whose bread he tears from their mouths. 'Tis there that his triumph awaits him. I am told, he has asked it as a reward for his services; he should have said, as wages; they are indeed worthy of his heart." At these words my tears began to flow; and the duke de Choiseul, as much affected as myself, said, embracing me: " My dear Marmontel, you wound me to the heart; I have perhaps done you much injury, but I will go and repair it."

Then taking his pen, with his natural vivacity, he wrote to the abbé Barthelemi:—" My dear abbé, the king has granted you the patent of the ' Mercure;' but I have just seen and heard Marmontel; he has touched me, he has persuaded me of his innocence; it would not become you to accept the spoil of an innocent man. Refuse the ' Mercure;' I will indem-

nify you for it." He wrote to M. de St Florentin:—
"You have received, my dear friend, the king's order to expedite the patent of the 'Mercure;' but I have seen Marmontel, and I want to speak to you about him. Press nothing till we have talked together." He read me these notes, sealed them, sent them off, and told me to go and see madame de Pompadour, giving me a note for her, which he did not read to me, but which was highly in my favour; for I was introduced as soon as she had cast her eyes on it.

Madame de Pompadour was indisposed and kept her bed. I approached her; I had first to endure the same reproof I had just experienced from the duke de Choiseul; and with still more mildness I opposed to it the same answers. Afterward, "These then," said I, "are the new crimes that are imputed to me, in order to induce the king, after eleven days imprisonment, to extend his severity so far as to pronounce my ruin! Had I been free, madame, I should perhaps have penetrated to you. I should have contradicted these falsehoods, and, by avowing to you my true and only fault, I might have found pardon in your eyes. But they begin by obtaining my detention within the walls of a prison; they profit by the time of my captivity to calumniate me with impunity quite at their ease; and the gates of the Bastile only open to me that I may see the abyss they have dug beneath my steps. But it is not enough to plunge me and my unhappy family into ruin; they know that a hand which delights in relief can again extricate us; they fear lest this hand, from which we have received so many benefits, should again become our aid; they take from us this last and only hope; and, because the pride of the duke d'Aumont is irritated, a crowd of innocent beings must be deprived of all consolation. Yes, madame, such has been the object of these falsehoods, which, by inducing you to think me either mad or malicious, stole from me your esteem. This is, above all, the sensitive part by which my enemies have contrived to pierce me to the soul.

"Now, that I may be without defence, they require that I should name the author of this parody, some verses of which I have retained and recited. They know me well enough, madame, to be very certain that I shall never name him. But not to accuse him, they say, is condemning myself; and, if I will not be infamous, I am ruined. Most certainly, if I can save myself only at this price, my ruin is fully decided. But in what age, madame, was it a crime to be honest? When was the accused obliged to prove himself innocent, and has the accuser been exempt from proof? Yet I am willing to repel by proofs an attack that has none; and my proofs are my writings, my known character, and my conduct through life. Since I have had the misfortune to be numbered among men of letters, all the satirical writers have been my enemies. There is no insolence that I have not received from them and patiently endured. Let any one cite an epigram, a touch of satire, an irony, in short a raillery, of mine, that approaches the character of this parody, and I consent to have it imputed to me. But if I have disdained such revenge, if my pen, always decent and temperate, has never been dipped in gall, why, on the word and faith of a man who is blinded with anger, is it to be believed that this pen has begun to distil its first venom upon him? I am calumniated, madame, I am so to you, I am so to that good king who cannot believe that he is imposed on; and but for the generous pity which I have just inspired in the duke de Choiseul, neither the king nor yourself would ever have known that I was calumniated."

I had scarcely finished when the duke de Choiseul was announced. He had lost no time; for I had left him at his toilette. "Well, madame," said he; "you have heard him; what do you think of all he endures?"—" That it is horrible," answered she, "and that the 'Mercure' must be restored to him."— "That is my opinion," said the duke de Choiseul. "But," replied she, "it is not fit that the king should appear to change so completely in a few hours. It is the duke d'Aumont himself who must take some steps . . . . "—" Ah! madame, you pronounce my sentence," exclaimed I: " he will never take the step that you are desirous he should take."—" He will do it," insisted she. " M. de St Florentin is with the king; he is coming to call on me, and I will speak to him. Go and wait for him at his hotel."

The old minister was not better pleased than myself with the turn that the weakness of madame de Pompadour took, and he did not dissemble to me that he thought it a bad omen. Indeed the obstinate pride of the duke d'Aumont was relentless. Neither the count d'Angiviller, his friend, nor Bouvart, his physician, nor the count of Duras, his comrade, could inspire him with any sentiment that was noble. As he had nothing in himself to command respect, he pretended at least to make himself feared; and he only returned to the court fully determined not to suffer himself to yield, declaring that he should consider those as his enemies who spoke to him of any step in my favour. None dared to oppose one of the men who approached nearest the person of the king; and all the interest they took in me was reduced to the securing me a yearly pension of one hundred and twenty guineas on the 'Mercure': the abbé Barthelemi refused the patent of it; and it was granted to one Lagarde, madame de Pompadour's librarian, the worthy protégé of Colin her steward.

Ten years afterward, the duke de Choiseul, in dining with me, recollected our conversations, to which, he said, he could well have wished that he had had some witnesses. I have been able to give you, from memory, only a short sketch of it, and my memory has long been cooled on this subject. But the circumstance must have inspired me very strongly; for he added, that he had never in his life heard a man so eloquent as I was on that occasion; and, talking on this subject, " Do you know," said he, " what prevented madame de Pompadour from getting you back the ' Mercure?' It was that knave Colin, to obtain it for his friend Lagarde." This Lagarde had so bad a fame that, in the society of *les Menus Plaisirs*, when he was admitted, they called him *Lagarde Bicêtre*. It was then, my dear children, to Lagarde Bicêtre that they sacrificed me; as the duke de Choiseul confessed.

As destitute of information as of talents, this new editor did his work so ill that the ' Mercure' was soon decried, and the affrighted pensioners perceived that it would be incapable of paying the pensions that were charged on it. They came to intreat me to consent to resume it, and offered to go in a body and request that it might be restored to me. But, having once quitted this heavy chain, I would not be loaded with it again. Fortunately, Lagarde dying, the ' Mercure' was conducted a little less ill, and fell more slowly into decay. But it at length became necessary to make it a bookseller's speculation, that the pensions might be paid.

BOOK VII.

My adventure with the duke d'Aumont had done me two essential services: it had induced me to renounce a project of marriage lightly formed, and of which I have since had reason to believe that I should have repented; and it had sown for me in the breast of Bouvart the seeds of that friendship which has been so salutary to me. But these good offices were not the only ones which the duke d'Aumont rendered me by his persecution.

In the first place, my mind, enfeebled by the dissipation of Paris, of Avenay, of Passy, and of Versailles, needed some adverse fortune to restore its ancient temper and the elasticity it had lost: the duke d'Aumont had taken care to give new vigour to my courage and character. In the second place, without employing me very seriously, the 'Mercure' never ceased to hold my attention captive, to consume my time, to steal me from myself, to prevent me from undertaking anything honourable to my talents, and to subject them to a minute and almost mechanical compilation: the duke d'Aumont had set them at liberty, and had restored to me the happy importunate want of making a worthy and noble use of them. In fine, I had resolved to sacrifice eight or ten of the best years of my life to this ungrateful journal, with the hope of amassing four or five thousand pounds, to which I limited my ambition. But the leisure which the duke d'Aumont had procured me, was worth nearly as much to me in the same number of years, without abridging any of my social pleasures in town, or in those delicious retreats where I passed the three gay seasons of the year.

I do not reckon the advantage of having been received at the French Academy sooner than I should have been, had I attended only to the 'Mercure.' It was not the intention of the duke d'Aumont to lead me there by the hand. Yet he did so without wishing it, and even against his inclination.

I have observed more than once, and in the most critical circumstances of my life, that, when fortune has appeared most adverse, she has served me more essentially than I myself should have asked. Here you behold me ruined; and, from this ruin, my dear children, you will soon see me rise in the enjoyment of the most equal, the most quiet, the most undisturbed happiness that a man of my profession can hope to possess. To establish it solidly, and on its natural basis, I mean on the repose of the mind, I began by freeing myself of my domestic inquietudes. Age or disease, that in particular which seemed to be contagious in my family, successively diminished the number of those dear relations to which I had so much pleasure in affording a comfortable subsistence. I had already persuaded my aunts to decline all trade, and, after having liquidated our debts, I had added pensions to the revenue of my little farm. Now these pensions of twelve guineas each, being reduced to five, I had a residue of half my pension of one hundred and twenty guineas on the 'Mercure;' I had beside twenty guineas interest on the four hundred guineas I had employed in giving security for M. Odde; to this I added an annuity of twenty-three pounds on the duke of Orleans, and, with what I had left on closing the accounts of the 'Mercure,' I bought some stock. So that, for my lodgings, my servant and myself, I had little less than one hundred and twenty guineas to spend. I never had spent more. Madame Geoffrin wished that the payment of my rent should cease from that time; but I begged her to let me try another year whether my faculties could not answer all my wants, assuring her that, if my rent oppressed me, I would confess it to her without blushing. I was not driven to this necessity. Most unhappily the number of pensions I paid diminished by the death of my two sisters, who were in the convent at Clermont, and who were torn from me by the same disorder of which our father and grandmother had died. A little time afterward, I lost my two old aunts, the only two who remained at home. Death left me only my mother's sister, my aunt d'Albois, who is still living. Thus, I every year inherited some of the benefits I had conferred. Besides, the first editions of my Tales began to enrich me.

Tranquil with regard to fortune, my sole ambition was the French Academy; and this ambition itself was temperate and peaceful. Before I should attain my fortieth year, I had still three years to give to my literary labours; and in three years I should have acquired new titles to this distinction. My translation of Lucan advanced; at the same time I was preparing materials for my Art of Poetry, and the celebrity of the Tales perpetually increased with every new edition. I thought the prospect before me mild and delightful.

You have seen in what a courteous way the friendly Bouret has begun with me. The acquaintance once made, the intimacy formed, his societies had been mine. In one of the tales of 'La Veillée,' I have painted the character of his fair and most intimate friend, the beautiful madame Gaulard. One of her two sons, an engaging man, held the place of receiver-general at Bordeaux; he had made a journey to Paris, and the day before his departure, one of the most beautiful days in the year, we were dining together at our friend Bouret's in good and charming company. The magnificence of this hotel, which the arts had decorated, the sumptuousness of the table, the nascent verdure of the gardens, the serenity of a pure sky, and, above all, the amiability of the host, who, in the midst of his guests, seemed to be the lover of all the women, the best friend of all the men, in fine, all that could spread good humour at a feast, had there exhilarated every soul. I, who felt myself the freest and most independent of men, was like a bird that, escaped from the net that held him captive, darts into the air with joy; and, to be sincere, the excellent wine with which they filled my glass contributed to give wings to my soul and fancy.

In the midst of this gaiety, the youngest son of

madame Gaulard took farewell of us; and, in talking of Bordeaux, he asked me if he could render me any service there. "Yes," said I; "that of kindly receiving me when I shall visit that beautiful port and opulent city; for, in the dreams of my life, that is one of my most interesting projects."—"Had I known that," said he, "you might have executed it tomorrow: I had a place to offer you in my chaise."—"And I," said one of the company (it was a Jew, whose name was Gradis, one of the richest merchants in Bordeaux) "I would have undertaken to send your trunks."—"My trunks," said I, "would not have been heavy; but how should I get to Paris again?....."—"In six weeks," replied Gaulard, "I would have brought you back."—"And is all this no longer possible?" I asked.—"Very possible on our part," they replied; "but we set off tomorrow." Then, whispering three words to the faithful Bury, who waited on me at dinner, I sent him to pack up my things; and instantly drinking the health of my fellow travellers, "you see me ready," said I, "and we are off tomorrow." The whole company applauded so active a resolution, and drank the health of the travellers.

It is difficult to imagine a more agreeable journey; an excellent road, and weather so beautiful and mild that we travelled all night, sleeping with the glasses down. The directors and receivers were everywhere eager to welcome us: I fancied myself in those poetic days and beautiful climates, where hospitality showed itself in *fêtes*.

At Bordeaux, I was received and treated as well as it was possible; that is, they gave me good dinners, excellent wine, and even salutes from the ships I visited. But, though there were in this city men of cultivated minds, and formed to engage, I enjoyed less of their intercourse than I could have wished. A fatal passion for gaming possessed them, clouded their minds, and absorbed their souls. I had every day the vexation of seeing some one oppressed with the loss he had sustained. They appeared to dine and sup together only to fall on each other with murderous hands when they rose from table; and this cruel cupidity, mixed with social enjoyments and social affections, was to me something monstrous.

Nothing could be more dangerous for a receiver-general than such society. However accurate he might be in his accounts, his sole quality of receiver should forbid him the gaming-table, as a rock, if not of his fidelity, at least of the confidence that is reposed in him; and I was not useless to my friend, in strengthening him in the resolution of never suffering himself to be affected by the contagion of example.

Another cause diminished the pleasure that my residence at Bordeaux would have given me; the maritime war made deep wounds in the commerce of that great city. The beautiful canal, that was full in my view, offered but the wrecks of it. But I easily formed an idea of what it must be in a state of peace and prosperity. The houses of some merchants, where there was no play, were those I most frequented, and that best suited me. But there was not one that had so much charm for me as that of Ansley. This merchant was an English philosopher, of a venerable character. His son, though then very young, announced those qualities that ennoble man; and his two daughters, without being beautiful, had a native charm in their mind and manners that delighted me as much and more than beauty would have done. The youngest of the two, Jenny, had made a lively impression on my heart. It was for her that I composed the romance of Pétrarque, and I sang it to her as I bade her farewell.

During the leisure that society left me in a town where, in the morning, each is occupied with his business, I indulged my taste for poetry, and composed my Epistle to the Poets. For my amusement too I had the humourous pleasantry that was then printing at Paris, against a man who deserved to be chastised for his insolence, and was so most severely; it was le Franc de Pompignan.

With a considerable literary fame in his province, and with little at Paris, yet with enough to be esteemed there, he might peaceably have enjoyed that esteem, if the excess of his vanity, presumption, and ambition, had not utterly intoxicated him. Unfortunately too much flattered at his academies of Montauban and Toulouse, accustomed to hear himself applauded there as soon as he opened his lips, and even before he had spoken, extolled in the journals, the favour of which he contrived either to gain or pay, he fancied himself a man of importance in literature; and, unfortunately again, he had added to the arrogance of the lord of a parish the pride of a president of the superior court in the town of Montauban; which altogether formed a most ridiculous personage. After the opinion he entertained of himself, he had thought it unjust that, at the first wish he had expressed of being admitted to the French Academy, they had not been eagerly desirous of receiving him there; and when, in 1758, Sainte-Palaye had been elected in preference to him, he had betrayed a proud indignation. Two years afterwards, the Academy had not ceased to grant him its suffrage; and in the unanimity of his election he might well have found grateful pleasure. But, instead of the modesty that even the greatest men affected, at least on entering there, he brought with him the sourness of offended pride, with an excess of affectation and arrogance that is inconceivable. The unhappy man had conceived the ambition of being I know not what in the education of the princes of the blood. He knew that, in his principles of religion, the dauphin did not like Voltaire, and that he looked with displeasure on the labours of the 'Encyclopédie;' he paid his court to that prince; he fancied he had recommended himself to his particular favour by his sacred odes, the magnificent édition of which ruined his bookseller; he thought he had highly flattered him, by confiding to him the manuscript of his translation of the Georgics: he did not know to whom he was exposing his vanity; he did not know that this translation, so painfully laboured in harsh, rough, and strained versification, without colour or harmony, compared to the masterpiece of Latin poetry, was, by the dauphin himself, submitted to the satirical eye of criticism, and turned into derision. He thought he had struck a deathblow, in attacking publicly, in the speech he made on entering the Academy, that class of men of letters who were called philosophers, and individually Voltaire and the Encyclopedists.

He had just made this attack, when I set out for Bordeaux; and that which was scarcely less astonishing than his arrogance, was the success it obtained. The Academy had listened in silence to this insolent declamation; the public had applauded it; Pompignan had retired triumphant, and inflated with his vain glory.

But a little while afterwards began against him the light skirmish of the ' Facéties Parisiennes'; and it was one of his friends, the president Barbeau, who called and told me that this poor M. de Pompignan was the fable of Paris. He showed me the first sheets that he had just received; they were the *when*, and the *wherefore*. I saw the turn and the tone that the pleasantry took. " You are then the friend of M. Lefranc?" asked I.—" Alas! yes," said he.—" Then I pity you; for I know the banterers who are at his heels. You have here the *when* and the *wherefore;* and the *if*, the *but*, the *for*, will soon follow in their train; and I can predict they will not quit him till he has passed through all the particles." The correction was still more severe than I had foreseen; they played upon him on every string. He wanted to defend himself seriously; he became the more ridiculous. He addressed a memorial to the king; his memorial was treated with contempt. Voltaire appeared to grow young again, in order to amuse himself at his expense; in verse, in prose, his satire was lighter, more pointed, more fruitful in original and comic ideas, than it had ever been. One sally trod on the heels of another. The public did not cease to laugh at the expense of the sad le Franc. Obliged to keep himself shut up at home, that he might not hear a pasquinade on himself sung in society, nor see himself pointed at, he finished by going to bury himself in his country-house, where he died, without ever daring to re-appear at the Academy. I confess that I felt no pity for him, not only because he was the aggressor, but because his aggression was serious and grave, and would even have gone, had he been believed, to the proscription of many literary men, whom he denounced and proclaimed as the enemies of the throne and the altar.

When Gaulard and I were on the point of returning to Paris; "Shall we again travel the same road?" said he; "would you not prefer taking the tour by Toulouse, Montpellier, Nîmes, Avignon, Vaucluse, Aix, Marseilles, Toulon, Lyons, and Geneva? We should then see Voltaire, with whom my father was acquainted?" You are very sure that I embraced this charming project with transport; and, before we set off, I wrote to Voltaire.

At Toulouse, we were received by an intimate friend of madame Gaulard, M. de Saint-Amant; a man of the old time, for frankness and politeness, and who occupied a place of considerable importance in that city. For myself, I did not find there a single person whom I knew. I had even great difficulty in recognising the city; so much to me did the objects of comparison, and the habit of seeing Paris, make it appear contracted and diminutive.

From Toulouse to Béziers, we were occupied with following and observing the canal of Languedoc. To me this was truly an object of admiration, because I there saw grandeur and simplicity united ; two characters that never show themselves together without causing astonishment.

The junction of the two seas, and the commerce from one to the other, were the result of two or three grand ideas combined by genius. The first was that of an immense mass of water, in the kind of cup formed by the mountains near Revel, a few leagues from Carcassonne, to be the perpetual source and reservoir of the canal. The second was the choice of an eminence, lower than the reservoir, but commanding on one side the space from that point to Toulouse, and on the other that from the same point to Béziers; so that the water of the reservoir, conducted thither by a natural slope, would there remain suspended in a vast level, and would only have to extend itself on one side towards Béziers, and on the other towards Toulouse, to supply the canal, and to deposit the barks in the Orbe on one side, and on the other in the Garonne. Finally, a third and principal idea, was the construction of the sluices at all the points where the barks would have to rise or descend; the effect of these sluices, being, as you know, to receive the barks, and, by being filled or emptied at pleasure, to serve them as steps for the double purpose of descending or rising to the level of the canal.

Though I spare you the details of foresight and industry, into which the inventor entered, in order to render inexhaustible the source of the canal, and to measure the volume of its water, without ever making it depend on the course of neighbouring rivers, or communicate with them, I neglected none of them myself. But the principal object of my attention was the basin of St Ferréol, the source of the canal, and the reservoir of its waters. This basin, formed as I have said by a circle of mountains, is two thousand two hundred and twenty-two fathoms in circumference, and one hundred and sixty feet in depth.

The narrow pass of the mountains that encompass it, is closed by a wall six and thirty fathoms thick. When it is full, its waters flow over in cascades; but in dry seasons these overflowings cease, and the water is then drawn from the bottom of the reservoir: the means employed for that purpose are these:—

In the side of the mountain, two long vaults are constructed at the distance of forty feet from each other, which run under the reservoir. To one of these vaults, three brass tubes are vertically adapted, whose bore equals that of the largest cannon, and by which, when their cocks are opened, the water of the reservoir falls into an aqueduct constructed along the second vault; so that when you reach to these tubes, you have one hundred and sixty feet of water above your head. We did not fail to advance thus far, by the glimmering light our conductor carried before us in a chafing-dish; for no ordinary light could have sustained the commotion of the air that the explosion of the waters soon excited under the vault; when suddenly with a strong iron lever, our guide turned the cock of one of the three tubes, then that of the second, and that of the third. At the opening of the first, the most dreadful thunder echoed beneath the vault; and twice, peal on peal, this roar redoubled. I thought I saw the bottom of the reservoir burst, and the mountains around shake from their base, and falling on our heads. The profound emotion, and, to speak the truth, the affright this noise had created, did not prevent us from going to see what was passing under the second vault. We penetrated there amid the sound of this subterraneous thunder, and saw three torrents rush from the three tubes. I know of no motion in nature that can be compared to the violence of the column of water that here escaped from the reservoir in floods of foam. The eye could not follow it; nor could it be looked on without giddiness. The border of the aqueduct, in which this torrent flowed, was but four feet wide;

it was covered with free stone, polished, wet, and very slippery. There we were standing, pale, motionless; and if our feet had slipped, the water of the torrent would have rolled us a thousand paces in the twinkling of an eye. We returned shuddering, and felt the rocks, which support the basin, tremble at the distance of a hundred paces.

Although quite familiar with the mechanism of the canal, I was again astonished, when from the foot of the hill of Béziers I saw, like a long staircase, eight contiguous sluices, by which the barks rose or descended with equal facility.

At Béziers I found one of my friends, M. de la Sablière, an old officer, who, after having long been accustomed to Paris, had come to pass the remnant of his days in his native city, there to enjoy the consideration which his services deserved. In the voluptuous asylum he had formed, he received us with that Gascon hilarity which was animated yet more by the comforts of a good fortune, an independent and tranquil mind, a taste for reading, a little ancient philosophy, and the renowned salubrity of the air that is breathed at Béziers. He enquired for M. de la Poplinière, at whose house we had passed many charming days together. "Alas!" answered I, "I never see him now. His fatal egotism has made him forget friendship. I will confide a secret to you which I have told to no one.

"Immediately after the marriage of my sister, I had obtained for her husband a place in the snuff-office at Chinon; a simple, easy employment, that my sister might have preserved had she lost her husband. This place was worth a hundred a-year. At the same time, la Poplinière had obtained for one of his relations the place of receiver in the custom-office at Samour, which, though of infinite detail and extreme difficulty, produced but fifty pounds a-year. La Poplinière intreated me to change with him, alleging conveniency, because his relation lived at Chinon. As he asked this service of me in the name of friendship, I did not hesitate to render it him. I even endeavoured to persuade myself that the talents of my brother-in-law would have been buried in a snuff magazine; whereas, in a receiver's place, which required a man of information, vigilance and application, he would be able to distinguish himself, and to deserve advancement. I thought then that I should do him no injury; and, generous at his expense I was to excess; for the place at Chinon, double the value of that at Saumur, la Poplinière offered me an annual indemnity of fifty pounds; and I insisted on no other compensation than the pleasure of obliging him. Well, this little place, in which my brother-in-law had re-established order, activity, exactitude, and which they had allowed him to join to that of the salt-office, was solicited by another person, without my knowledge, and my brother-in-law lost it."—" And did la Poplinière suffer it to be torn from you?"— "What could he do?"—" Why! bless me! was he without credit in his company? At least ought he not to have acknowledged and pleaded what you had done for him?"—" What will you say, then," added I, " when I tell you, that he himself, without saying a word to me, has solicited this employment for his secretary, and stolen it from the husband of my sister?"—" That cannot be."—" It is but too true: the farmer-generals themselves have told me so." La Sablière remained for some time in silent astonishment; and then, " My dear friend," said he, " you and I have both loved him: let us think but of that, and cast a veil over the rest." And indeed we did nothing but retrace those happy days when la Poplinière was our engaging host, and that moving gallery of pictures and characters which we had so often witnessed at his house. " I still love the memory of those days," said he; " but 'tis like a dream from which I awake without regret."

Montpellier offered nothing interesting to us but the botanic garden; and that again afforded us only an agreeable walk; for in botany we were both equally ignorant; but, as we were connoisseurs in pretty women, we had the pleasure of following with our eyes some charming brunettes, who had an engaging air. What distinguishes the women here, is an animating look, an active walk, and an alluring eye. I particularly observed that they had delicate feet, which, in every country, is a happy presage.

At Nîmes, we expected, on the faith of travellers and artists, to be struck with admiration; but nothing surprised us. There are things whose grandeur and beauty have been so exaggerated by fame, that the idea we conceive of them, at a distance, can but decrease when we behold them near. The amphitheatre did not appear vast to us, and its structure only astonished us by its massive heaviness. The square house gave us some pleasure, but it was the pleasure afforded by a small object, regularly constructed.

I will not forget that at Nîmes, in the cabinet of a naturalist, M. Segnier, we saw a collection of grey-coloured stones, which, broken in layers, like slate, present the two halves of an incrusted fish, whose form is very distinct; and this did not much surprise. But I beheld it with wonder, when this naturalist assured me that these stones are found on the Alps, and that the species of fish they inclose is not known in our seas.

"Quærite, quos agitat mundi labor."—LUCAN.

We only saw Avignon as we passed through it, to go and be in raptures at Vaucluse. But here again it was requisite to lower the idea we had formed of the enchanted residence of Petrarch and Laura. It is with Vaucluse as with Castalia, Peneus, and Simois. Their renown is due to the muses; their true charm is in the verses that have celebrated them. It is not that the cascade of the fountain of Vaucluse is not beautiful, both for the volume and charming bounds of its waters among the rocks that break their fall: but the poets who have described it, must allow me to say that its source is absolutely destitute of the ornaments of nature; both sides of it are naked, barren, steep, without shade; it is only at the bottom of the cascade that the river, which it forms, begins to clothe its borders with smiling verdure. Yet, before we quitted the source of its waters, we seated ourselves, meditated, and, without speaking to each other, with our eyes fixed on the ruins, that seemed to us to be the remains of Petrarch's villa, we ourselves indulged for some moments in poetic fiction and thought we beheld, wandering round these ruins, the shades of two lovers from whom the fame of Vaucluse is derived.

But what is more essentially formed to delight the eyes is the local position and exterior of a little town, that is embraced by the river of Vaucluse, and by which its walls are bathed; and this has given it the name of L'Isle. We fancied that we really beheld an enchanted island, as we walked around it, under two rows of mulberry trees, and between two canals of spring water, pure and rapid. Some pretty groups of young Jewesses, who were walking like ourselves, added to the illusion that the beauty of the place created; and some excellent trout, with some fine cray-fish, that were brought us for supper at the inn, which terminated this charming walk, added the gratification of another sense, to the pleasures of the imagination and of the view.

The fine weather, that had so agreeably accompanied our journey since we left Paris, abandoned us on the confines of Provence. The country, where it so rarely rains, was rainy. The city of Aix lay on our road to Marseilles and Toulon, and we thought ourselves obliged to pay the customary visit to the governor of the province who resided in that city. This governor, the unworthy son of marshal Villars, received me with a politeness, that in any other, would have flattered me. He insisted on keeping us till after the *Fête Dieu*. We refused; but he made us promise that we would return to Aix the day before the fête, to see the procession of king René.

The commercial and maritime ports of Marseilles and Toulon, were to me two objects of very lively interest and eager attention; and though, at Marseilles the new city, most magnificently built, was worthy of occupying us, the little time we were there was wholly employed in visiting the port, its fortifications, magazines, and all the great objects of that commerce which the war almost annihilated; but which would again become flourishing in peace. At Toulon, the port was again the only object of our thoughts. We there recognized the hand of Louis XIV in the superb establishments that bore the stamp of his grandeur, and in which, both for the building and armament of vessels, all recalled the idea of a respectable power.

Here, what it should seem ought most to have imposed on me, was what astonished me least. One of my desires was to behold the open sea. I saw it, but calm; and the pictures of Vernet had so faithfully represented it to me, that the reality caused me no emotion; my eyes were as accustomed to it as if I had been born on its shores.

The duke de Villars had appeared desirous that we should witness the gala he intended to give at his house the day before the Fête Dieu. We arrived there in the evening, and found all the best company of the city, a ball, card assembly, and supper. The next day, the bad weather deprived us of the sight of the procession, which they had represented to us as very brilliant. However, we saw some specimens of it: for instance, a drunken porter represented the queen of Sheba; another, king Solomon; three others, the Magi, and all up to the ears in dirt. The queen of Sheba nevertheless jumped about in cadence, and king Solomon bounded after the queen of Sheba. I admired the gravity of the people of Provence at this sight, and we took great care to imitate the respect they paid. However I had sometimes extreme difficulty in refraining from laughter. Among others, I remarked one of these personages, who carried a white rag at the end of a pole, and behind him three other dirty fellows, who made all kinds of drunken motions in the street, whenever the man with the white rag threw down his pole. I asked, what was the mystery that this represented to us.

"Don't you see," said the mayor, to whom I spoke, "that they are the three Magi conducted by the star, and who lose their way as soon as the star disappears." I contained myself. Nothing moderates an inclination to laugh, like the fear of being stoned.

The governor insisted that we should not leave Aix the next day, till after we had dined with him. At this dinner, he made a point of assembling men of merit, with M. de Monclar at their head. I had conceived the highest esteem for this great magistrate. I expressed it to him with that ingenuousness of sentiment that has no resemblance to flattery. He appeared sensible of it, and returned it with kindness. Soon after we rose from table, I took leave of the duke de Villars, as grateful as I could be, for the attentions and favours of a man whom I did not esteem.

On our road from Aix to Lyons, there was nothing remarkable but a trait of honesty in the woman who kept the inn at Tain, a village near *Côte de l'Hermitage*, which is so celebrated for its wines. At this village, while we were changing horses, I said to the hostess, giving her a louis d'or, "Madame, if you have any excellent red hermitage, give me six bottles of it, and pay yourself out of this louis." She looked at me with an air of satisfaction, pleased at the confidence I was willing to repose in her.

"As for excellent red wine," said she, "I have none; but I have some white of the very best." I confided in her; and this wine, for which she took only two shillings a bottle, proved to be nothing less than nectar.

Eager to get to Geneva, we did not even give ourselves time to see Lyons; reserving for our return the pleasure of admitting the master-pieces of industry in that great workshop of luxury.

Nothing can be more singular, or more original, than the reception Voltaire gave us. He was in bed when we arrived. He extended his arms to us, and wept for joy while he embraced me. He embraced the son of his old friend, M. Gaulard, with the same emotion. "You find me dying," said he: "do you come to restore me to life, or to receive my last sighs?" My companion was alarmed at this preface; but I, who had a hundred times heard Voltaire say he was dying, gave Gaulard a gentle sign of encouragement. And, indeed, a moment afterwards, the dying man, making us sit down by his bed-side, said, "My dear friends, how happy am I to see you! particularly at the moment when I have a man with me whom you will be charmed to hear. It is M. de l'Ecluse, the surgeon-dentist of the late king of Poland, now the lord of an estate near Montargis, and who has been pleased to come to repair the irreparable teeth of madame Denis. He is a charming man: but don't you know him?"—"The only l'Ecluse that I know," answered I, "is an actor of the old comic opera-house."—"'Tis he, my friend—'tis he himself. If you know him, you have heard the song of the 'Grinder,' which he plays and sings so well." And there was Voltaire instantly imitating l'Ecluse, and with his bare arms and sepulchral voice, playing the 'Grinder,' and singing the song:

> "Oh! where can I put her?
> My sweet little girl!
> Oh! where can I put her?
> They'll steal her and . . . ."

We were bursting with laughter; and he quite serious: "I imitate him very ill," said he; "'tis l'Ecluse that you must hear, and his song of the 'Spinner;' and that of the 'Postillion;' and the 'Quarrel of the Apple-woman with Vadé!' 'Tis truth itself. Oh! you will be delighted. Go and speak to madame Denis. Ill as I am, I will get up to dine with you. We'll eat some wild fowl, and listen to M. de l'Ecluse. The pleasure of seeing you has suspended my illness, and I feel myself quite revived."

Madame Denis received us with that cordiality which made her so charming. She introduced M. de l'Ecluse to us; and at dinner Voltaire engaged him, by the most flattering praises, to afford us the pleasure of hearing him. He displayed all his talents, and we appeared charmed with them. It was very requisite; for Voltaire would not have pardoned us a feeble applause.

The walk in his gardens was employed in speaking of Paris, the 'Mercure,' the Bastile (of which I only said a word), the theatre, the 'Encyclopédie,' and of that unhappy le Franc, whom he still teazed; his physician having ordered him, as he said, for exercise, to hunt le Pompignan every morning for an hour or two. He charged me to assure our friends, that they should every day receive from him some new pleasantry. He was faithful to his promise.

When we returned from our walk, he played a game or two at chess with M. de Gaulard, who respectfully let him win. Afterwards, he again spoke of the theatre, and of the revolution which mademoiselle Clairon had introduced. "Is then the change that has taken place in her somewhat prodigious?" said he. "It is," I replied, "a new talent; it is the perfection of art, or, rather, it is nature herself, such as your imagination can paint her in her greatest beauty."

My mind and language being warm, I endeavoured to make him comprehend the natural and sublime manner in which she performed Camille, Roxane, Hermione, Ariane, and Electre. I exhausted the little eloquence I had to inspire in him that enthusiasm for Clairon with which I was filled; and enjoyed, while I spoke, the emotion to which I gave birth. At last, addressing himself to me, "Well! my dear friend," said he, with transport; "'tis just like madame Denis; she has made an astonishing, an incredible progress. I wish you could see her play Zaïre, Alzire, Idamé! Talent can go no further." Madame Denis playing Zaïre! Madame Denis compared with Clairon! I was thunderstruck: so true it is, that taste accommodates itself to the object it can enjoy; and that this wise maxim,—

"When we have not what we love,
We must love what we have,"—

is, indeed, not only a lesson of nature, but a means she husbands to procure us pleasures.

We returned to walk, and, while M. de Voltaire was talking to M. Gaulard of his ancient friendship for the father of this young man, I, on my side, was conversing with madame Denis, and recalling the good old times to her memory.

In the evening, I put Voltaire on the chapter of the king of Prussia. He spoke of him with a kind of cold magnanimity, like a man who disdained a too easy revenge, or as an undeceived lover pardons in the mistress he has left, the rage and indignation she has excited.

At supper, the conversation turned on the men of letters he most esteemed; and in the number it was easy for me to distinguish those he loved from the bottom of his heart. They were not those who most boasted of being in favour with him. Before he went to bed, he read to us two new cantos of 'La Pucelle,' and madame Denis informed us that, since he had been at les Délices, it was the only day he had passed without retiring to his closet.

The next day, we had the discretion to leave him at least a part of his morning, and sent him word that we should wait till he rang. He was visible about eleven. He was still in bed. "Young man," said he, " I hope you have not renounced poetry: let us see some of your new productions; I conceal nothing; each should have his turn."

More intimidated before him than I had ever been, whether it were that I had lost the ingenuous confidence of early youth, or that I felt more intimately than ever, how difficult it is to write good verse, I resolved, with difficulty, to recite to him my Epistle to the Poets: he was highly pleased. He asked me if it were known at Paris. I answered that it was not. "Then," said he, "you must send it to the Academy; it will make some noise there." I represented to him, that I had allowed myself a licence of opinion in it, at which many would be alarmed.

"I know an honourable lady," returned he, "who confessed that one day, after having proudly reproved an imprudent lover, the tender words escaped her—'Charming, impudent wretch!' The Academy will do the same."

Before dinner, he took me to make some visits at Geneva; and, talking of the way in which he lived with the inhabitants, "It is very grateful," said he, "to live in a country where its sovereigns send to ask you for your carriage, that they may come and dine with you."

His house was open to them; they passed whole days there: and, as the gates of the city were shut at the close of day, not to open till the morning rose, those who supped at his house were obliged to sleep there or at the country houses that cover the borders of the lake.

On our way, I asked him how, almost without territory, and without any facility of commerce with foreign countries, Geneva had enriched itself. "In manufacturing watches," he replied; "in reading your gazettes, and profiting by your follies. These people know how to calculate the profits on your loans."

As we were talking of Geneva, he asked me what I thought of Rousseau. I answered, that in his writings he appeared to me only an eloquent sophist; and, in his character, only a false cynic, who would burst with pride and indignation if the world ceased to gaze on him. As to the earnest desire he had conceived of giving a fair exterior to the part he acted, I knew the anecdote, and told it to him.

In one of the letters of Rousseau to M. de Malesherbes, you have seen in what a transport of inspiration and enthusiasm he had conceived the project of declaring himself against the arts and sciences. "I was going," says he, in the recital he has made of this miracle,—"I was going to see Diderot, then a prisoner at Vincennes; I had in my pocket a 'Mercure de France,' which I turned over as I went along. I fell on the question of the Dijon Academy, which has given rise to my first work. If anything ever resembled sudden inspiration, it is the emotion that this question excited in me. Suddenly my mind is dazzled with a thousand lights; crowds of vivid ideas press on me at once, with a degree of force and confusion that throw me into inexpressible disorder. I feel my head seized with a giddiness that resembles intoxication. A violent palpitation oppresses me, and heaves my bosom. No longer able to breathe as I walk, I fall at the foot of one of the trees of the avenue, and I there pass half an hour in such an agitation, that, on rising, I perceived all the front of my waistcoat wet with my tears, without having been sensible that I had shed any."

You have here a transport eloquently described. I will now tell you the fact, in its simplicity, such as Diderot related it to me, and such as I related it to Voltaire.

" I was,"—'tis Diderot who speaks,—" I was a prisoner at Vincennes; Rousseau came to see me there. He had made me his Aristarchus, as he has said himself. One day, as we were walking together, he told me that the Dijon Academy had just proposed an interesting question, which he was desirous of treating. This question was—" Has the re-establishment of arts and sciences contributed to the improvement of morals? Which side will you take?" asked I. " The affirmative," answered he. " 'Tis the asses' bridge," said I; " all ordinary talents will take that road; and you will there find only commonplace ideas; whereas the contrary side presents a new, rich, and fertile field for philosophy and for eloquence."

" You are right," returned he, after a moment's reflection; " and I'll take your advice." Thus, from that moment, added I, his part has been decided, and the mask worn.

" You do not astonish me," said Voltaire; " that man is factitious from head to foot: he is so in his mind and soul. But it is in vain for him to play now the stoic and now the cynic; he will eternally belie himself, and his mask will stifle him."

Among the inhabitants of Geneva that I saw at his house, the only men who pleased, and who were pleased with me, were the chevalier Hubert, and Cramer the bookseller. They were both of easy converse, and of a jovial temper, and having wit without affectation; a rare thing in their city. Cramer, I was told, played tragedy tolerably well; he was the Orosmane of madame Denis, and this talent had won him the friendship and the custom of Voltaire;

that is to say, thousands. Hubert had a talent less useful, but amusing and very curious in its futility. You would have said he had eyes at his fingers' ends. With his hands behind his back, he would cut out a portrait in profile as like, and even more like, than he could have drawn with a pencil. He had Voltaire's face so strongly impressed on his imagination, that, absent or present, his scissars represented him meditating, writing, in action, and in all attitudes. I have seen landscapes cut out by him in white paper, where the perspective was preserved with prodigious art. These two amiable neighbours were very assiduous in their visits to Les Délices, during the little time I staid there.

M. de Voltaire insisted on showing us his country house at Tornay, where his theatre was, a quarter of a league from Geneva. This was the end of our ride in the afternoon in his carriage.—Tornay was a little neglected country seat, but the view from it was admirable. In the valley was the Lake of Geneva, bordered by country houses, and terminated by two large cities, beyond, and in the distance, a chain of mountains of thirty leagues in extent, and that Mont Blanc! loaded with eternal snows and ice that never melts.—Such is the view that Tornay affords. There I saw the little theatre that tormented Rousseau, and where Voltaire consoled himself for no longer visiting the theatre of Paris, which nightly resounded his fame.

The idea of this unjust and tyrannical privation filled me with grief and indignation. Perhaps he perceived it; for, more than once, by his reflections, he answered my thoughts; and, on the road, as we returned, he talked to me of Versailles, of the long residence I had made there, and of the kindness that madame de Pompadour had formerly expressed for him.

"She still loves you," said I; "she has repeated it often to me. But she is weak, and dares not, or cannot, effect all she wishes; for the unhappy woman is no longer loved, and perhaps she now envies the lot of madame Denis, and would willingly be at Les Délices."—" Let her come," said he, with transport, " and play tragedy with us. I will write characters for her, and characters of queens. She is beautiful— she should know the play of the passions."—" She knows too," said I, " the torments of profound grief and bitter tears."—" So much the better! that is just what we want," exclaimed he, as it were enchanted at having a new actress; and in truth, you would have said that he thought he saw her arrive. " Since she suits you," said I, " leave the rest to me: if she can no longer succeed on the theatre of Versailles, I will tell her that your's awaits her."

This romantic fiction amused the company. They found some probability in it; and madame Denis, indulging the illusion, entreated her uncle not to oblige her to yield her parts to the new actress. He retired to his closet for a few hours; and in the evening, at supper, kings and their mistresses being the subject of our conversation, Voltaire, in comparing the spirit and gallantry of the old and new courts, displayed to us that rich memory which nothing interesting ever escaped. From madame de la Vallière to madame de Pompadour, the anecdotic history of the two reigns, and in the interval that of the regency, passed in review with a rapidity and a brilliancy of beauty and colouring that dazzled us. Yet he reproached himself with having stolen from M. de l'Ecluse moments which, he said, he would have occupied more agreeably to us. He begged him to indemnify us by a few scenes of the ' Apple-women,' and he laughed at them like a child.

The next day (it was the last we were to pass together), he sent for me early in the morning, and giving me a manuscript: " Go into my closet," said he; " and read that; you shall give me your opinion of it." It was the tragedy of ' Tancrède,' that he had just finished. I read it, and returning with my face bathed in tears, I told him he had written nothing more interesting. "To whom," asked he, "would you give the part of Aménaïde?"—"To Clairon," answered I; "to the sublime Clairon, and I will answer for a success at least equal to that of Zaïre." —"Your tears," replied he, "tell me most eloquently what I was most desirous of knowing; but the action,—did you find nothing that stopped you in its march?"—"I found that it only wants what you call criticisms of the closet. The public will be too much moved to be occupied with them at the theatre." Fortunately, he said nothing of the style; I should have been obliged to conceal my sentiments; for, in my opinion, 'Tancrède,' in point of style, was very far from being written like his best tragedies. In 'Rome Sauveé,' and in 'L'Orphelin de la Chine,' I had still found the beautiful versification of 'Zaïre,' of 'Merope,' and of 'La Mort de César;' but in 'Tancrede' I thought I saw a decline in his style; weak, tedious verses, loaded with redundant words that disguise the want of force and vigour; in a word, the age of the poet: for in him, as in Corneille, the poetry of style was the first that declined; and after 'Tancrede,' where the fire of genius still emitted some sparks, it was wholly extinguished.

Afflicted at our departure, he would not steal from us one moment of this last day. The desire of seeing me received at the French Academy, the eulogy of my 'Tales' which formed, he said, their most agreeable family reading, then my 'Analysis of Rousseau's Letter to d'Alembert on the Stage,'—a refutation which he thought unanswerable, and which he appeared to esteem very highly,—were, during our walk, the subjects of his conversation. I asked him whether Geneva had been deceived on the true motive of this letter of Rousseau. "Rousseau," said he, "is better known at Geneva than at Paris. We are here neither the dupes of his false zeal nor of his false eloquence. It is against me that his darts are directed, and that is obvious to every one. Possessed of an unbounded pride, he would wish that, in his native country, no one should occupy any place in the public mind but himself. My residence here eclipses him; he envies me the air I breathe here, and above all he cannot suffer that, by amusing Geneva sometimes, I should steal moments that might be employed in thinking on him."

As we were to set off at the dawn of day, as soon as the gates of the city should be open and we could get horses, we resolved in company with madame Denis, M. Hubert, and M. Cramer, to prolong till that hour the pleasure of sitting up and conversing together. Voltaire would be of the party, and we pressed him in vain to retire to bed; more awake than ourselves, he read to us some cantos of the poem of 'Jeanne.' This reading was to me an inexpressible charm; for if Voltaire, in reciting heroic verse, affected, in my mind, an emphasis too monotonous, a cadence too strongly marked, no one read familiar and comic verse with so much natural delicacy and grace: his eyes and smile had an expression that I have never seen but in him. Alas! it was for me the song of the swan, and I was only to see him again as he expired!

Our mutual adieus were tender even to tears, but much more so on my part than on his: that was natural; for, independently of my gratitude and all the motives I had for loving him, I left him in exile.

At Lyons, we gave one day to the family of Fleurieu, who expected me at la Tourette, their country-house. The two following days were employed in seeing the city; and, from the spinning-house of gold and silk to the perfection of the richest tissues, we rapidly followed all the operations of art that made the riches of that flourishing city. The manufactories, the town-hall, the beautiful hospital of la Charité, the library of the Jesuits, the convent of the Chartreux, and the theatre, each attracted our attention.

Here, I recollect that, as I passed on my way to Geneva, mademoiselle Destouche, the directress of the theatre, had sent to me to ask which of my tragedies I should wish to see played on my return. I sensibly felt this civility; but I only returned her my thanks, and requested her to gratify me with that tragedy of Voltaire's which her performers played best. They gave 'Alzire.'

While my epicurean philosophy was enjoying itself in the provinces, the hatred of my enemies did not sleep at Paris. I learnt, on arriving there, that d'Argental and his wife were spreading the report that I was lost in the king's esteem; and that it would be in vain for the Academy to elect me; because his majesty would not confirm my election. I found my friends struck with this opinion; and, had I been as impatient to be of the Academy as they were to see me there, I should have been very unhappy. But, while assuring them that in spite of intrigue I should obtain this place from which my enemies were so desirous to exclude me, I also declared that my pride would be well satisfied if I deserved it, even without obtaining it. I applied myself then to finish my translation of the 'Pharsalia,' and my 'Poétique Française;' I sent my 'Epître aux Poëtes' to the Academy; and as the editions of my 'Tales' succeeded each other, I added new ones.

The success of the 'Epistle to the Poets' was such as Voltaire had predicted; but it was not without difficulty that it bore the prize in preference to two other excellent rival works, one was Thomas's 'Epistle to the People;' the other, Delille's 'Epistle on the Advantages of Retirement for Men of Letters.' This circumstance of my life was remarkable enough to deserve a few words.

I had scarcely sent my epistle to the Academy,

when Thomas, according to his custom, came to show me that which he was about to send. I thought it beautiful, and of so noble and firm a tone that I believed it at least very possible that it would be preferred to mine. "My dear friend," said I, after having read and warmly applauded it; "I have a confidence to make to you in my turn; but on two conditions: one, that you will observe the most absolute secrecy; the other, that, after having heard what I am going to say to you, you will make no use of it, that is, that you will act just as if I had not told it you. Give me your promise." He gave it to me. "Now," continued I, "I will tell you that I have sent an epistle to the Academy."—"In that case," said he, "I withdraw mine."—"That is what I cannot consent to," replied I; "and for two reasons: one, because it is very possible that my work may be objected to as heretical, and that the prize may be refused it,—you shall judge of it yourself;—the other, because it is not decided that my epistle is preferable to your's, and that I will not steal from you a prize that perhaps belongs to you. I therefore rely on the promise you have given me. Here's my epistle." I read it to him; and he agreed that there were bold and perilous passages in it. Behold us then the confidential rivals of each other, and competitors with the abbé Delille.

One day when the Academy were sitting in judgment on the rival epistles, in order to determine the prize, I met Duclos at the opera, and asked him whether it were decided. "Don't mention it," said he; "I believe this competition will set fire to the Academy. Three pieces, such as are rarely seen, dispute the prize. There are two whose merit is not doubtful; on that all are agreed; but the third turns our heads. It is the work of a young madman, full of fervour and boldness, who respects nothing, who braves all literary prejudices, who speaks of poets like a poet, and who paints them in all their proper colours with an entire frankness; dares to praise Lucan and censure Virgil, reprobate the contempt of Boileau for Tasso, appreciate Boileau himself, and reduce him to his just value. D'Olivet is furious; he says that the Academy dishonours itself, if it adjudge the prize to this insolent work, and yet I am persuaded that it will be so." And so it was. But, when I presented myself to receive the prize, d'Olivet swore that he never would forgive me as long as he lived.

It was, I think, at that time that I published my translation of the 'Pharsalia:' from that moment rhetoric and poetry divided my studies; and to my Tales, at intervals, a few moments were devoted.

It was particularly in the country that I found this kind of meditation was favourable; and occasion sometimes presented me with happy subjects. For example, one evening at Besons, where M. de St Florentin had a country house, being at supper with him, and the conversation turning on my Tales: "There has happened," said he, "in this village, an adventure of which you could perhaps make something interesting." In few words he then related to me, that a young peasant and his lass, cousins-german, had made love and the girl had proved with child; that, as neither the rector nor the judge of the Bishop's court would marry them, they had had recourse to him, and that he had been obliged to procure a dispensation from Rome. I agreed that indeed this subject, well developed, might have its interest. At night, when I was alone, it recurred to my fancy, and seized so forcibly on my mind that, in an hour, all the pictures, the scenes, and the characters themselves, such as I have painted them, were designed, and as it were, present to my view. At that time, the style of this kind of composition cost me no labour; it flowed as from its source; and, when the tale was once well conceived, it was written.

Instead of sleeping, I meditated all night on this. I saw, I heard 'Annette and Lubin' as distinctly as if this fiction had been the fresh recollection of an event I had just witnessed. On rising at daybreak, I had only to commit rapidly to paper what I had meditated; and my tale was written such as it is printed.

After dinner, before our walk, I was asked, as I often was in the country, whether I had not something to read, and I read 'Annette and Lubin.' I cannot express the surprise of the whole company, and particularly the joy of M. de St Florentin, at seeing in how short a time I had painted the picture of which he had given me the outline. He wanted to send for the real Annette and Lubin. I entreated him to excuse my seeing them in reality. However, at one of the representations of the comic opera that was taken from this tale, the Annette and Lubin of Besons were invited to come and see themselves on the stage. They were present at this performance in a box that was given them, and they were very much applauded.

My imagination, directed to this species of fiction, was, to me, in the country, a kind of enchantress, who, from the moment I was alone, enveloped me in her witchcraft; sometimes at Malmaison, on the border of that rivulet which, by a rapid slope, rolls from the summit of the hill, and winding under green bowers goes to revive the verdure of the flowery lawn; sometimes at Croix Fontaine, on those banks that the Seine waters, is describing an immense semicircle, as it were to please the eye; then again those beautiful alleys of St Assise, or on that long terrace that commands the Seine, and from whence the eye measures in its distant majestic bed the tranquil course of the stream.

At these country seats, my friends had the kindness of appearing to desire my company, to welcome me with joy, never like myself to think the days that we passed there tedious, and never to see me go away without expressing some regret. For myself, I would willingly have been able to unite all my societies together, or to multiply myself that I might quit none of them. They had no resemblance to each other; but each had for me its peculiar charms.

Malmaison then belonged to M. Desfourniels: the society was that of madame Harenc; and I have sufficiently described the close ties of friendship and gratitude that there engaged my heart. The woman to whom I have been most dear, my mother excepted, was madame Harenc. She appeared to have inspired all her friends with the tender interest she took in me. To love and to be loved, in this intimate society, was my habitual life.

At St Assise, at the house of madame de Montulé, friendship was not without reserve, nor without distrust; I was young, and young women thought they ought to be circumspect with me. On my part, I had with them only a measured liberty, that was respectfully timid. But, in this constraint itself, there was something very delicate and very charming. Besides, the life of rule and agreeable application that was led at St Assise, suited my taste. A father and a mother, constantly occupied in rendering instruction easy and attractive to their children; the former making for them with his own hands, that curious extract from the 'Memoirs of the Academy of Sciences,' of which I preserve a copy; the latter abridging and reducing Buffon's Natural History to what might be read by them without danger, and with propriety; a governess for the two daughters, teaching them history, geography, arithmetic, Italian, and still more carefully, the rules of the French language, by exercising them every day in writing correctly; in the afternoon, the brush in the hand of madame de Montulé, and pencils in those of her daughters and their governess; and this occupation animated by smiling remarks or agreeable reading, serving them for recreation; in our walk, M. de Montulé exciting and directing the curiosity of his children to the knowledge of trees and plants, of which he formed for them a kind of herbal, where the nature, properties, and use of these vegetables were explained; finally, in our games themselves, ingenious artifices and continual excitements to emulation, to render pleasure profitable, by insinuating information even into their amusements; such was for me the picture of this domestic school, where study never had the air of constraint, nor teaching the tone of severity.

You may conceive, that a father and mother who instructed their children so well, had themselves cultivated minds. M. de Montulé did not study to be engaging, that was the least of his cares; but madame de Montulé had, in her mind and disposition, that grain of genteel coquetry, which, mixed with decorum, gives to the agreeable qualities of a woman more vivacity, brilliancy, and charm. She used to call me philosopher, well persuaded that I scarcely deserved that title; and to laugh at my philosophy was one of her pastimes. I perceived it, but it was a pleasure of which I would not deprive her.

With more cordiality, the good and all simple madame de Chalut attracted me to St Cloud; and to keep me there she had an irresistible charm, that of a friendship, which from the bottom of her heart poured into mine, without reserve, its most secret cares, its most intimate feelings, and its dearest interests. She was not necessary to my happiness I must confess it; but I was necessary to her's. Her soul needed the support of mine; it reposed on mine, and there it forgot its sorrows and its griefs. She had one, the horror of which is inexpressible: it was that of seeing those she had lately served, her patrons, her benefactors, her friends, the dauphin, the dauphiness, struck at the same time, as by an invisible hand, and consumed, by what she called a slow poison, languish, wither, and die. It was I who soothed her sorrows at this slow death. She mixed with them some confidential communications, which she made only to me, and the secret shall follow me to the silence of the tomb.

But of the country houses at which I successively passed the gay seasons of the year, Maisons and Croix Fontaine were those that had the most charm for me. My visits at Croix Fontaine were short: but all the voluptuousness of luxury, all the refinements of the most ingenious and delicate gallantry, were united there by the enchanter Bouret. He was acknowledged to be the most obliging and most magnificent of men: the grace with which he conferred his obligations was proverbial. Alas! you will soon see into what an abyss of misery this engaging and fatal passion led him. At the same time, as he held two important financial places, that of farmer-general and that of farmer of the posts; as he had besides, by his correspondents and his couriers, every facility of procuring himself, for his table, whatever was most exquisite and rare in the kingdom; as he received from every side presents from those he patronised, or whose fortune he had made, his friends saw in his profusion only the effects of his credit, and the use of his riches.

But madame Gaulard, who probably saw better, and farther into the affairs of her friend than we, and who was afflicted at the expenses in which he lavished his fortune, determining to be no longer either the cause or the pretext for them, had taken at Maisons, on the road to Croix Fontaine, a simple, modest house, where she lived habitually solitary, with a niece of a lovely disposition, and the gaiety of fifteen. I have painted the character of madame Gaulard in one of the tales, 'La Veillée,' where I have introduced myself under the name of Ariste. Her plain and simple disposition, so mild, so natural, and of so peaceful an equality, harmonized so readily with mine, that she had scarcely known me at Paris, and at Croix Fontaine, when she chose me for her intimate companion in her retreat at Maisons; and I insensibly found myself so happy there that I, at last, not only passed the summer months with her, but whole winters, when she preferred the silence and tranquillity of the country to the noise and tumult of the town. What a charm had this solitude for me! You suspect it, and I would tell it without mystery; for nothing was more legitimate than my intentions and views. But as they did not succeed, they are but as one of those dreams the remembrance of which has nothing interesting, except to him that has dreamed. It suffices to know that this quiet retreat was that in which my days glided on with most calm and rapidity.

While I thus forgot the world, the Academy, and myself, my friends, who thought literary honours usurped by all those who obtained them before me, were indignant at seeing in one single year new academicians pass over my head, without my being moved at it; while, at every new election, my enemies, besieging the doors of the Academy, redoubled their manœuvres and their efforts to keep me from it.

In speaking of the parody of Cinna, I have forgotten to say that there was a severe word in it for the count de Choiseul Praslin, then ambassador at Vienna. You know that Augustus says to Cinna and Maximus,—

"You who serve me instead of Agrippa and Mecænas."

This line was parodied thus:—

"You who serve me instead of the blackbird and my wife."

Now this name of 'the Blackbird' was a nickname given to the count de Praslin. It is for this reason, that, when he had taken la Dangeville for his mistress, Grandval, who had been her favourite, and whom she wished to preserve as an auxiliary, answered her:

> "The blackbird has sullied that cage,
> Which the sparrow will enter no more."

This verse of the parody, then, had been represented to the duke de Choiseul as another crime; and in one of our conferences, he quoted it to me as an insult offered to his cousin. I had the weakness to answer, that this line was not among those that I had known. "And what then was the line you knew?" insisted he.—I answered, to rid myself of my embarrassment:

"You who serve me instead of my deceased wife."

—"Fye!" exclaimed he; "that line is flat; the other is much better; there is no comparison." Praslin was not a man to take a joke so gaily. He had a low and melancholy soul; and, in men of that character, wounded pride is inexorable.

On his return from his embassy, he was made minister of state for foreign affairs. Then, like a profound politician, he consulted with d'Argental and his wife on the means of preventing, at least for some time to come, my admission into the Academy.

Thomas bore away the prizes of eloquence there, with a great superiority over all his rivals. They resolved to oppose him to me; and for that purpose, the count de Praslin began by taking him as his secretary, and by procuring him the place of secretary interpreter to the Swiss republic. This was giving to himself the honourable appearance of patronising a man of merit. Thus the littleness of the revenge he was exerting against me adorned and thought itself ennobled; and the moment only was waited for to put Thomas forward, in order to bar my way to the Academy.

In the meantime, my friends and I, while we rejoiced at Thomas's good fortune, thought only of removing the obstacle that, in the opinion of the academicians, opposed my election. " So long as they shall believe," said d'Alembert to me, " that the king would refuse you, they will not dare to elect you. D'Argental, Praslin, the duke d'Aumont, assure us that we should experience this refusal. We must absolutely destroy this idea."

Restored to the good graces of madame de Pompadour, I communicated my fears to her, entreating her to learn from the king, whether he would be favourable to me. She had the kindness to ask him, and his answer was, that if I were elected, he would confirm my election. " May I then, madame," said I, " assure the Academy of it?"—" No," replied she; " no, you would compromise me; you must only say that you have reason to hope for the king's approval."—" But, madame," insisted I, " if the king has formally said to you . . . . ."— " I know what the king has said to me," replied she with vivacity; " but do I know what those about him may make him say?" These words silenced me; and I returned to d'Alembert with the vexatious account of what had just passed.

After having inveighed bitterly against feeble minds, it was decided between us that I should only announce hope, but in such a tone as plainly to indicate that it was well founded: and, indeed, the death of Marivaux, in 1763, leaving a vacant place, I made the usual visits, with the air of a man who had nothing to fear from the court. At the same time, the inquietude of madame de Pompadour on the influence courtiers might have in directing the king's decision, disturbed me; I laboured to imagine some means of assuring myself of his favour: I thought I discovered one; but at that moment I could not employ it. My 'Poétique' was in the press; but some months would still elapse before it could be published: and it was the instrument of the design I had formed. Fortunately, the abbé de Radouvilliers, formerly under teacher to the French princes, presented himself, at the same time with me, as a candidate for this vacant place; and it was doing something agreeable to the dauphin, and perhaps to the king himself, to resign it to him. I went then to Versailles, to declare to my competitor that I withdrew from the contest. I had but little merit in it, he would have carried it against me; and such was his modesty, that he was sensible of this deference, as if he had owed to me alone all the suffrages united in his favour. A very remarkable circumstance, at this election, was the artifice employed by my enemies, and by those of d'Alembert and Duclos, to render us odious to the court of the dauphin. They had begun by spreading the report that my party would be adverse to the abbé de Radouvilliers, and that if, on the first scrutiny, he obtained the majority, at least on the second, he would not escape the affront of some black balls. This prediction being made, the question was how to verify it; and they attempted it thus. There were at the Academy four men distinguished by the name of philosophers, an odious title at that time. These noted academicians, were Duclos, d'Alembert, Saurin, and Watelet. The worthy chiefs of the opposite party, d'Olivet, Batteux, and probably Paulmi and Séguier, formed a plot to give four black balls, which would most assuredly be attributed to the philosophers; and indeed four black balls were found on the scrutiny.

Great astonishment and murmurs were heard among those who had given them; and with their eyes fixed on the four on whom the suspicion rested, the impostors said loudly, that it was very strange that a man so faultless and so estimable as the abbé de Radouvilliers, should experience the affront of four black balls! The abbé d'Olivet was indignant at so shameful, so public a scandal; the four philosophers looked confounded. But the chances quickly turned in their favour, and to the shame of their enemies. The unexpected stroke was this: the custom of the Academy on beginning the ballot, was to distribute to each of the electors, two balls, one black and one white. The box into which they fell, had likewise two capsules, and two cups above, one white and the other black. When you would vote in favour of the candidate, you put the white ball into the white cup, the black ball into the black cup; and when you would vote against him, you put the white ball into the black cup, and the black ball into the white cup. Thus, on examining the balls, the whole number should be found, and as many white in the black capsule as there were black in the white capsule.

Now, by a species of divination, one of the philosophers, Duclos, having foreseen the trick that their enemies were about to play them, had said to his comrades, " Let's keep our black balls in our hands, so that if those knaves have the malice to give any, we may be able to produce the proof that the black balls do not come from us."

As soon, then, as they had suffered d'Olivet and the other impostors to burst out into murmurs against the malevolent; " It is not I," said Duclos, opening his hand, " who have given a black ball; for I have fortunately kept mine, and there it is!"—" Nor is it I," said d'Alembert; " here's mine!" Watelet and Saurin said the same in showing theirs. At this sudden blow, the confusion was reflected back on the authors of the artifice. D'Olivet had the simplicity to think it unfair to have parried the blow by keeping back the black balls, alleging the laws of the Academy, on the inviolable secrecy of the ballot. " M. abbé," said d'Alembert to him, " the first of laws is that of personal defence; and we had only this method of arming ourselves against the suspicious light in which you have endeavoured to place us."

This trait of foresight on the part of Duclos became current in society, and the d'Olivets, caught in their own trap, were the ridicule of the court.

At length the printing of my 'Poétique' being completed, I entreated madame de Pompadour to obtain from the king that a work which was wanting in our literature might be presented to him. "It is," added I, "a favour which will cost nothing either to the king or the state, and which will prove that I am well liked and well received by the king." I owe this testimony to the memory of this beneficent woman, that, at this simple and easy method of publicly deciding the king in my favour, her beautiful countenance beamed with joy. "Most willingly," said she, "will I ask for you this favour of the king, and it will be granted." She obtained it without difficulty, and, in announcing it to me, "You must give," said she, "all possible solemnity to this presentation; and, on the same day, all the royal family, and all the ministers must receive your work from your own hand."

I confided my secret only to my most intimate friends; and my copies being very magnificently bound (for I spared no expense in it) I went one Saturday evening to Versailles with my packets. On my arrival, I entreated madame de Pompadour, through Quesnai, to engage the king to receive me kindly.

The next day I was introduced by the duke de Duras. The king was at his levee. I never saw him so engaging. He received my homage with an enchanting look. I should have been at the summit of joy if he had said one word to me; but his eyes spoke for him. The dauphin, whom the abbé de Radouvilliers had predisposed in my favour, had the kindness to speak to me. "I have heard much in praise of this work," said he; "I think highly of its author." As he pronounced these words, he smote my heart with grief, for I saw death on his countenance and in his eyes.

In all this ceremony the good duke de Duras was my conductor; and I cannot tell with what interest he exerted himself to have me well received.

When I went down to madame de Pompadour's, to whom I had already presented my work, "Go to M. de Choiseul's," said she, "and offer him his copy, he will receive you well; and leave me that of M. de Praslin; I will offer it him myself."

After this business was over, I went quickly to d'Alembert and Duclos, to announce to them the success I had just had; and the next day I made a present of my book to the Academy. I distributed some copies of it to those academicians whose sentiments I knew to be favourable to me. Mairau said, that in this work I had laid a mine under the door of the Academy, in order to blow it up, if it were shut upon me; but all the difficulties were not yet removed.

Duclos and d'Alembert had had some strange altercation in full Academy, on the subject of the king of Prussia, and of cardinal de Bernis; they had so violently fallen out that they no longer spoke to each other; and, at the moment when I was likely to need their harmony and good intelligence, I found them enemies to each other. Duclos, the more hasty of the two, but the less lively, was likewise the less offended. The enmity of such a man as d'Alembert gave him pain; he wanted to be reconciled; but he wished that I should engage d'Alembert to make the first advances.

"I am indignant," said he, "at the oppression under which you have groaned, and at the secret and sordid persecution you still experience. It is time that it should finish. Bougainville is dying; you must have his place. Tell d'Alembert that I desire nothing more than to secure it to you; let him speak to me about it at the Academy: we will arrange this business for the next election."

D'Alembert stamped with rage, when I proposed to him to speak to Duclos. "Let him go to the devil," answered he, "with his abbé de Bernis: I will have no more to do with the one than the other."—" In that case, I give up the Academy; my only regret," said I, "is that I ever thought of it."—" Why so?" replied he with warmth; " do you want Duclos, in order to be of it?"—" And who should I not want, when my friends abandon me, and when my enemies are more eager to injure me, and more active then ever? Ah! they would speak to the devil, to deprive me of a single vote; but what I have formerly said in verse, I experience myself:

"Friendship desponds, but, frozen by misfortune,
Hatred, implacable, never tires."

" You shall be of the Academy in spite of your enemies," replied he. " No, sir, no, I shall not be of it; I will not be of it. I shall be played the fool with, supplanted, insulted by a party already too numerous and too strong. I prefer living in obscurity; for that, thank heaven, I shall want no one."—" But, Marmontel, you are angry, and I don't know why . . . . ."—" Oh! I well know why; the friend of my heart, the man on whom I reckoned most on earth, has but one word to say to extricate me from oppression . . . ."—" Well! Good God! and I'll say it; but nothing ever gave me so much pain in my life."—" Has Duclos then so seriously offended you?"—" What! don't you know then, with what insolence, in full Academy, he has spoken of the king of Prussia?"—" Of the king of Prussia! and what does this king regard the insolence of Duclos? Ah! d'Alembert, tell me that you have need of my most cruel enemy, and that to serve you it is only requisite to pardon him; I'll go and embrace him instantly."—" Well," answered he, " this evening I'll be reconciled to Duclos; but let him serve you well ; for it is only at that price, and for love of you . . . . ."—" I am sure he'll serve me well," said I; and indeed, Duclos, enchanted to see d'Alembert return to him, was as active and as warm in my favour as he himself.

But, at the death of Bougainville, and at the moment when I flattered myself that I should succeed him without any obstacle, d'Alembert sent for me. " Do you know," said he, " what they are plotting against you? They oppose to you a competitor, in favour of whom Praslin, d'Argental and his wife, are soliciting votes both in town and at the court. They boast of having engaged a great number of them, and I believe it; for this competitor is Thomas."—" I do not believe," I replied, " that Thomas consents to be the instrument of this manœuvre."—" But," said he, " Thomas is very much embarrassed about it. You know that they have entangled him by favours and gratitude; besides, they have long persecuted him to think of the Academy; and, on his representing to them that his quality of private secretary to the minister would be an obstacle to his election, Praslin had obtained for him from the king a patent that ennobled his place. Now that the obstacle is removed, they require that he should offer himself, and make themselves responsible for a great majority of votes. He is at Fontainbleau with the minister, and beset by d'Argental. I advise you to go there and see him."

I set off, and on arriving I wrote to Thomas, to request a rendezvous. He answered that, at five o'clock, he would be on the border of the great bason. I waited for him there; and, in coming up to him, " You surely conjecture, my dear friend," said I, " what brings me here. I come to know from you whether what I am told be true;" and I repeated to him what d'Alembert had said to me.

"Yes, it is true," answered Thomas; "and it is also true, that M. d'Argental has signified to me this morning, that M. de Praslin insists on my offering myself; that he requires of me this mark of attachment; that such has been the condition of the patent he has procured me; that in accepting it, I must have understood why it was granted to me; and that if I disoblige my benefactor out of regard for a man who has offended him, I lose my place and my fortune. This is my position. Now tell me what you would do in my place."—" Are you really serious," said I, " when you ask that question?"—" Yes," he replied, smiling, and with the air of a man whose resolution was fixed.—" Well then," answered I, " in your place I would do what you will do."— " Nay, irony apart, what would you do?"—" I don't pretend," said I, " to give myself for an example; but am I not your friend? Are you not mine?"—" Yes," returned he; " and I say it openly,—

" I have told it to earth, to heaven, to Gusman himself."—

" Well," replied I; " if I had a son, and if he had the misfortune to serve the hatred of a Gusman against his friend, I would . . . ."—" Stop there," said Thomas to me, shaking me by the hand; " my answer is made and well made."—" Ah, my friend," said I, " do you think I doubted it?"—" Yet you are come to assure yourself of it," added he, with a gentle reproof. " Certainly not," answered I; " it is not for myself that I needed this assurance, but for those who do not know your heart so well as I know it."—" Tell them," replied he, " that if ever I enter the Academy, it shall be by the door of honour. And with respect to fortune, I have enjoyed it so short a time, and have done without it so long, that I hope I have not now to learn to live without it." At these words, I was so moved that I would have resigned the place to him, if he would have accepted it, and if he could have done it with decency. But the hatred of the minister against me was so declared, that we should have been supposed, he to have served it, and I to have sunk under it. We therefore adopted that free and frank conduct that became us both. He did not offer himself as a candidate; and he lost his place as secretary to the minister. However, they had not the impudence to deprive him of that of secretary interpreter to the Swiss republic. He was received by the Academy immediately after me, he was received by acclamations, but after a long interval; for from 1763 to 1766 there was no vacancy, although the average number of deaths in the Academy was three in two years.

I ought to tell, to the shame of the count de Praslin, and to the glory of Thomas, that the latter, after having refused to commit an act of slavery and meanness, thought it his duty not to withdraw from the house of a man who had done him some service, till he should be dismissed. He remained with him another month, presenting himself as usual every morning at his levee, while this vain, unfeeling man never said a single word to him, or even deigned to look. To a soul naturally proud and noble, like that of Thomas, judge how painful this humble trial must have been! At length, after having given to gratitude even more than its due, seeing how irreconcilable was the vile arrogance of this minister, which modest patient attention could not overcome, he sent him word that he felt himself obliged to take his silence for a dismissal, and left him. This conduct completely made known his character; and even on the score of fortune he lost nothing by having acted like an honest man. The king was pleased with him for it; and he not only obtained afterwards a pension of eighty guineas on the royal treasury, but a handsome apartment at the Louvre, which was procured for him by the count d'Angiviller, his friend and mine.

END OF VOLUME I.

LONDON:
PRINTED BY C. B. REYNELL, BROAD STREET, GOLDEN SQUARE.

Printed in the USA
CPSIA information can be obtained
at www.ICGtesting.com
LVHW050322011224
798030LV00009B/586